Forbes®

GREATEST
INVESTING STORIES

Forbes®
GREATEST
INVESTING STORIES

RICHARD PHALON

John Wiley & Sons, Inc.

New York • Chichester • Weinheim • Brisbane • Singapore • Toronto

Copyright © 2001 by Forbes Inc. All rights reserved.
Forbes is a registered trademark of Forbes Inc. Its use is pursuant to a license agreement with Forbes Inc.
Published by John Wiley & Sons, Inc.
Published simultaneously in Canada.

This publication is designed to provide accurate and authoritative information in regard to the subject matter covered. It is sold with the understanding that the publisher is not engaged in rendering professional services. If professional advice or other expert assistance is required, the services of a competent professional person should be sought.

PICTURE CREDITS: Page xiv: ©Bettman/Corbis; Page 26: Courtesy Third Avenue Funds, New York, NY; Page 50: T. Rowe Price, Baltimore, MD; Page 74: Courtesy Janus, Denver, CO; Page 96: ©Bettman/Corbis; Page 126: ©John Abbott; Page 148: Brown Brothers, Sterling, PA; Page 174: Courtesy Muriel Siebert & Co., Inc.; Page 190: Courtesy Baker Library, Harvard Business School, Boston, MA; Page 206: ©Jim Bush

Library of Congress Cataloging-in-Publication Data
Phalon, Richard
    Forbes greatest investing stories / by Richard Phalon
      p. cm.
    Includes index.
    ISBN 0-471-35624-7 (cloth : alk. paper)
      1. Finance, Personal—United States—Case studies. 2. Investments—United States—Case studies. 3. Success in business—United States—Case studies. I. Forbes. II. Title.

HG179.P4498 2001
332.6—dc21

2001017828

Printed in the United States of America.

10 9 8 7 6 5 4 3 2 1

For Nancy Hoepli-Phalon

CONTENTS

WHY INVESTORS SHOULD KNOW THEIR HISTORY

—— ⚎◆⚎ ——

"History doesn't repeat," said Mark Twain, "but it sure does rhyme." Sam Clemens wasn't talking about Wall Street in particular but he could have been—after all, he was an active, if not very successful, investor.

At any rate, Twain's aphorism fits the stock market nicely. On Wall Street the dates, the industries, the personalities, and the names change, but the big themes remain constant. That's what this book is about: the persistence in finance of certain patterns through changing times.

The author of this book, Dick Phalon, has covered The Street for almost a half century for some of the nation's leading periodicals. To create a sort of tableau vivant for the edification of investors, he has selected a rich cast of characters, some living, some dead. This is not a history of Wall Street in the twentieth century. It is an impressionistic and affectionate job of storytelling that instructs as it amuses. The stories gain insight from the fact that Phalon burned shoe leather covering several of the stories back when they were breaking news. He has met many of the actors. He witnessed a good deal of the drama close up.

As any such book must, this one includes Ben Graham, Warren Buffett's respected teacher. Graham took a rather cynical view of Wall Street. Paraphrasing the famous put-down of the French Bourbon monarchs, Graham once said: "Wall Street people learn nothing and forget everything." Graham died more than 30 years ago, but I remembered those words when the tech-heavy NASDAQ Index was pushing toward 5000. Many of The Street's most respected houses were floating sales pitches for hot tech stocks, issues that were already levitating without visible support from profits and/or assets or much in the way of sales. How Bourbon that was! How right Graham was neither for the first time nor the last. Alas, Wall Street served investors badly because it failed to remind them how disastrously such levitations always end.

End this one did. The new millennium had scarcely begun when many of the brokerage community's darlings shed 90 percent and more of their price, amidst margin calls and deflated reputations. The Street's susceptibility to obtuse amnesia was demonstrated once more in what can only be described as a classic crash that took the tech-heavy NAS-DAQ Index down 50 percent.

Classical scholar, womanizer, arbitrageur, and investment philosopher, Ben Graham comes to life in these pages as we realize how relevant his old ideas are in today's "New Economy." In a subsequent chapter, Phalon introduces us to Marty Whitman, who applies with great skill Ben Graham's principles to investing in the twenty-first century.

Had The Street, collectively, been less like the Bourbon Kings, it would have remembered what one of the inventors of growth stock investing, T. Rowe Price, said about growth stocks: "Buy them at an early stage of growth, stick with them as long as earnings are demonstrably on the rise, sell when the growth cycle begins to mature."

Somehow all those tech stock fanatics forgot the "sell" side of T. Rowe Price's advice. That's why they were blindsided when PC sales "suddenly" slowed and Lucent revealed that it had been—if not cooking the books, at least heating them up quite a bit. Price certainly wouldn't have been blindsided by the tech stock disaster. The turn-of-the-twenty-first century tech favorites had their match in the Nifty Fifty growth stocks of the late 1960s and early 1970s. Price correctly identified many of these as true growth stocks but by the time the Nifties collapsed in 1974—some losing 90 percent and more—Price was well out of them. He saw correctly that the kind of stocks he liked to own had become too expensive. The time to sow was past. It was time to reap. A few years before the end came, Price was predicting "a bear market of indeterminate extent and duration." Was he ever right. That bear market didn't end until the Dow Industrials were down 45 percent from their former highs. The bull market didn't resume for a full decade.

In yet another chapter, Phalon visits the Janus Mutual Fund people. For a long time, Tom Bailey and his sidekicks at Janus were careful not to overpay for growth. They were finicky about assuring themselves that the growth was going to continue. But they overplayed their hand amidst a flood of new money attracted by their great success in the earlier stages of the tech bull market.

Cendant sort of rhymes with Lucent. And well it might. Lucent fell through the floor in 2000, shedding nearly 85 percent of its price, a thoroughbred that became a dog. Out went its CEO and down, down, down went its stock after it became apparent that the company had seriously overstated its earnings. The Street was pretty much taken by surprise. This was a great company. And so was Cendant, The Street once thought. In chronicling that onetime Wall Street darling's fall from grace, Phalon reminds us how easy it is, CPAs and the SEC notwithstanding, for unscrupulous or frightened managers to bend the numbers to their wills.

The book abounds in such useful lessons. Should you always sell stocks on bad news? Those who believe in momentum investing would usually say "yes." But history shows that bad news often creates terrific buying opportunities. Just ask Warren Buffett. He made one of his earliest coups by taking a big position at American Express at a time when many professionals feared the company was heading for Chapter XI. Phalon tells that story in intriguing detail.

Hetty Green, "the Witch of Wall Street," was generally loathed in her time as Warren Buffett is esteemed in our time, but in some ways they thought alike. Hetty prided herself on dressing and living frugally and her contempt for fashion extended to stocks. The less fashionable the better. "When I see a thing going cheap because no one wants it," she told an interviewer, "I buy a lot of it and tuck it away. Then when the time comes, they have to hunt me up and pay me a good price for my holdings." However, like Buffett, Green was only interested in unfashionable merchandise of good quality. She simply understood that "price" and "value" aren't the same thing in the short run.

How do you tell the difference between price and value? "Before deciding on an investment I seek out every kind of information about it," Hetty Green liked to say. If that sounds trite, ask yourself: How carefully did I research all the stocks I own?

Talking about doing your homework, Georges Doriot dealt in companies where there wasn't any of the kind of value that Green and Graham sought out. A French-born Harvard Business School professor, he was the father of public venture capital and in many ways the progenitor of the tech stock boom in the 1960s and 1970s. Doriot was interested in start-ups. They had no visible assets. To judge the deal, concentrate on the entrepreneur, Doriot advised. He wasn't interested in people who talked about how much money they could make him. He wanted people who were burning to create a great enterprise. "I view capital gains as a reward for a job well done, not as a goal," Phalon quotes Doriot. "The interesting ideas are research, development, production, and distribution and sales." He wanted intense young people with interesting ideas for whom getting rich was secondary. Familiar advice but recently more honored in the saying than in the selection of IPOs.

Dig into this book and you will learn more about investing and about picking stocks than you could get in a year of listening to the talking heads on TV. The stock market may not repeat itself exactly, but it sure does rhyme.

James W. Michaels
Editor Emeritus
Forbes Magazine

Forbes®
GREATEST
INVESTING STORIES

Ben Graham codified a classic approach to investing. With a few new wrinkles of their own, disciples like Warren Buffett follow it to this day.

CHAPTER 1

Value Avatar

Benjamin Graham

BENJAMIN GRAHAM'S ARRIVAL on Wall Street in that summer of 1914 was not much more than a chance encounter, a light reconnaissance of the world of money. There were no telltales that Graham would live in that world for the next four decades, synthesize a dominant theory of value investing, and in the process create a class of thousands of superinvestors like himself. Among the chief disciples is one-time student and employee Warren Buffett, who graces Graham with the ultimate accolade. Graham, he says, had more influence on him than any man except his father.

Buffett underscored the link through his own son's middle name—Howard Graham Buffett. Among other expressions of filial gratitude, Buffett has unabashedly told fellow Berkshire Hathaway shareholders, "I benefited enormously from the intellectual generosity of Ben Graham, the greatest teacher in the history of finance."

Buffett doesn't burn incense at Graham's shrine simply because he was a nice guy. Graham has been dead for more than three decades now, but there are still uncanny touches of his style in the discipline that has made Buffett and dozens of other disciples very rich men.

What did Graham so lastingly teach this school of brilliant portfolio managers? The simple hardheaded principle that is at the heart of value investing: the need to cut through market prices to reality. When you buy a stock, you are not buying a piece of paper; you're buying part of a business. There is often a huge spread between the "intrinsic value" of the business and the price that a frequently manic stock market is putting on the paper. Buy a stock significantly above intrinsic value and you court a loss. Buy below intrinsic value and you have a good chance of making money over the long haul, with little risk of taking a permanent hit on your capital. The basic bet is that market value and intrinsic value will ultimately converge.

In one of a number of lead articles he wrote for *Forbes*, Graham thought of his strategy as "buying dollar bills for 50¢." It was a strategy that enabled him to survive the bad years of the 1929 crash while others were sinking and it brought him returns of 20 percent or more over many good years.

The touchstone is intrinsic value. How to establish it? Graham, an irrepressible polymath who loved puns, dancing at Fred Astaire studios (mainly for the pulchritude of the female instructors), and Latin verse, worked at refining his formula almost literally to his dying day in 1976 at age 82. First he concentrated on undervalued assets. Then he began working earnings and dividends into his risk/reward equations. His formula in its final form, a distillation to ten critical elements, took shape as Graham's "Last Will & Testament" in the *Forbes* of August 1, 1977 (see box, next page).

The refinements evolved out of his own experience in Wall Street, three decades of teaching at the Columbia Graduate School of Business, and the writing of his multiedition best-sellers, *Security Analysis* and *The Intelligent Investor*.

Graham had little time for the hype and hyperbole of Wall Street. Talking of growth stock fads and high-tech cults shortly before he died, Graham noted that the Bourbon Kings were said "to forget nothing and learn nothing." "Wall Street people," he added, "typically learn nothing and forget everything." It's fashionable in these high-flying days to dismiss Graham as irrelevant. If Graham is irrelevant, so is Warren Buffett.

The education of Ben Graham, Wall Streeter, began that summer in 1914. Graham was 20, a star young graduate and classics scholar who sometimes thought of himself as the wandering Ulysses. He had already turned down flattering but low-paying teaching offers from three different departments at Columbia University. He had missed out on a job touring Europe as an assistant to the high-powered author Norman Angell and had even taken a fling at writing advertising jingles ("There Was a Young Woman from Winona Who Never Had Heard of Carbona").

Ten Points: Ben Graham's Last Will and Testament

In his last years, Ben Graham distilled six decades of experience into ten criteria that would help the intelligent investor pick value stocks from the chaff of the market.

The Ten:

1 An earnings-to-price yield of twice the triple-A bond yield. The earnings yield is the reciprocal of the price earnings ratio.

2 A price/earnings ratio down to four-tenths of the highest average P/E ratio the stock reached in the most recent five years. (Average P/E ratio is the average stock price for a year divided by the earnings for that year.)

3 A dividend yield of two-thirds of the triple-A bond yield.

4 A stock price down to two-thirds of tangible book value per share.

5 A stock price down to two-thirds of net current asset value—current assets less total debt.

6 Total debt less than tangible book value.

7 Current ratio (current assets divided by current liabilities) of two or more.

8 Total debt equal or less than twice the net quick liquidation value as defined in No. 5.

9 Earnings growth over the most recent ten years of seven percent compounded—a doubling of earnings in a ten-year period.

10 Stability of growth in earnings—defined as no more than two declines of five percent or more in year-end earnings over the most recent ten years.

Together, Ben's ten points construct a formidable risk/reward barrier. The first five point to potential reward by pinpointing a low price in relation to such key operating results as earnings. The second five measure risk by measuring financial soundness and stability of earnings.

Backtesting has shown that concentrating on stocks that meet just two or three of these criteria can produce good results. Changing market conditions and business practices (see text) make it unlikely that many stocks will get by these screens, which Graham worked out together with James Rea, an aeronautical engineer. Six years after Graham died, Rea tucked the formula into a mutual fund known as the American Diversified Global Value Fund. Run by Rea's son, James Jr., it turned out to be a clunker.

Now, carrying a recommendation from Columbia Dean Frederick Keppel, Graham was pacing anxiously in front of Trinity Church, waiting for the hands on the steeple clock to creep to 3:10 P.M. That was his cue to cut across the street to 100 Broadway and an after-the-market-close interview for a job as a junior bond salesman with the partners of the New York Stock Exchange firm of Newburger, Henderson & Loeb.

The reception was a bit starchy. Senior partner Alfred Newburger—"Mr. A.N." as he was known in the firm—seemed surprised that Graham, despite a fistful of distinctions in math, English lit, and philosophy, had dropped out of the only economics course he had taken. Graham had whizzed through Columbia on a scholarship in two and a half years, working the while at such odd jobs as a night shift manager for the U.S. Express Co. and peddling cut-rate photograph coupons door-to-door. Graham hurriedly told Mr. A.N. he just hadn't been able to reschedule the economics course, and then demonstrated his practical grasp of the subject by talking up the starting salary on his new job from $10 to $12 a week. "We always start our young men at $10 a week, but in view of your necessities we'll stretch a point and make it $12," Mr. A.N. told the new recruit.

Newburger knew something of Graham's background. Graham's father had died when Ben was nine. The family's prosperous chinaware import business had quickly gone bust in the hands of uncles, bringing a precipitous drop in fortune. A household that had included a cook, a maid, and a French governess had literally become a boarding house, a forlorn last-ditch stab at making ends meet. To Graham's shame, the enterprise failed so badly that even the furniture had to be auctioned off. As the family mathematician, it was 12-year old Ben's job to tally the proceeds room by room, right down to the upright piano that sold for $150.

Ben's "necessities" as Newburger called them, included not only helping with the support of his widowed mother, but such chronic financial emergencies as the failure of a suburban movie house that older brother Leon had bought only a few months before.

Playing to Ben's needs, Mr. A.N. expanded on the opportunities Wall Street might unfold for a young bond salesman with the right stuff. He ended the interview, recalled Ben, with a warning. "If you speculate, young man, you'll lose your money. Always remember that." It was a warning that young Ben took to heart—but only after getting blind-sided a couple of times by his own enthusiasms. When he talked spec-ulation, Mr. A.N. didn't mean the threat of a paper loss. He was talking about getting wiped out.

Learning the business from the ground up—matching buy and sell orders in the back office, swapping checks and stock certificates with other runners—Graham jauntily hung his newly arrived Phi Beta Kappa key to the watch chain across his vest, and went right on working two after-hours jobs. One of them was tutoring army officers' sons on Governors Island; the other teaching English to foreigners at night school.

All told, Ben was bringing in $28 a week—a decent sum in a time when you could buy a workshirt for 75¢ and beef steak for 26¢ a pound. Counting what brothers Leon and Victor earned, there was now enough to move the Grossbaums (the family name was changed after the out-set of World War I) to what Ben in his memoirs describes as the "rather exclusive apartment complex called the Hunts Point Complex." "One of the less desirable five-room apartments," continued Ben, "could be had for a mere $45 a month," only $10 more than the old flat in down-at-the-heels Kelly Street. The move to Hunts Point in the southwest Bronx, then a predominantly Jewish neighborhood graced by fine apartment houses with marquees, uniformed doormen, and tennis courts, was a big step up.

"Imagine with what pride the Grossbaum family took up their abode in this huge and glistening palace. No blasé experience of the past could chill our enthusiasms nor could any deeper wisdom tell our triumphant hearts that all these things were only baubles," recalled Ben. "Dreamy and impractical," he had often fantasized of restoring the family fortunes. Now Graham was savoring the first of many rewards that would come from the trade-off of his university teaching ambitions against a commitment to Wall Street never quite reconciled in his clas-sicist soul.

Working his way out of backoffice chores to a slot in the Newburger bond department, Ben needed no repetition of Mr. A.N.'s warnings on the perils of speculation. He had learned of them at his mother's knee. Mrs. Grossbaum had a small margin account and, among other stocks, had been trading odd lots of U.S. Steel. As a small boy, recalled Ben, he had checked the financial pages to keep tabs on how the stock was doing—knowing just enough "to be glad when the price advanced, and sorry when it was down." His mother's account was wiped out in the panic of 1907, adding to the anxiety Graham often felt when Mrs. Grossbaum sent him to the bank to cash a personal check. "Is Mrs. Grossbaum good for five dollars?" the tellers would whisper.

At Newburger, Henderson & Loeb, Graham was beginning to formulate the crux of his theory of value investing. All investments are tinged with some element of speculation, he thought. The trick was to limit the level of risk. Always look for a margin of safety. Ben's theories did not spring full-blown, like Minerva from the brow of Jupiter. They grew by trial and error—some wins, some fearful losses—and maturation.

Did the family's business misfortunes help to forge Graham's conviction that the margin of safety was the supreme rule of the investment road? At age 20 he had already tasted what for many would have been a lifetime of exiguous bad luck—with plenty more to come.

Take the summer of 1910, spent after graduation from Boys High School in Brooklyn on a hard scrabble dairy farm in upstate New York. Ben was working a 60-hour week, pitching hay, slopping the pigs, mucking out stables. The pay: $10 a month and board. After chores at night, Ben was teaching himself ancient Greek by lantern light, certain that he had won a Pulitzer scholarship that would give him a full four-year ticket through Columbia.

Then came the devastating word. He thought he had sailed through a final interview only to be told that he had not made the cut after all. Graham's fallback was tuition-free City College of New York. CCNY was at its zenith then, tough to get into on merit, a powerhouse of the poor but hugely talented. Graham saw going there after the rejection at socially upscale Columbia as "the acceptance of inferiority, the admission of defeat." He soon dropped out, and drifted through a couple of monotonous assembly-line jobs, easing the tedium by reciting to himself passages from the *Rubaiyat* and the *Aeneid*.

Then came a stunning note from Columbia's Dean Keppel. Through some administrative mix-up, Ben's name had been confused with that of cousin, Louis Grossbaum, who already had a Pulitzer. Ben's award, with inexorable bureaucratic logic, had gone to the next person in line. "But I've lost a whole year," Ben told Dean Keppel. Then, characteristically, he set about cramming for placement exams that enabled him to catch up on lost time and then some.

Thus, by the time he had nodded acquiescence to Mr. A.N.'s caution on speculation, two elements of young Ben's nascent theory of value investing were already in place: Anticipate the unexpected; prepare for it with rigorous study.

In spare moments at Newburger, Ben set about memorizing descriptions of the bonds on the firm's recommended list, jotting them down in a loose-leaf notebook. What was at first an indistinguishable blur of items like "Atchison, Topeka and Santa Fe General 4s, Due 1995" settled into a pattern that made Ben something of a walking manual on railroad securities.

He began looking for deeper patterns behind the raw numbers, a challenging task in a time when companies were only reluctantly beginning to disclose at least window dressing on their operations, and stock prices were more often as not a product of rumor and manipulation.

One of Ben's early reports—an analysis showing that Missouri Pacific Railroad bonds had slipped below investment grade—was so penetrating that it drew a job offer from a competing brokerage firm. Newburger preempted the bid by raising the upstart's pay from $12 to $18 a week. He was shifted out of bond sales (where he'd generated very little in commissions) and breveted the firm's first "statistician" (i.e., a security analyst).

Ben never did cotton to the sales side of the business. The upgrade did so much for his confidence levels that he for a time affected a walking stick. Though cautious, Graham was by no means risk averse, and quite willing to take a flutter on his own recommendations.

At one point, he projected improving earnings for the Missouri, Kansas & Texas Railroad. The stock seemed cheap at $12 a share. Ben went into a joint account with one of Newburger's customers men on 100 shares and was showing a small profit when authority intervened in the person of Mr. A.N. ("He seemed to know everything about everybody in the firm," recalled Ben.) Newburger ordered Ben to unwind the deal and chewed him out.

"If you are going to speculate in something, you should have better sense than to pick a run-down, no good road like the M.K.T." It was another lesson in the need for rigorous analysis. Mr. A.N. had taken a hard look at the interest coverage on the road's bonds. Graham hadn't, distracted for the moment by what proved to be only a temporary (and suspiciously fortuitous) bulge in the M.K.T.'s profits.

In the end, Mr. A.N. was right, but so was Ben. The M.K.T. did indeed flounder into bankruptcy, but the Newburger firm made good money on a new piece of Graham analysis. On his suggestion, it bought stock at 50¢ a share that on the road's reorganization brought new stock worth twice as much.

The M.K.T. call launched Ben's career as a risk arbitrageur—a pursuit requiring a quick mathematical turn of mind, and an eye keen enough to distinguish two discrete bits of information: market price on the one hand and underlying value on the other.

Ben's first big such hit lay in the perception that the market was grossly underpricing the liquidation of the Guggenheim Exploration Company. It owned major interests in four Big Board–traded mining companies. As reconstructed by colleague (and fellow superinvestor) Irving Kahn in a study for the Financial Analysts Research Foundation, Guggenheim's going-out-of-business arithmetic looked like this: Each share of the holding company would receive .7277 shares of Kennecott Copper; .1172 shares of Chino Copper; .0833 shares of American Smelting; and .185 shares of Ray Consolidated Copper.

All told, the package carried a market value of $76.23. Guggenheim Exploration, on the other hand, was selling at a bargain $68.88. Ben recommended that Newburger simultaneously sell the pieces and buy Guggenheim for a clear gross profit of $7.35 a share.

The spread was there because of the risks: Shareholders might turn down the deal in the three months before it was scheduled to fall into place; the deal might get tied up in litigation or some regulatory hang-up; prices on the small pieces might rise sharply before they were distributed to Guggenheim holders, thereby wiping out the profit spread. Ben had assessed the dangers and decided they weren't substantial. Ben was right and won himself another raise. On the strength of the Guggenheim coup, he began to develop a personal following and a deepening sense of value investing: *When you spot intrinsic value at a discount, go for it!* Ben's margin of safety: the strong likelihood that Guggenheim would trade up to the value of the pieces.

Among his new followers was Algernon Tassin, one of Ben's favorite professors at Columbia. Tassin put his lifesavings—about $10,000 in blue-chip utility stocks—into a joint account. Ben would run the book; profits and losses would be split 50-50. Ben's reputation was anchored in the idea that he had tamed speculation. There was risk, but you weren't betting on some vague evanescent turn in the market to make you rich. You were buying a piece of hidden value the market would recognize soon or late and price accordingly.

The Tassin account was doing well, but much else was on the boil. The United States had entered World War I. British-born Ben—the family had emigrated from London to New York when he was little more than a year old—tried to enlist in Officers Candidate School. Turned down because he wasn't a U.S. citizen, Ben did manage to gate-crash a New York Guard outfit. He was also settling into marriage with Hazel Mazur, a sweet but assertive elocution and dance teacher he had met when double-dating with brother Leon.

Reciprocally enough, Ben was financing a new venture of Leon's (he of the movie house failure). This involved the purchase of the Broadway Phonograph Shop, located uptown at Broadway & 98th St. The cost, about $7,000, had come out of Ben's share of the profits of the Tassin account. The record shop failed to live up to its promise. Unfortunately for Ben, its swan song coincided with a sharp peace scare sell-off in the stock market.

The peace scare—a flash that the Germans were about to surrender—was a hiccup typical of runaway bull markets. Traders glorying in war-driven prices had no confidence in the underlying economy.

In its full dimension, Ben's value theory holds that safety-minded investors (as distinguished from speculators) should shift proportionately more money out of stocks and into bonds as equity prices boom. The point is to be able to get back into stocks when bear market bargains reappear. Ordinarily, Ben would have been buying as peace scare prices fell. But with all his cash tied up in Broadway Phonograph and its Vocalion brand record inventories, he was in a liquidity bind. He had no buying power. Worse yet, he couldn't meet margin calls on the money borrowed to leverage the Tassin account.

To cover the calls, he was forced to sell of some of his old professor's treasured blue chip, American Light & Traction stock.

In his memoirs, Graham recalls wandering the Financial District in bleak despair: "I had a debt to the account which I could not repay; what was worse . . . My management of Tassin's capital had failed abjectly."

The old tutor stuck with Ben, though it was almost two years before he was fully repaid at the rate of $60 a month—all Ben could afford. What comes around goes around. Tassin's continuing trust in Ben made him a rich man. And Ben, who subsequently bought a substantial piece of a bankrupt Aeolian Company preferred stock at distress prices, finally managed to squeeze a profit out of the record business. The Tassin failure burned, though. And while it made him much more conservative about borrowing money, Ben was about to get another lesson in humility that reinforced the innate caution of his still evolving market strategy.

A friend arranged for Ben to be let in on the ground floor of a heavily promoted new issue for an outfit called Savold Tire. The draw was high-tech stuff: Savold's revolutionary new process for retreading automobile tires. The stock opened at 10 and zipped to 35. Within a week, recalled Graham, his initial stake of $5,000 brought a check for three times that amount.

Graham clamored for more, getting himself and friends in for $20,000 on a Savold affiliate floated four weeks later. Inside price: $20. The stock opened at $50, and Graham celebrated his twenty-fifth birthday in a "blaze of excitement": a check for the original contribution, plus some 150 percent in profits.

Disappointingly, Graham and his friends were shut out of the next Savold offer. Sorry, just not enough stock to go 'round, Ben was told. Then came the good word—yet another affiliate was about to hit The Street. Last call! Graham quickly put together $60,000, half of it anted up by three friends, and got ready to pop the champagne on another smash debut.

The offering didn't go off as scheduled. Administrative delays, Ben was told. Anxious days went by. Then, like a puff of smoke, bids on all the Savold companies totally disappeared in the raucous outcry of the old outdoor Curb Market.

The only thing real about these will-o'-the-wisps, reckoned a chastened Graham, was the big electric sign that appeared over Columbus Circle, "as if by magic," soon after the first stock offering. It flashed "Save," then "Old," and then "Savold." Stunned by his own cupidity, Graham took the pledge. Moral: Late bull market IPOs are all part of the high-octane speculative environment. The game hasn't changed very much.

Generations of hot new issues have come to market since Savold, pushed to "levels little short of insane," wrote Ben, only to collapse in very short order. Today's promotional techniques may be different—Internet chat rooms instead of neon signs over Columbus Circle—but the results are the same. Dozens of hotshot dot-coms have vaporized with attrition rates that make it plain you can do better at the blackjack table.

Ben, at least, had direct recourse. He ultimately collared the promoter and succeeded in squeezing out of him about 30¢ on every dollar that had been plunged on the last Savold offer. A chagrined Graham had done no homework on the issue—a lamentable breach of the advice handed down in a series of pamphlets ("Lessons for Investors") he had been writing for Newburger clients. Graham had put heavy emphasis in the pamphlets on the need to search for intrinsic value priced well below the market. Don't follow the crowd, he preached.

This was pretty cocky stuff coming from a "statistician" of less than a decade's standing on The Street, but Graham had backed his rhetoric with a rare talent for sniffing out value. In recognition, he'd been elevated to junior partner, with a modest share of the Newburger profits. His arbitrage operations had expanded to the point where they were absorbing more capital than Mr. A.N. wanted to divert from the firm's highly profitable margin business.

The impasse was resolved when Ben, just nine years after he had talked his way into a $12 a week starting salary, turned independent money manager. He kept his office at Newburger and continued to trade through the firm, but had signed on to run a $250,000 account for a group of well-to-do clients who were principals in a thriving raincoat business. Ben's end of the deal: a salary of $10,000 a year and 20 percent of the profits after a minimum 6 percent return on the clients' money.

Ben quickly covered the 6 percent bogey with underpriced finds like DuPont. DuPont then held a huge stake in General Motors. Pierre du Pont, in fact, the patriarch of the family, was about to become head of the automaker. Each share of DuPont was backed by seven shares of GM—precisely the value a grossly inefficient market was putting on the stock. A sharp trader could buy DuPont for the price of its GM stock alone, in effect, getting the combine's fast growing chemicals business for nothing. Graham seized on the spread with an elegant turn of the math—buy DuPont, sell short seven times as many shares of GM against it. When the market finally caught up with imbalance, Graham profited by selling DuPont and covering his short position in GM.

Latter day macro hedge funds, such as the notoriously ailing Long Term Capital Management LP, nearly swamped by heavy leverage and sophisticated mathematical formulas that misfired, could have benefited from Ben's plain-vanilla approach.

By 1926, Ben's reputation as a value player and the runaway bull market had brought new affluence to the young Grahams. There were three children now, and a spacious apartment at 86th St. and Riverside Drive, in a neighborhood that to Ben "spoke of financial success." The family summered in the carefully manicured enclave of Deal, on the New Jersey shore, and Ben began to take squash and golf lessons at the City Athletic Club.

The new affluence was a direct result of the under-valued situations Ben continued to dig up, sometimes almost by sixth sense. Working with $450,000 in capital now, much of it his own, Graham was winnowing through an Interstate Commerce Commission annual report on railroads one day when he did a double take on a footnote reference to a group of pipeline companies.

Graham was soon on a train to Washington, D.C. In the records room of the ICC, he requested documents he hadn't known existed before spotting the footnote reference in some of the pipeline financials.

Eight of these pipelines had come out of the breakup of the Standard Oil Company in 1911. Their job was to move crude oil from the wellheads to the refineries. Tankers had taken over much of their business and Wall Street was paying them little attention, as evidenced by the junk bond–like nine percent yield on Northern Pipeline Company common stock.

Dividend payout had already been cut some, and the yield was signaling that Wall Street expected still more trouble ahead. The mingy one-line income statement the pipelines made public did little to dispel this apprehension.

Sifting through the full balance sheets he found on file at the ICC— documents other "statisticians" had missed—Ben made a startling discovery. The pipelines were loaded with prime railroad bonds, which in the case of Northern Pipeline amounted to about $95 a share. The stock was selling at $65 and paying a $6 dividend. Ben began nibbling at the stock and slowly acquired 2,000 shares, making him and his partners in the Graham Joint Account the biggest holders of record after the Rockefeller Foundation.

Ben confronted the Standard Oil management with the unwelcome idea that all this surplus capital clearly not needed in the business ought to be distributed to shareholders. Not surprisingly, he was told to get lost and smothered in Robert's Rules of Order when he tried to make his point heard at an annual meeting.

Ben responded by buying up much more of Northern than his partnership could afford. He began lobbying other stockholders, and succeeded in getting himself elected to the board—something no outsider had ever managed to do before. It took two years, and some behind-the-scenes nudging by the puissant Rockefeller Foundation, but a restructuring finally brought Ben and his followers total value of about $110 on their shares. Ben's forte of rigorous research had once again carried the day. Ben didn't particularly like being portrayed as a self-serving outsider in the pipeline struggle—a "raider"—but he had learned another important lesson. It is one thing to perceive value; often another to capitalize on it.

The value of the Graham Joint Account was approaching $2.5 million, much of it reflecting Ben's reinvested profits. Some new money had come from fellow Boys High and Columbia grad Jerome Newman. Newman, a shrewd negotiator and businessman, was beginning to play Mr. Outside to Ben's cerebral Mr. Inside in a partnership destined to last more than 30 years.

Ben was sharing some of his investment ideas with Big Names. One of them was mover and shaker Bernard Baruch, who rather condescendingly (Ben thought) offered Graham a junior partnership. Ben was happy to be able to turn him down. The stocks that Baruch got aboard were typical Graham picks. They were rather stodgy solid franchises like Pepperell Manufacturing (sheets and pillowcases) and Heywood & Wakefield (baby carriages), selling well below going business value, ignored in the great bull market rush for glamour items like Radio Corporation.

Though still able to cherry pick values, Graham was certain a grossly overpriced market was riding for a fall—a point sounded often in the once-a-week, two-hour-long security analysis classes he had begun to teach at the Columbia Business School.

Ben had been talking about writing a book on security analysis for some time now and thought that preparing a lecture series would help him put one together. Ben's classes were liberally salted with Wall Street professionals, who happily swapped market tips. The classes focused on current market case studies (Pepperell Manufacturing, for one) and were wildly popular. As the market mounted to its 1929 peak, more than 150 students were absorbing the Graham keys to income statements and balance sheets, with particular emphasis on the ambiguities of corporate accounting practices.

The Graham family affluence was mounting, too. This was evidenced by the ten-year lease (at $11,000 a year) Ben had signed on a new duplex with a great view of Central Park. The domestic staff included a valet-butler whose duties included a daily massage for the master of the house. The new affluence was little solace for the loss of first-born son Isaac Newton, who died of meningitis at age eight— roughly Ben's age when his own father had died.

There was still pain 40 years later in Ben's recollection of the child's death. A new son would soon be born, but the marriage with Hazel was beginning to unravel. As to the book, Ben was about to live through a market chapter that would provide him with plenty of new material. It was 1929, and the excesses of the great bull market were coming home to roost.

After a spectacular 1928 (up 60 percent versus 51 percent for the Dow Jones Industrials), Ben had come into 1929 with what he thought was a cautiously hedged position—about $2.5 million in convertible preferred stock offset by a short position in an equal amount of common stocks. If the market dropped, the common would fall faster than the preferred and Graham could close out the hedge with a profit.

In addition, he was carrying common stocks with a market value of about $4.5 million on borrowed money—margin of about $2 million. By the standards of the day (you could buy stock with as little as 10 percent down) Graham was looking at the world from behind what seemed to be a solid bulkhead. The painful memory of unmanageable debt in the Tassin account was never far from his mind. The waves of Black Tuesday, however (October 29, 1929), struck with unprecedented ferocity. Some $14 billion in market value got wiped out on huge volume.

With the ticker running hours behind trades on the floor, prices were mainly guesswork. Exhausted clerks were catnapping nights in the office in a vain effort to keep the paperwork abreast of the flood. Peak to trough, the Dow Jones Industrials in 1929 sank from a wonderful nonsense 380 to under 200. Graham made money on the short side of the market, but still came out of the year with a 20 percent loss. The licking he took in 1930 was even worse—50 percent (versus 29 percent for the Dow Jones Industrials). Ben was struggling to pay down debt and at the same time hold on to stocks he saw as having solid potential.

He was in double jeopardy. Though he and partner Jerry Newman valiantly continued to pay quarterly distributions of 1 1/4 percent out of their own capital, the return was not enough to keep partners with troubles of their own from pulling money out of the account. The only injection of new money—a heartening gesture and ultimately a highly profitable piece of bottom fishing—came from Jerry Newman's father-in-law. By the end of 1932, the fund was down to less than 25 percent of the $2.5 million with which it had entered 1929. Fearful that the losses would never end, sick that he had failed friends and family, Ben wrote a poem that asked:

Where shall he sleep whose soul knows no rest
Poor hunted stag in wild woods of care?

Though haunted by uncertainty, Ben had actually done amazingly well. From the depths of the 50 percent loss in 1930, he was down only 16 percent in 1931 (versus minus 48 percent for the Dow Jones Industrials) and down only three percent (versus minus 17 percent DJIs) in 1932. Ben was battered but alive. If Graham had done as badly as the market as a whole, he would have been wiped out. His margin of safety: relatively conservative borrowing, a cautiously hedged position that produced major profits on the downside.

Still a lot better off than he had been 10 years before, Ben began to retrench. "The crash reaffirmed parsimonious viewpoints and habits that had been ingrained in me by the tight financial situation of my early youth," he recalled in his memoirs. The duplex was rented (though not at the full rate) to a member of the Neiman-Marcus retailing family; the ten-year lease wiggled out of at some modest penalty; and the Graham family resettled in the cheaper if not exactly low-rent quarters of the El Dorado at 91st Street and Central Park West. The domestic staff was cut and Ben's mother was asked to give up the car and driver he was providing.

On the business side, the partners wrung a settlement from underwriters who had sold them bonds on a zinc mine whose earnings had been outrageously inflated in the prospectus. As major holders of Universal Pictures eight percent preferred, they even confronted Max Laemmle, president and founder of the movie maker. Universal had stopped paying dividends, the preferred had dropped to 30¢ on the dollar, and where the hell did Laemmle get off, paying himself three thousand smackers a week while stockholders were doing without?

The ploy didn't work, but it was a measure of how desperate Graham was to pay off margin debt and get the account back into the black. Both were a must, since his own compensation was keyed to a percentage of the profits. Worse yet, he and Newman were entitled to no money at all until all the capital losses were made up.

The agreement was later modified, but Ben had to scurry for other sources of cash. He got serious about the book, hiring young David Dodd, a former student at Columbia, to help with the research, and stepped up his outside writing. A series of three articles for *Forbes* summed up what he had learned from the Great Crash.

The *Forbes* pieces packed into one explosive kernel everything that was to make Ben Graham's reputation as the Von Clausewitz of value investing. They were at the core of the strategy that made his open-end mutual fund, Graham Newman Corporation, a star performer for three decades. Their findings were at the heart of his best-selling books, *Security Analysis* and *The Intelligent Investor*. The *Forbes* series also helped to showcase the extraordinary quality of the training he gave three generations of up-and-coming money managers at the Columbia Business School, including such reigning Grahamites as Warren Buffett and the Sequoia Fund's Bill Ruane.

Ben's intuitive sense of value right along had focused on such great finds as Guggenheim Exploration and Northern Pipeline—situations where he spotted underlying riches at well below market prices.

Graham had to work hard to dig up ten strikes like those. Now, suddenly, after the Great Crash that had put him in such hot water, value was everywhere and going begging. Ben set a cadre of his students to matching market prices and values for all 600 industrials listed on the

New York Stock Exchange. This was foot slogging work in the pre-calculator, pre-computer age, but the results were startling: One out of every three of the 600 could be bought for less than net working capital. More than 50 were selling for less than the cash (and marketable securities) they had in the bank.

Montgomery Ward, for example, was trading for less than half of net quick assets. For $6.50 a share, you got $16 in working capital and the whole of this great retailing franchise—catalog business and all—for nothing. With issues like American Car & Foundry and Munsinger, $20 and $11 would bring $50 a share and $17 a share, respectively, in cash alone. The rest of the businesses—bricks, mortar, machinery, customers, and profits—was a free ride.

It was clear "that in the best judgement of Wall Street, these businesses are worth more dead than alive," Ben told *Forbes* readers. Liquidated in a private sale, they would at least fetch working capital, which was a lot more than what they were bringing on the floor of the New York Stock Exchange.

Yes, there was a bear market. Busted booms, continued Ben, always bring "unduly low prices." There had been a bear market in 1921, too, "but with respect to cash assets alone, present prices are relatively six times lower" than in the deep sell of eight years earlier.

Ben's students' research showed that corporate operating results were not "materially poorer," so why weren't investors stepping up to the plate on these bargains? "50 Cents on the Dollar," read the *Forbes* headline. Why were they selling out for a fraction of such real values as cash in the till?

Good question. It is a question—yet another of the many parallels in their lives—that Warren Buffett raised in *Forbes* 40 years later after go-go stocks cratered in the sell-off of 1973–1974. Prices were so low that Buffett felt "like an oversexed guy in a harem." "This is the time to start investing," he told *Forbes* readers. You had to be patient and wait for buying times like these, he added, echoing the value precepts of his mentor Ben Graham. "You're dealing with a lot of silly people in the marketplace; it's like a great big casino and everyone else is boozing. If you can stick with Pepsi, you should be OK."

Prices soon took off in one of the sharpest rallies ever, but Buffett was back in *Forbes* again five years later, preaching Grahamisms to pension managers in yet another sell-off. Why were they stampeding into bonds, asked Buffett, instead of bargain-basement equities "aggregating book value or less?"

His answer was not very different from Graham's take on the Great Crash 50 years earlier. Graham's diagnosis: The "new era madness" of 1928–1929 had brought deep psychological changes in the "proverbially weak" logic of Wall Street. Investors who used to routinely screen values in terms of balance sheet numbers had been carried away by the "excessive emphasis being laid" on reported or much ballyhooed antici-pated earnings. Lost in the bull rush was the idea that rising earnings might be only a temporary one shot, or even deceptive, thanks to "purely arbitrary differences in accounting methods." "The opportunities for downright crookedness are legion, nor are they ignored," wrote Graham.

Among the prime examples: a Big Board company that had "turned an operating loss into a profit by the simple expedient of marking up its goodwill and adding the difference to earnings, without bothering to mention this little detail."

Apparently, continued Ben, management "not unreasonably" reck-oned a market besotted with rising earnings would never "examine the balance sheets closely enough to detect their charming artifice."

The environment was so superheated that "a mere $1 increase in profits, from $4 to $5 a share, raised the value of a stock from 40 to 75, on the joyous assumption that an upward trend had been established which justified a multiple of 15 instead of 10," Graham told *Forbes* readers. "The basis of calculating value thus became arbitrary and mainly psychological, with the result that everyone felt free to gamble unrestrainedly under the respectable title of 'investment.'"

If this Grahamism sounds as though it could have been lifted straight from *Forbes* 2001 instead of *Forbes* 1932, it's because Ben had a grip on some timeless truths. Yes, earnings are important, but they should be taken into account with a jaundiced eye. As Ben saw it, the best guide to "real value" was net current assets. Without too much to worry about on the downside, you could afford to wait for earnings to build. Research for the *Forbes* series helped to sharpen this perception. "Sub-asset" bar-gains, many snapped up for as little as two-thirds of working capital, became a major element in the investment mix of what was now the publicly traded investment company, Graham Newman Corporation.

Ben focused mainly on secondary companies with solid past records—stocks that for one reason or another, he wrote, had "no charm for the public." In bear markets, the bargains did less well than some of the hedges and liquidations Ben pursued, but the long-term record is an enviable one.

At well below market risk levels, Graham Newman, betweeen 1948 and its liquidation in 1956, delivered shareholders an average annual appreciation of 11.4 percent. A round lot (100 shares) of Graham Newman, bought for $11,413 at the beginning of 1948 was worth $70,400 when the fund closed shop. A similar investment in the Standard & Poor's 500 stock average would have returned only $30,968.

Those returns do not take into account the peak gains of a master stroke—the buyout of a 50 percent stake in a special situation that literally just walked in the door. Government Employees Insurance Corporation, had been founded a dozen years before by Leo Goodwin, Sr., a Fort Worth accountant with a deceptively simple idea: Cut out the middle man. The concept was to sell auto insurance by direct mail to a select low-risk group (first to the military and then government employees generally). Bypassing the standard agency structure gave the company a competitive edge in low rates. By 1948, GEICO had grown from a Mom 'n Pop operation into one turning good profits on about $3 million in premiums. The one drawback was that Goodwin and his family owned only 25 percent of the company. Their majority owners wanted to cash in on success while it was there for the grasping.

The day he walked into Ben's office, attorney David Kreeger had for a while been trying—with no success—to place a chunk of the controlling stock in sympathetic hands. Ben Graham and Jerry Newman sensed potential, but worried about risk. The asking price seemed fair enough in terms of earning power and assets, but there was a serious question of exposure. Half the company would cost about $720,000—nearly a quarter of Graham Newman's assets. For a strategy built around broad diversification—Ben's stake in bargain issues was spread over dozens of companies—GEICO would mean a drastic change in style.

It was a gutsy call. The GEICO stock was spun off to Graham Newman stockholders on a share-for-share basis at a value of around $27 a share. As GEICO powered its way to rank among the top five auto underwriters in the country, the Graham Newman shares rose to the equivalent of $54,000 a share.

Among the early stage buyers: one of Ben's students, 21-year-old Warren Buffett. Following his master's dictate of rigorous research, as part of a paper he was doing, Buffett journeyed to GEICO's Washington D.C. office on a Saturday afternoon. The janitor sent him up to talk to the only other person in the office that day—investment officer (and subsequent chief executive) Lorimar Davidson. The two chatted for five hours and Buffett came away a believer. He popped about three-quarters of his $9,000 net worth into the stock and sold a year or two later for a 50 percent profit.

It was clearly love at first sight. In 1976, after Ben had retired as chairman, GEICO had over-expanded pell-mell to the edge of bankruptcy. Over the next five years, in yet another demonstration of his own bargain hunting skills, Buffett put more than $47 million into the company. Ultimately tucked into Berkshire Hathaway, GEICO now boasts assets of more than $9 billion.

Ben Graham's call on GEICO brought in more than the total of all his other investments. It was a call that broke some of his own long-standing investment rules and left Graham with somewhat ambivalent feelings. The moral? "There are several different ways to make and keep money in Wall Street," he wrote.

Ben's record demonstrates that one of the best and least risky ways to make money in Wall Street is to focus on cheap assets. Is this a formula for all seasons? Ben had no difficulty finding working capital values from the Depression 1930s into the mid-1950s—a long enough period to validate the idea that there was good money to be made in focusing on assets.

Ben himself conceded there would be times when bargains would be scarce, and that the conservative investor could be left on the sidelines of a raging bull market. That's okay with Warren Buffett. "Sometimes it's a good idea to go to the beach," he says. It's a reminder that Buffett himself sat on the sidelines for a while after liquidating his partnership in 1969, precisely because he felt prices were out of sync with the value discipline.

From the mid-1950s on, as pension and mutual fund money sluiced into stocks, bargains got thinner on the ground. There were, of course,

those market breaks that left Warren Buffett feeling so oversexed—
opportunities when 20 or more sub-asset plays could be cherry picked
on the New York Stock Exchange alone. Buffett seems certain that the
New Paradigm of the 1990s has not legislated those opportunities out
of existence. Not long ago he told shareholders "When the market
plummets—as it will from time to time—neither panic nor mourn. It's
good news for Berkshire." And so it has been.

Ben himself rarely tried to push profits, cautiously selling (except
for GEICO) when he saw a 50 percent profit.

As Buffett notes, Graham had no real intensity for money. Truly a clas-
sicist, his deepest satisfactions were intellectual—working the numbers,
watching them come out. Graham Newman liquidated largely because
Ben was no longer feeling challenged.

He had married again (for the third time), started a new family,
moved to Beverly Hills and began teaching at the UCLA Graduate
School of Business in a tenure that lasted 15 years. He tinkered with
inventing an improved version of the slide rule, translated a favorite
novel from Spanish, and continued to refine his value strategies
through successive editions of his books.

Ben began to focus more on earnings and dividends than assets. As
published in *Forbes*, the new look was designed as a handy pocket tool for
the average investor and produced superior results for five of the six ten-
year market periods that Graham matched it against (see box, page 3).

More recent—if limited—backtesting comes from Henry R. Oppenheimer, professor of finance at the State University of New York,
Binghampton. Tracking the years from 1974 to 1981 in an article for the
Financial Analysts Journal, Oppenheimer found that stocks picked on
the basis of two or three of Ben's criteria would have brought mean
annual returns of at least 26 percent. That was double the 14 percent
return on an index of Big Board and American Stock Exchange issues.

Graham's risk reward screens are so demanding it's often hard to
find companies that meet more than a few of his criteria. Changes in
business practices—a switch from high-dividend payouts to open market stock buy-backs, for example—have altered the relationship that
Graham liked to see between stock and bond yields.

Other criteria have withstood the test of time. Minimum earnings
growth and stability are certainly two of the hurdles any stock should

clear before making the buy list. And while you may not be able to find any discounts at the moment, Graham's tests will help you determine whether the price you are being asked to pay is within reasonably conservative parameters or totally out of sight. As Mr. A.N. warned, "If you speculate, young man, you'll lose your money."

Graham was more than just a number cruncher. His shrewd insight into emotional swings in the marketplace anticipated by decades what behavioral psychologists are only now documenting: Investors tend to overreact on both good and bad news.

Take "Mr. Market," a tongue-in-cheek construct designed to help investors keep the foibles of price movements in perspective. This obliging character of Ben's stands ready every minute of the trading day to tell you what your piece of the business is worth and "offers either to buy you out or sell you an additional interest on that basis." Sometimes Mr. Market is plausible enough in terms of fundamentals. Other times he is manic—"his enthusiasm or his fears run away with him and the values he proposes seem little short of silly," said Ben.

Why let Mr. Market's emotional swings determine your view of value? asks Graham. You might be happy to sell to him if his quote is "ridiculously high, or buy if his quote is low." But to do so simply because of what the voluble Mr. Market seems to be signaling is a losing game. Better to filter out the noise and concentrate on basics like operating results.

Value investors by definition are contrarians, but that doesn't mean the canon is frozen in time. Look at how differences in master/protégé style have evolved. Buffett's search for under-valued assets has turned to intangibles like brand names and franchises—potential Ben Graham would have dismissed as just so much overpriced good will.

When Buffett first bought into Coca-Cola Company and the Gillette Company a decade ago, he did so at what were for him uncommonly rich multiples. His assessment was that the companies' global reach was an unassailable competitive edge that would keep earnings growing well into the future. Monopoly positions have value, too—hence Buffett's investment in newspapers like the *Washington Post* and the *Buffalo Evening News*. The applications may be new (as were the changes Ben brought in his day), but the search for value at a discount is a constant.

There are other generational differences. With the notable exception of GEICO, where he served as chairman, Graham tended to look on companies as abstractions. Buffett gets deeper into them as businesses, in many cases first buying pieces of them—as if for a laboratory sample—and then snapping up the rest.

Growing stylistic nuance hasn't dimmed Graham's legacy. One of his lasting bequests is the tradition of rigorous research. Ben's doggedness in digging out documents on the Northern Pipeline rail bond holdings, for example, is mirrored in Buffett's Saturday descent on the GEICO janitor, or his counting chemical tank car shipments to get a line on sales of gasoline additive sales.

Graham himself thought all he had learned in six decades of tracking the market could be summed up in three words: margin of safety. The concept got lost—to considerable pain—in the super-heated environment of the last several years. Off-the-chart prices can be justified only if everything in an unpredictable future goes exactly right. By Graham's standards, the margin of safety on runaway stocks can be measured only in imaginary numbers.

The margin of safety is really a comfort factor—the idea is to cut some slack against such X-factors as bad judgement, bad luck, and the unpredictables always lurking around the corner. In an era of lower market multiples and interest rates, comfort factors were easier to come by. To cite one of Ben's examples, a more or less typical stock would be selling at an earnings yield of nine percent—the reciprocal of a price earnings ratio of 11. With high-quality bond yields at four percent, you had a margin of five percent going for you. Compounding the margin over a long-term investment in a company with reasonably predictably earning power, you would likely have no trouble sleeping nights.

This Grahamesque exercise remains a useful tool. It won't generate comfort levels of anything like five percent, but will nonetheless provide a realistic measure of the depth of the waters you're about to plunge into.

The touchstone is still intrinsic value—the discounted present value of the cash that can be taken out of a company over an investment period of a decade or so. Buy below intrinsic value, and you've got a margin of safety. Buy above it, and you may be looking for trouble.

Central value asks questions like: What is this company worth as a going business? How much have other companies like it sold for? What would it go for in a liquidation? Value-oriented outfits like the Legg Mason Value Fund routinely do such analyses. They start with a sophisticated sense of both a company's potential earning power and a realistic discount factor. Though the term has an air of permanence, intrinsic value is a horseback estimate, varying with interest rates and the fudge factors of the people making the estimates.

Buffett, for example, won't touch high-tech stocks with a barge pole. Famously, he says he won't invest in companies he doesn't understand. Neither—not coincidentally—will he invest in companies that do not yield "a reasonably predictable earnings pattern a decade or more out."

Some value players who have ventured into high-tech stocks like America Online (AOL), usually at bad-news prices, have done so by cranking very high safety rates into the equation. William H. Miller, III, for example, a portfolio manager for Legg Mason's Value Trust, for a time tacked a 30 percent discount on AOL—about three times the rate he put on IBM.

In short, the margin of safety lies in minimizing business risk. For value players like O. Mason Hawkins and G. Staley Cates, chairman and president, respectively of the Memphis, Tennessee-based Longleaf Funds, that means looking for such competitive edges as low costs, entrenched brand names, and dominant market share.

You need to measure financial strength, too—low debt levels, limited liabilities, and plenty of free cash flow reinvested at high margins. The trick, of course, is to find at least some of these attributes in a package selling well under the market.

It can be done. In his noted essay on the "Superinvestors of Graham-and-Doddsville," commemorating the fiftieth anniversary of the publication of *Security Analysis*, Buffet cites the amazingly consistent performance of nine of Graham's former students and intellectual heirs. Besides his own sterling numbers, Buffett puts up for inspection the records of such well-known Grahamites as Sequoia Fund's Bill

Ruane, and Tom Knapp and Ed Anderson (who founded the money management firm of Tweedy Browne Partners). Their styles differ somewhat, but they all adhere to yet another of Ben Graham's tenets, a paraphrase of Spinoza: Value is best approached from the viewpoint of calamity.

Marty Whitman, sometime "Vulture Investor," likes nothing better than combing the wreckage of the bankruptcy courts in search of the low-risk bargains that are his trademark.

CHAPTER 2

Value with a Difference

Marty Whitman

"OF COURSE I'M DIFFERENT. I know I'm different."
That's the combative Martin J. (for Jacob) Whitman speaking.
As a guy who runs some $2 billion of other people's money with one of
the most eclectic value strategies in the business, Whitman makes quite
a point of differentiating himself from the Wall Street mainstream.

No Savile Row tailoring or maundering over efficient market theories here. This is the plain, unvarnished Marty Whitman. What you see
is what you get. Slouched in an armchair, sneakered feet crossed on a
glass-topped coffee table, Whitman is in his customary office casual—
plaid flannel shirt open at the neck; blue, mail-order corduroy jeans just
a few miles short of fraying at the knees.

Whitman's office overlooking Third Avenue is chock-a-block with
such treasures as a bronzed bear copulating with a bull. Significantly,
there is nowhere in sight that most common artifact of Wall Street environment, the manic flicker of a stock market monitor.

Whitman's laid-back air can be read as a political statement. It goes
with his conviction that Wall Street fixation on such supposed predic-
tives as the higher economics, investor psychology, and short-term
earnings swings is just so much noise. "We don't carry a lot of excess
baggage," he says in the flatted vowels of his native Bronx. "A lot of
what Wall Street does has nothing to do with the underlying value of a
business. We deal in probabilities, not predictions."

Like Warren Buffett and other spiritual heirs of Dr. Value himself,
Benjamin Graham, Whitman aims to buy "safe and cheap." Basically,
that means buying assets and earnings at a discount. Typically, value and
growth stocks outrun the market at different phases of the economic

cycle. Value stocks (think low prices to earnings and book value) tend to outperform in periods of no to slow expansion. Growth stocks (think fast rising earnings, high price earnings ratios) tend to outperform when the economy is on the move.

Whitman, in the main, breaks the mold. His Manhattan-based Third Avenue Fund did lag the market in the final stages of the now busted great growth stock craze, but over the last decade he nonetheless managed to crank out an average annual return of 19 percent—a point above the market, with a third less volatility.

The record entitles him to argue that "There are only two kinds of passive investing, value investing and speculative excess." "For the last two years, like 1928–1929 and 1972–1972," continues Whitman, "we've had nothing but speculative excess."

OK, so reports of the death of value are greatly exaggerated. What do you do if "safe and cheap" stocks are thin on the ground, as they were for much of the decade in which Whitman did so handily? Surprisingly, he pulled off deep bets against the market in bummed out high-tech stocks, mainly depressed chip equipment manufacturers. He burrowed away to the point where tech stocks got to be a third of his portfolio. "If you had told me seven years ago I would be so heavily involved as a value investor in small-cap high-tech plays, I would have said forget about it," says Whitman with a pleased grin. In the manic twists of the market, there are times—and prices—at which growth stocks become value stocks.

Whitman has also opportunistically been scouring the deep discount markets of Japan for "cheap and safe." In the larger strategic sense, he has been pushing an updated model of Ben Graham's value strategies into the far more complex world of latter-day financial engineering.

In Graham's pre-Internet time, you bought shares below what seemed to be a company's value as a going business, counted on a rising tide of earnings and dividends to bring the price up, and ultimately looked to open market sale to take you out at a profit.

Life is no longer that simple. Look at the long-term profits investors have pulled out of the now struggling AT&T. In the years since the company was broken up by an antitrust fiat, the big money has come not from the Grahamesque fundamentals of earnings and dividends, but from a dizzying and far less predictable succession of mergers, acquisitions, and spin-offs. What Graham thought of as "extraordinary events" have become the ordinary, and a major point of departure for Whitman's brand of value investing.

Over any three- to five-year period, he says, most of the stocks in his biggest investment pool, the $1.8 billion open-end Third Avenue Value Fund, the biggest of his three funds, will be overrun by some major happening. The possibilities crackle off Whitman's tongue: "mergers and acquisitions, hostile takeovers, divestitures, spin-offs, refinancings, and going private."

Casting a mordant eye over 22 companies in which Third Avenue owned major positions lately, Whitman counts 13 in the throes of some sort of "resource conversion." The prospects go like this: two cash sales of control and one exchange of stock; three attempts at hostile takeovers; five acquisitions of smaller companies; one partial liquidation; one sale of a new issue of common stock.

All these deals were cooking at a premium above going market prices. Whitman typically tries to capitalize on such sleights of financial engineering by putting more emphasis on quality assets and less on operating earnings than Graham fundamentalists. These days, argues Whitman, management has to be appraised not only as operators of a going business, "but also as investors engaged in employing and redeploying assets."

This is in some ways an extension of Warren Buffett's dictum that "being a businessman makes me a better investor, and being an investor makes me a better businessman."

Whitman digs into personal experience to amplify the point. In the late 1980s, he helped put together a prepackaged bankruptcy for Nabors Industries, now one of the world's biggest and best capitalized oil drilling contractors. Whitman saw to it that Nabors came out of the reorganization debt free, with an all-equity base. When hard times hit the industry, Nabors had no difficulty raising the money it needed to buy up debt-ridden competitors at bargain prices. "Other industry participants did not have the financial wherewithal to bid against Nabors for those assets," notes Whitman.

The result was that Nabors was able to turn operating losses of more than $20 million into positive cash flow of better than $200 million. Among the beneficiaries of the move: longtime holder Whitman and his Third Avenue Value Fund. Whitman's point on the Nabors' success—one frequently ignored on Wall Street—is that shrewd analysis of balance sheet potential is a better tool for predicting future earning power than a study of past earnings patterns.

As a long-term investor looking to a number of possible exit strategies, Whitman glories in the freedom to ignore near-term earnings predictions and results. Acidly, he argues that Wall Street spends far too much time "making predictions about unpredictable things."

His search is for companies backed by strong financials that will keep them going through hard times ("safe"), selling at a substantial discount below private business or takeover value ("cheap"). Buying quality assets cheap almost invariably means that the company's near-term results are rocky enough to have turned off Wall Street. "Markets are too efficient for me to hope that I'd be able to get high-quality resources without the trade-off the near-term outlook not being great," says Whitman. He chuckles and runs a hand through a fringe of white hair. "When the outlook stinks, you may not have to pay to play."

Whitman's penchant for seizing on opportunities left for dead by Wall Street has won him some celebrity as a "vulture investor." Whitman likes this journalistic tag line. "It's a lot better than being called an indexer or an asset allocator," he says, taking another poke at standard Wall Street dogma.

Whitman learned the dogma from the ground up. He started on Wall Street as an analyst in the late 1940s after a three-year hitch in World War II as a Navy pharmacist's mate, and a post-graduate year in economics at Princeton. He says his education in distress merchandise didn't start until several years later when he began picking up retainers as an expert witness on valuation in bankruptcy cases. Whitman made his first big money in the early 1970s, buying up senior mortgage bonds of the busted Penn Central Railroad. "The bonds were cheap because not too many people realized they were safe," recalls Whitman.

Trolling troubled waters for bargains, Whitman offers a cheery insight into the limits of risk.

From the 1970s through the 1990s, he says, severe recessions have whipped through a baker's dozen of industries without grossly affecting the economy as a whole. Among the victims: energy, banking, real estate, savings and loans, retail trade. Semiconductor equipment and other high-tech capital goods producers now crowd the casualty list. Typically, many stocks in these depressed industries trade down to ultra-cheap levels as

Wall Street walks away from grim near-term prospects. It's a combination that brings out the vulture in Whitman.

He argues that scouting depressed industries is not a particularly dangerous way to live. Every investment, he contends, has something wrong with it. Whitman's job is to sniff out what is wrong, and figure out the trade-offs against what is right, particularly in terms of some form of potential asset conversion. Mutual fund management companies, for example, throw off huge amounts of cash, but because entry costs are low, they are vulnerable to new competition that keeps barging into the business. Capital intensive companies such as oil refiners, on the other hand, do not have to worry overmuch about new competition, but tend to take their lumps in the down end of the business cycle.

Among the most common wrongs Whitman tries to avoid:

❋ Attractive-seeming highly liquid cash positions that on inspection prove to be in the custody of managements too timid to put surplus assets to good use;

❋ Seductively high rates of return on equity that often signal a relatively small asset base;

❋ A combination of low returns on equity and high net asset value that may simply mean that asset values are overstated;

❋ High net asset values that may point to a potentially sizable increase in earnings, but which just as often point to swollen overhead.

Whitman's willingness to take on companies like the stereotypical "sick, lame, and lazy" he treated as a pharmacist's mate—the old salt, in Navy slang, still thinks of himself as having been a "pecker checker"— is not unalloyed. Buying seeming trouble at a discount, Whitman ignores market risk (current price swings). Whitman worries all the time, though, about investment risk (the possibility he may have misjudged a temporary illness that will prove terminal).

Two critical elements Whitman focuses on in weighing investment risk are the "quality and quantity of resources." The dynamics behind these seemingly bookeeperish abstractions show in the long run that Whitman has made at semiconductor equipment manufacturers. Outfits like Applied Materials, Electroglas, and KLA-Tencor produce the highly specialized tools needed to shape the ubiquitous microchip, increasingly embedded in everything from credit cards and greeting cards to telephones and toys. Despite its expansive reach, the chip business is highly cyclical for end producers and suppliers alike.

Whitman first started nibbling at the manufacturing stocks some five years ago at the beginning of an indeterminate down cycle he thought might last anywhere "from two quarters to three years, or maybe even longer." It was hard to get a handle on the negatives. Global growth was slowing, the personal computer market for integrated circuits was approaching saturation, and business was demonstrably lousy.

To Whitman's great satisfaction, Wall Street took the customary short-term view and began dumping the stocks. That's when Whitman started his move, buying much of the time at less than a 50 percent premium over book value ("cheap"). He dove into the equipment producers rather than their customers, chip makers such as Intel, mainly because they were cheaper.

As smallish niche producers, often protected by proprietary techniques, the equipment manufacturers seemed less vulnerable to shake out, and had better "quality" assets. Unlike the far more capital-intensive chip makers, with their heavy investments in bricks and mortar, the equipment producers operate out of comparatively low-cost clean rooms, and buy, rather than make, most of their components. Research and development costs are high, but Whitman cannily focused on companies that expensed rather than capitalized them. Those running charges understated earnings, making them seem particularly weak in the down cycle. So much the worse for Wall Street.

Whitman was looking at hard book value (few intangibles) that gave him a high level of "quality" resources. He was unsettled for a bit when a minor bull market perversely erupted in the stocks, but his worst case estimate of how long the downturn would last proved to be bang on. Major Third Avenue Value holdings like Electroglas were reporting straight-line quarterly sales and operating earnings declines of 60 percent or more. Predictably, the stocks continued south to the point where many plunged to well under book value.

Whitman continued to buy a cross section of equipment producers at quotes he regarded as "better than even first stage venture capitalists have to pay, and for companies already public and very, very cash rich."

So Whitman's "cheap" stocks got even cheaper, but were they still "safe?" That question loomed ever larger as Whitman pushed his stake in the equipment producers to as high as 22 percent of Third Avenue Value's assets. Whitman was averaging down, a key part of his strategy, but anathema to Wall Street's momentum players.

Whitman was betting turnaround. The question was when it would materialize. He showed shareholders a stiff upper lip: "Explosive growth" lay ahead, thanks to expanding applications and basic advances in technology. "The use of smaller and smaller circuits to achieve increased density," Whitman expostulated, "will in and of itself result in semiconductor manufacturers having no choice but to replace equipment simply in order to remain competitive. They have to ante up for the latest tools as a cost of doing business."

That was Whitman, talking up the stocks for public consumption. Underneath the rhetoric, he was assessing values with his customary gimlet eye. Whitman spread some $300 million over a mix of close to a dozen equipment-makers, hardheadedly diversifying because it was clear that not all the smaller company stocks he had picked up would make it on their own. "Most," he thought, "ought to do okay and a few ought to be huge winners, but there would be a few strikeouts." The exit strategy for the strikeouts, in a consolidating industry, would almost certainly be acquisition.

Beyond diversification, Whitman protected himself by loading up on management that fit his two acid tests: good at day-to-day operations and equally good as asset managers. His biggest holdings were among the likes of Applied Materials, companies that had been riding high in the up cycle, and capitalized on their then popularity on Wall Street to sell stock.

"Lots of these guys were quite smart," says Whitman. "Even though they didn't need the cash at that time, when the market was terrific, they took advantage of the opportunity to raise a lot of money." Looking at stocks like Electroglas, with cash-to-asset ratios of 35 percent or more a share, Whitman felt well-fortified to ride out adversity. The one nagging question of course, was the "burn rate." Would the industry-wide depression go so deep and continue so long that much of the cash would he siphoned off by attrition? Operating losses were mounting as the big chip makers, fighting hard times of their own, were pressing on the prices of the limited amount of new equipment they were buying, and putting off orders on the next generation of tools the equipment-makers were spending so much money to develop.

The impasse prompted stomach-churning sell-offs of 40 percent or more in at least three of Whitman's equipment producers—Clare Corporation, FSI International and SpeedFam-IPEC. Two (FSI and SpeedFam) were sitting on extremely solid cash positions. Seemingly thriving on adversity, Whitman rated them (along with eight other portfolio issues down 25 percent or more) as either promising "very good operating results," or likely candidates for some form of financial engineering. And, in fact, that was exactly what happened. Several, including Whitman's biggest holding, Silicon Valley Group, were acquired at substantial premiums.

Once again scoffing at market risk, Whitman underlines the comforts of being cushioned by strong financials. "When you're in well-capitalized companies, if they do start to dissipate, you get a chance to get out." "On the other hand," he continues, "when you're in poorly capitalized companies, you better watch the quarterly reports very closely."

As a buy-and-hold investor, with one of the lowest portfolio turnover rates in the business, Whitman is the first to admit that he is slow on the sell side. He is quick to unload obvious mistakes, but is often in a quandary with stocks that seem "grossly overpriced."

That's because he thinks in terms of multiple markets. What may seem to be a very rich price to an individual investor can be a perfectly reasonable one for control buyers looking to an acquisition. They can afford to stump up a premium because of the advantages control brings. Among them is the ability to finance a deal on easy terms with what Whitman calls "OPM" (Other People's Money) and "SOTT" (Something Off The Top) in the form of handsome salaries, options, and other goodies that come with general access to the corporate treasury.

Thus, through long experience, Whitman has decided that his analytical sense works better on the buy side than the sell side. "I've held securities for three years and sold them for a double only to see them triple over the subsequent six months," he says. Moral: "Just sitting around is a better way to make money." That conclusion helps to explain why so many of Whitman's exits are by acquisition rather than outright sale.

There is another angle to this. Whitman thinks of himself as being in the business of "creating wealth" rather than managing money as such. That means keeping as big a chunk of the profits at work for as long as you can. Whitman's waiting game and trademark low turnover, besides catching financial engineering premiums, help to keep tax liabilities down.

The waiting game certainly paid off with the chip equipment producers. The turnaround Whitman was looking for finally did materialize. Wall Street tastemakers like Morgan Stanley, in the Millennium, once again began posting "outperform" stickers on the stocks. Whitman once again laughed his contrarian way to the bank. His profits sweated out over several years, demonstrates the essence of the Whitman strategy—ignore market swings, except to average down; ignore Wall Street's accepted wisdom. Shop depressed industries for strong financials going cheap and hang on. By strong financials Whitman means companies with little or no debt and plenty of cash. What's cheap? No hard and fast rules. "Low prices in terms of the resources you get," he generalizes.

For industrial companies, Whitman tries to pay no more than 50 percent to 60 percent of takeover value. One value indicator is the multiple of price-to-book—stock price divided by book value. The lower the multiple, the better. Book value, of itself, doesn't tell the whole story, but as a best-case example, Whitman was more than happy averaging down on some of the chip equipment producers at as little as 40 percent of very hard book.

Some of his other pricing rules of thumb:

❋ For small cap, high-tech companies, a premium of no more than 60 percent over book—about what venture capitalists would pay on a first stage investment.
❋ For banks, Whitman's limit is no more than 80 percent of book value.
❋ For money managers, Whitman looks to assets under management (pay no more than two percent to three percent).
❋ For real estate companies, he zeros in on discounted appraised values rather than book.

Whitman, thumbing his nose at convention, has clearly established himself as an outside force on Wall Street. Despite the philosophical linkage, he even backs off from identification with what he calls Graham & Dodd Fundamentalists. The basic similarities are striking: long-term horizons, a rigorous analytic approach to the meaning behind reported numbers, and an unshakeable belief that probabilities favor those who buy quality at the lowest possible price. Like Ben Graham, Whitman scoffs at the academicians who hold that stock prices are set by a truly knowledgeable and efficient market. Acknowledging his debt to Graham, Whitman argues that his calculated exploitation of exit strategies has added a new dimension to value investing. Graham, he insists, was far more preoccupied with market risk and macroeconomic factors that he simply ignores.

Give Whitman an edge. He has moved value investing into the new century, but in personal terms he is not as far from Graham as he contends. Like Graham, Whitman grew up in a family business. His parents, who emigrated from western Poland in 1920, made felt underbodies for women's hats. Whitman grew up in the middle-class enclave of the Grand Concourse in the Bronx, not far from Yankee Stadium. He helped with deliveries and did odd jobs, but was not particularly interested in the family shop. His passions were basketball and baseball. He was such an indifferent student in high school that his sister Phyllis, a Pennsylvania Superior Court Judge, at Whitman's seventy-fifth birthday party, reminded everyone of the family fear that he would never amount to much.

Whitman traces his value orientation in part to the windup of his father's business. "He liquidated and then did a lot of speculating." recalls Whitman. "I couldn't see myself doing that, buying and selling all the time." Still ruminating, Whitman says, "I couldn't be a trader. I'm very slow with numbers. I have to understand what they mean."

Whitman sees value investing as a "good enough" business—no swinging for the fences. "It's the art of the possible," he says. "The aim is not to maximize profits, but to be consistent at low risk. I never mind leaving something on the table."

Out of the Navy, Whitman struggled through an early marriage that lasted only six months. He finished his undergraduate work at Syracuse with distinction in 1949 ("I guess I was finally maturing," he laughs), ran out the rest of his GI Bill eligibility with a graduate year at Princeton, and then gravitated to Wall Street. Much of the work he did on his first job as an analyst at Shearson Hayden Stone quickly festered into disenchantment with Wall Street's myopic view of value.

"It was ridiculous," recalls Whitman. "Ninety-eight percent of the emphasis was on short-term earnings and the near-term outlook." "One company came my way," he continues, "a lumber company that had little or no visible earning power, but plenty of timber. I couldn't analyze it, so I knew there had to be some other way of doing things."

Whitman's sense of something else—a long-term view and the assets side of a business as a store of value—sharpened when he moved on to the Rosenwald Foundation. That charitable repository, funded by a Sears, Roebuck founding family, held controlling interests in a number of other companies, including Western Union. "That's when I began to get a glimmering that whatever you did, it was $10 million of your own money, and that it would be committed on a permanent or a semipermanent basis for a long time," recalls Whitman.

It was a vital part of Whitman's education. The virtues of buy and hold were beginning to crystallize. The distinction between market risk and investment risk was beginning to take on a new dimension, too. In yet another parallel with Ben Graham, Whitman began to pick up retainers as an expert witness, among other cases testifying for the government in an investigation of misdoing in the Teamsters Union investment practices. Whitman soon developed a reputation for smarts in stockholder litigation and bankruptcy cases. "The less respectable areas of corporate law," laughs Whitman. The key question in his work for bankruptcy trustees often centered on valuation. How to put a price on this security? What is this company worth?

"Preparation, preparation, preparation" for his stints in the courtroom gave Whitman an object lesson in how skewed market prices and their underlying asset values could become. Panicky creditors or bondholders, stampeding through a very narrow exit in anticipation of a bankruptcy, were truly at the peril of the market. Opportunists picking up the pieces at distress prices got the benefit. They were pretty well-insulated from market risk. How much further could prices drop? The monkey on their back was investment risk. Would their business plan work? Could they control a redistribution of assets that would turn their cheap paper into gold?

The rewards were persuasive enough to turn Whitman the theorist into an activist. Hired as an advisor by a group of creditors, Whitman in the early 1970s bought $100,000 of the egregiously busted Penn Central Railroad senior first mortgage bonds at a deep discount. He made five times his money when the fully secured paper was paid off at face value. It was a splendid opener for Whitman's advent as a vulture investor.

As an expert witness, Whitman had been getting a thorough grounding in utility finance. He testified as a rate expert in the Senate hearings on the breakup of AT&T, and subsequently served as financial adviser to the Presidential Commission named to investigate the near meltdown of the General Public Utilities Three Mile Island nuclear plant.

Whitman put the technical background to good use for clients of the newly established brokerage and advisory firm of M.J. Whitman & Company. The specialty, of course, was distressed utility paper.

Working for partners like Citicorp, Whitman analyzed the prospect of bankruptcy workouts on such troubled nuclear power companies as the Michigan-based Consumers Power Company and the even more controversial Public Service Company of New Hampshire. Ecological problems and the heavy leverage of idle nuclear capacity hung over the securities of both companies like a mushroom cloud. Weighing the values, Whitman bought into the utilities' heavily sold mortgage bonds, calculating he could come out ahead even if the companies did go through the bankruptcy wringer.

In a cliffhanger, both companies scraped by—at least for the moment. In a little over two years, Whitman doubled his money, coming out with a gain of some $15 million. The profit was a gratifying testament to the distinction between market risk and investment risk. When the fix at Public Service of New Hampshire proved to be only temporary, Whitman went back for more. The second helping centered on third mortgage bonds trading at around 60¢ on the dollar and yielding around 13.75 percent.

Fronting for a major Citicorp investment, Whitman worked out and presented to creditors a well-publicized reorganization strategy: a consensual prepackaged bankruptcy that would permit the utility to shed debt in a quick turn through bankruptcy court. The plan had something for everybody except PSNH management.

Whitman and his clients had carefully assembled enough voting power to block any other reorganization plan put on the table, including one backed by management. Pressing heavily on a Nativist PR pedal, PSNH responded by picturing Whitman as plotting a "complete takeover by New York bankers for a whopping profit." Chivvied by dozens of other creditors, and denied a critical rate increase, the utility lurched into bankruptcy on its own. Three years and dozens of lawsuits later, the utility emerged with a huge rate increase and a merger bid from neighboring Northeast Utilities Holding Company.

Acceptance of Whitman's consensual prepackage would have speeded the reorganization immeasurably, but he couldn't quarrel with the wrap-up. Citicorp and a number of Whitman appendages split an $80 million profit on a $100 million investment. Trophies all around! Whitman presented his partners with navy-blue caps sporting a vulture triumphantly perched on a nuclear cooling tower. Citicorp presented Whitman with his prized bronze of a bull fornicating with a bear.

Whitman went on to other analytical triumphs with distressed merchandise, demonstrating what he thinks is yet another distinction between his value approaches and that of Graham fundamentalists. Grahamites, argues Whitman, look to a credit against the probability of a default. He looks beyond the credit to see what can be got when it does default—yet another variant on "safe and cheap."

Whitman does go on about what makes him so different from Ben Graham. He goes on so often that it makes you wonder why. One easy inference is that he is scrambling to get out of the shadow of some powerful antagonist.

The scramble makes the similarities seem all the sharper. Like Ben Graham, Whitman turned early to teaching. He has been a visiting professor at the Yale School of Organization & Management for more than a quarter century, relishing the cut and thrust of the debates that flare in his heavily attended seminars on investment. "They ask good questions, these young people," he says. "Half the time I think I'm back in a bankruptcy court witness chair."

Some former students—Curtis Jenson, for one, who runs Third Avenue's Small Cap Fund—have gone to work for the old professor. Others are part of the Mafia that Whitman swaps information and deals with. There is Kwon Ho Sung, for one, president of Joonghoo Industry of Korea, who studied with Whitman 20 years ago. He and other members of his influential Korean family were major stakeholders in yet another of Whitman's efforts to capitalize on cheap and safe Asian assets. That was an abortive attempt in a $500 million buyout of the bankrupt Hanbo Steel Company, Korea's second biggest producer of grey metal. Though the bid failed, it is yet another illustration of the arithmetic that stokes Whitman's fires. Hanbo had come out of reorganization with all equity and no debt. "It's the only way to structure these deals," says Whitman.

Connections aside, teaching broadens Whitman's perspective. "If I had known in 1951 what I learned interacting in the classroom," he says, "I would have been able to analyze the asset side of that lumber company with no trouble at all."

Lecturing has helped Whitman systematize his value theory. "It forced me to sit down and think about what I do," says Whitman, "a hell of an opportunity for a money grubber like me." Like Ben Graham, he has expanded this theory into two books, *The Aggressive Conservative Investor*, coauthored in 1979 with Yale Professor Martin Shubik; and Whitman's own *Value Investing*, published in 1999. Neither is likely to achieve the best-sellerdom of the Master's *Security Analysis* or *The Intelligent Investor*. That doesn't trouble Whitman. "I did what I wanted to do," he says. "I showed Wall Street and the academicians, all those efficient market guys, that they don't know what they're doing."

Whitman backs this contention with a notably unsentimental view of how Wall Street really works. He argues that heavy reliance on short-term earnings predictions as the key to market values makes trend players of money managers. Such linkages are the stuff of stock market columns. The Genesco shoe chain allows that fourth quarter earnings will "meet or exceed" analysts' estimates, and the stock pops with a gain of almost 25 percent. Sykes Enterprises, a call-center specialist, signals that earnings will be down, and the stock falls by a third.

Typically, argues Whitman, analysts spend far more time on "field work"—management interviews aimed at eliciting earnings forecasts—than digging into audit reviews that can provide real clues to underlying values. For high-turnover portfolios consisting of hundreds of stocks, contends Whitman, traditional spadework has become a high cost no-no. Bad enough that estimates are often wildly inaccurate. Worst yet, investors are given "target" prices in which error is compounded. Applied to the estimates are equally evanescent multiples cobbled out of notional industry trends and management appraisals. "Making forecasts about future general market levels," writes Whitman in *Value Investing*, "is much more in the realm of abnormal psychology than finance."

Analysts who focus on earnings trends to the exclusion of asset values, continues Whitman, tend to think laterally. "The past is prologue;

therefore, past growth will continue into the future, or even accelerate." Unfortunately, the "corporate world is rarely linear," and becomes a particularly dangerous place for trend players who leave no margin of safety in concentrating on high multiple growth stocks.

Whitman is looking back at a market in which most of the growth shown by one key measure—Standard & Poor's 500 stock index—was generated by only 30 companies. Almost all these key performers were technology stocks, leaving on the list only a corporal's guard of "old economy" stocks regularly canvassed by traditional value investors. To make money outside technology, you had to go with the biggest and the best—American International Group, for example. Multiples on these stocks soon soared beyond conservative buy limits, leaving value investors with fewer places to go and putting them at a still deeper competitive disadvantage with growth.

One advantage to Whitman's strategy is his skill with distressed credits. When equity discounts are hard to find, Whitman can turn to discounted debt like the $52 million in Kmart's unsecured debentures and trade credits he picked up not long ago.

The package looked cheap enough. Whitman paid about 74¢ on the dollar for securities yielding 18 percent to maturity. Cheap yes, but safe? Like Barneys, Jamesway, Bradlees, and other major chains, Kmart was making heavy weather in a retailing world made ever more uncertain by the advent of interactive cyber shopping.

The earnings prognosis was shaky at best. Wall Street was totally down on the common stock. Whitman—as usual—was looking beyond the short term to depth of assets. Kmart's Big Box stores of 100,000 square feet or more were comparatively new or recently refurbished. True, the chain was loaded down with about $2 billion in long-term debt, most of it unsecured. But Whitman reasoned that as long as Kmart continued to have access to new capital, his credits—bought at discount mainly from the chain's worried suppliers—would get paid off with interest.

Whitman felt safe even if Kmart, worst case, went into bankruptcy. His credits were way up in the pecking order, and reorganization would enable the chain to close out the worst of its 2,500 stores at minimal cost. Landlords holding long-term leases would be entitled to a maximum of three years rent. Going-out-of-business sales, Whitman reasoned, would bring in some cash, and with Big Box space in brisk demand, Kmart might even be able to sublease some of its standalone stores to other retailers

A major investment risk: the prospect that Kmart might bumble along for a couple of years more, getting deeper into debt that might prove senior to Whitman's holdings. Certain he would do no worse than break even, Whitman continued to average down to the point where Kmart paper accounted for more than 10 percent of Third Avenue Value assets. As it turned out, bankers shared Whitman's sense of the chain's staying power and confidence in the new management that had just taken over the company. As part of a court-ordered restructuring, the bankers pumped some $3.5 billion into Kmart.

Good news for the chain; not such good news for Whitman. His trade credits dropped from a priority position to a junk bond rating behind the bank debt. Playing conservatively, Whitman opted out, selling his paper at a decent profit. He could have held out for more. "Admittedly there are huge profit potentials in owning junk," Whitman told shareholders, but sticking with the stuff just did not comport with his definition of safe.

Significantly, though the Kmart scenario did not work quite as well as he hoped, Whitman had built enough safety in his calculations to come away with a profit. He shrugged off disappointment with a touch of humor. He had shopped Kmart stores and found them good, but Third Avenue Value "would be in deep trouble if it had to base its investment decisions, even in part, on my personal shopping experiences."

In fact, some of the fund's investment decisions are so idiosyncratic that they could be personal shopping expeditions—Whitman seeing "safe" and "cheap" in far-out opportunities that even he sometimes has second thoughts about. Look at the $200 million he has put in a cluster of Japanese stocks, mainly casualty insurance companies.

Unlike their American counterparts, these companies actually make money writing automobile and fire coverage, profits that give them a solid going concern value. Their chief appeal to Whitman, though, is the "surplus surplus" on the balance sheet—a pile of cash and securities not needed to run the basic business. The reserves themselves generate a steady stream of dividend and interest income. Carried at portfolio values well under going prices, these reserves also reflect a huge call on stock profits. Think of these casualty underwriters as closed-end investment companies with an insurance front.

Attacking across his customary broad front, Whitman has bought into a half dozen of the carriers at discounts of as much as 60 percent below net asset value. The jewel of the collection, a stock he began nibbling at $44 a share in 1997, is Tokio Marine & Fire Insurance Company, Limited. The biggest of Japan's casuality underwriters, Tokio Fire dominates the field with an 18 percent share of the market. A look at the vital statistics shows what caught Whitman's eye: a portfolio of top Japanese stocks with a cost basis of about $9.6 billion. The market value when Whitman bought in: some $31.5 billion. Counting up total assets, without putting a value on the operating side of the company, Whitman figured he was getting about $105 worth of value at a cost of well under half that amount.

In quick succession over the next couple of years, happily averaging down in a sliding Tokyo market, Whitman bracketed most of the other big names in the industry at equally deep discounts. Most of these buys were also so deep in assets, he was sure that they were impervious to purely economic wipeout.

In venturing onto foreign turf, though, Whitman was exposing his value theory to a whole new level of unexplored risk. The carriers seemed cheap. Were they truly safe? Among the new X-factors: currency risks and the high transaction costs—all part of the game in playing savvy locals on the home ground.

Most unfathomable of all were the cultural and regulatory risks peculiar to Japan. The currency risk could be hedged readily enough. Price spreads on the floor of the Tokyo Exchange could be monitored. But how to weigh the uncertainties of dealing with the Mandarins of the all-powerful Ministry of Finance, the murky imperatives of the conglomerate business groups that control the casualty companies, or the flagging efforts of a crony-ridden government to reverse a chronic recession?

The X-factors were critical because Whitman wasn't just one more passive outside investor looking for long-term growth to take him out of the casualty stocks at a profit. He had done his homework before buying into Tokio Fire and confirmed his numbers through intermediaries such as the accounting firm of Peat Marwick Japan. He was blinking Mammon at what he saw as one huge asset play. His hope: that financial engineering would burst into full flower in Japan.

The parallel in Whitman's mind was the United States of the 1960s. A feast of "surplus surplus" old-line casualty companies like Reliance

Insurance Company and Home Insurance disappeared at premium prices into the maws of predators like Leasco and City Investing. The acquisitors could well afford the premiums. Paying up gave them access to huge pools of liquidity they were quick to redeploy. It had happened in the United States. Why not Japan?

After all, outfits like GE Capital and AXA, the French insurance giant, were buying up huge chunks of ailing Japanese life insurance companies, mainly as a detour around regulatory restrictions limiting access to Japan's rich but untalented pension fund management business. Conceptually, couldn't the casualty companies spin off some of their surplus assets into the life business and do joint ventures with other Westerners itching to break into the pension market? That was Whitman conjuring up his favorite theme of "resource conversion." Some of this is happening. Tokio Marine, for example, is in the throes of merging two competitors into a holding company, thereby diversifying its product line.

This is a very modest start on large hopes. Given the muddled state of Japan's two-steps-forward-three-steps-back approach to deregulation and the nontransparency of its regulators, Whitman candidly admits he doesn't know what kind of exit strategies he can realistically contemplate. Acquisition and diversification seemed to be high among the possibilities. Was it too farfetched to think that Japanese capital markets might see financial engineering as an answer to the structural rigidity that has been throttling economic growth for a decade?

Whitman was a man in search of catalysts. Early on, he had to concede "we do not know if anyone is thinking in these terms." There were few signs that the American example would take. Playing for the long term, sure that something would break, Whitman continued building his position in Japan. He had plenty of money to play with. Seen as a hot fund by such major distributors as Charles Schwab and Fidelity Management, Third Avenue Value was awash in sales to new investors. Further, a number of cushy credit plays like Kmart had been closed out, pushing Whitman's cash position to a very rich 40 percent of assets. He had to hustle to put his own surplus assets to use. His best idea, after semiconductors, was Japan. From the initial bite at Tokio Fire & Marine, the Japanese initiative swelled to almost 10 percent of Third Avenue Value assets.

Systematically adding to his casualty company holdings, Whitman also picked up a 3.5 million share piece of Toyoda Automatic Loom Works (a major holder of Toyota Motors), and a slug of three Japanese banks. All seemed "cheap," snapped up at attractive-looking discounts.

There was one red flag. One of the banks, conceded Whitman, the Long Term Credit Bank, was a bit off quality standards. It was certainly "cheap" (bought at 50 percent or more below book), but maybe not all that "safe." As a major lender to a big swatch of industrial Japan, the bank was loaded with nonperforming deadbeat loans. Further, it might not be able to roll over a tranche of maturing debentures, but the rationale for the buy seemed solid. A strategic alliance with Swiss Bank Corporation would project the Long Term Credit Bank into the richer preserves of investment banking and asset management with a world-class partner.

Other opportunities were opening up. "Preliminary and indirect conversations with several Japanese banks," Whitman told shareholders, held the promise that TAVF might be able to repeat in Japan what it had done in the United States in the 1990s. The hope was that the fund could buy new Treasury stock directly from the banks, thus bucking up their shaky capital positions—but at an appropriate discount, of course.

Whitman held up this transfusion, a classic piece of financial engineering, as a prospect. At bottom, it had an air of wishful thinking. "Whether this (the stock buy) is possible in actuality is hard to say, but conceptually the banks ought to be very interested," Whitman told shareholders.

Whitman was caught up in a concept of his own, of course—notably that the dynamics of money are much the same everywhere. It was only a matter of time before the immutable law of convergence began to push Japanese market prices into line with investment values. Also, of course, there was that pile of new money burning a hole in his pocket.

There was a textbook case to be made for a $60 million holding in Toyoda Automatic Loom Works. Toyoda, which founded Toyota Motors in 1933, is a major supplier of engines, castings, and air conditioner compressors to the automobile company. It still owns five percent of Toyota, along with a $1.9 billion pot of other securities, mainly other Toyota suppliers. Toyota, in turn, in a cross holding typical of Japanese industry, owns 22 percent of Toyoda. At around $17 a share, Whitman figured he was buying assets (including the business) of $28 a share—a discount of some 37 percent.

Buying a call on one of the world's best automotive companies that far under the market is a hard strategy to fault. As ever, Whitman was weighing exit strategies beyond a simple long-term hold. As a major supplier, Toyoda might be acquired by Toyota. Again, conjecturally, Toyota's portfolio—including the Toyota stock—might be spun off to shareholders.

As an exercise in financial engineering, all this makes sense. Financial engineering, however, does not appear to play all that well with the ruling Toyota family. It gave Whitman a sharp lesson in how easy it is for control stock to make hash of the B-School logic he was bringing to bear on the complexities of the Japanese business culture.

Whitman was holding seven million shares of yet another Toyota control situation—the Chiyoda Fire & Marine Insurance Company, Limited. Toyota owned 37 percent of Chiyoda. One of Whitman's exit thoughts was that Toyota might want to buy up the rest of the company—at a premium, of course—and thus diversify directly into the automobile insurance business.

It was easy to infer that something like that was in the wind. Toyota had already made a small move or two in the direction of financial products and Whitman's hunch was right—partly. Toyota did increase its stake in Chiyoda to 47 percent with the direct purchase of a new issue of stock. For Toyota, the price could not have been more right. It paid 500 yen for stock with a net asset value of 875 yen.

By Whitman's lights, this was an outrageous steal—dilutive, and an evil precedent if the rest of Chiyoda was to be bought up. Goodbye to any thought of a premium. Whitman was sufficiently exercised to yell foul. He was agreeably surprised when his letter actually brought a reply: Toyota, if it did go for an acquisition, would consider the "entire fairness" of the situation.

It came down to a ritualistic "so sorry" for that elbow in the ribs. Whitman, playing the game of Japanese politesse, allowed that he was mollified by the Toyota response. He might even have meant it if similar asset grabs had not been engineered at two of his other casualty holdings.

In all, the Japanese initiative has been a hard learning experience for Whitman—"cheap," but not without a couple of blindside hits that are hard to equate with "safe." Getting preempted in Chiyoda was a mere slap on the wrist compared to the jolt Whitman took with the Long Term Credit Bank. The rationale—the bank's joint venturing with Swiss Bank Corporation—destructed when the Swiss walked from what now proved to be a tangle of highly politicized loan defaults on the LTCB books. Debate on how to liquidate them raged in the Diet as the pols jockeyed to keep deadbeat constituents from being forced to pay off their loans or go to the wall. Ultimately, LTCB was auctioned off to Ripplewood Holdings, a New York-based investment group that pledged not to use too much muscle in trying to recoup from the bank's weakest borrowers.

There was some consolation in the windup—but not much. Timothy Collins, head of the Ripplewood Group, was one of Whitman's students at Yale and part of his Mafia.

Unhappily for Whitman, there just wasn't enough cash in the Ripplewood bid for LTCB to do anything for common shareholders. Zeroed out with a stub holding, Whitman took a $46 million writeoff on LTCB and two smaller banks that he'd also latched on to. The hit cost TAVF stockholders 89¢ a share, dropping the fund's total return for 1998 to a minus 3.7 percent—its first negative in eight years of operation. Ominously, redemptions began to roll in, putting Whitman—despite his generally good long-term performance—very much on the defensive. To cover the redemptions, he had to start selling stocks he would just as soon have held on to.

Redemptions soon reversed, but Whitman was almost Japanese in the fulsomeness of his apology. In acquiring LTCB, he told shareholders he had hoped to replicate the profits he had been able to pull out of U.S. banks in the 1990s. "This seems to have been especially faulty analysis on my part," he said. "There was never any chance that LTCB could have been like its U.S. counterparts. Though I now have the benefit of hindsight, I really should have known better."

Is the misreading a harbinger? Does it mean that the other exit doors Whitman hopes to see open in Japan will also remain nailed shut? The questions go to one of Whitman's favorite aphorisms: "If after 10 minutes at the poker table you do not know who the patsy is, you are the patsy."

Whitman is now far less sanguine that Japan's slow drift to deregulation is going to turn its capital markets into a hotbed of financial engineering any day soon. "If I had the same opinion of managements in Japan when we started investing over there as I do today, I don't know if we'd gone in as heavily as we did, despite the fact that things were so cheap." The concession goes to yet another Whitman aphorism: "A bargain that stays a bargain isn't a bargain."

It's clear that Whitman has overreached on his theory in Japan. His own doctrine says that everything that seems "safe" and "cheap" isn't necessarily either. Maybe value strategists can afford to ignore macroeconomic factors, but in Japan Whitman badly misread well-defined political and cultural currents. A consensus society governed by the need to avoid confrontation, Japan is nowhere ready to embrace the pain of financial engineering, U.S style. As Whitman's Japanese initiative shows, value investing is a useful tool, but not quite ready for universal export.

Patient as ever, Whitman is rolling with the punches. "It's a business of probabilities," he says. "Things like LTCB go with the territory." "After all," adds Whitman, brightening into his customary cockiness, "Peter Lynch (of Magellan Fund fame) had Crazy Eddie and Warren Buffett had USAir. We all make mistakes. You have to consider the long term."

Long term, Whitman stacks up pretty well, consistently doing better than the market. Third Avenue returns are largely a function of what is happening in the depressed contrarian regions Whitman likes to track. The long-term orientation needed to capitalize on them helps to explain why Whitman is so adamantly against playing the comparative performance game. In this inside-out world, Third Avenue Value is in fact a best buy when asset values are flat on the deck. That's when quality assets generally are going cheap.

Whitman pops up frequently enough among *Forbes* top-rated funds not to be accused of sour grapes when he argues that the significance of comparative performance as an investment guide is "vastly overrated." Few can beat the market consistently over the short term. "Money managers who strive to maximize performance consistently pretty much have to be traders, acting and reacting based on market judgements." That's not Whitman's game, or the game of other value strategists with somewhat similar styles. Whitman will take superior performance if he can get it, but not at the cost of raising long-term risk levels. His goal: an average return of at least 20 percent a year.

Can he do that? Not always. Whitman thinks of himself as very like the managements of many of the companies in which he invests—

willing to trade return against safety. This formula of controlled opportunism has certainly worked for Whitman personally. It has led him profitably through the ambushes of bankruptcy plays to control of a mutual fund management cluster—Third Avenue Value with its small cap, high yield, and real estate siblings—with assets of some $2.6 billion.

Irreverent as ever, Whitman figures he is in a great business. "Mutual fund management is a license to steal" he whoops. "I was thinking about going into semiretirement, but with all these deals around, I don't have the time."

Who says value is dead?

T. Rowe Price pioneered growth when the nation was in the
dumps and made it pay. No doctrinaire, he knew what to
do when growth got overpriced—sell.

CHAPTER 3

_____ ≖♦≖ _____

Growth Avatar
T. Rowe Price

I N HIS OFFICE HIGH above the bustle of Baltimore Harbor, David
Testa—chief investment officer of the $130 billion T. Rowe Price
Mutual Fund group—is musing over the peculiar genius of his com-
pany's founder.

"The important thing to remember about Mr. Price is that most
investment managers are like passengers on a ship," says Testa. "As long
as the ship is going in the right direction, everything is fine. But when
you get an unexpected change in direction, there's panic. Nobody has
any idea of what to do next. With just one good idea about how to manage that change, you can make a brilliant career." Testa pauses and
smiles. "Mr. Price had at least three good ideas."

Three brilliant ideas about critical changes in market direction and
hundreds of smaller ones—all focussed on the growth stocks that were
Price's ruling passion. A roll call of the companies Price turned up while
developing his growth stock theory in the 1930s shows some amazingly
prescient picks—perennials that have persisted on "Nifty Fifty" lists
through nearly seven decades of good times and bad. Among them:
Abbott Laboratories, Black & Decker, and GE.

There were some clunkers, of course. An insomniac—driven, competitive, autocratic—Price had few close friends, no small talk, and was
as hard on himself as on his associates.

"Will I ever learn a few basic fundamentals?" Price railed in a diary
entry after a too cautiously placed limit order forced him to pay up two
points on a stock he had been following. "Buy and sell at the market,"
he admonished himself.

David Testa, as a young analyst, recalls Price poking his head in the door one day and demanding, "What's a growth stock?" The startled Testa stammered something about compounding earnings. "You haven't learned a thing!" snapped Price. A couple of days later, Testa found in the middle of his desk, underlined in red ink, the Full Monty from one of Price's pamphlets: "Growth stocks can be defined as shares in business enterprises which have demonstrated favorable underlying long-term growth in earnings and which, after careful research study, give indications of continued secular growth in the future."

Testa thinks of the encounter as an object lesson in the need "to learn substance before you start spouting off about things." "I admired Mr. Price," he continues, "and wanted to be as smart as he was."

Growth stocks are so closely tied to the investment strategy Price pioneered that he often seems to have invented them. In fact, Price was not so much Edison as Henry Ford, systematizing bits and pieces of existing lore the way that Ford's idea of standardizing parts revolutionized the assembly line.

Price was the consummate pragmatist. He wrote often about his growth stock theory, but its essential points could be bulleted on the back of a post card. Price was not a theorist in the way that Ben Graham was. He liked to think of himself as relying on "what my grandmother called gumption, my father called horse sense, and most people call common sense."

Operating in the backwaters of Baltimore, deliberately aloof from the trendiness of Wall Street, Price loved going against the crowd. As his son Thomas Rowe Price, III, put it, "He would sometimes go the other way out of sheer obstinacy." Price pursued growth when mainstream investors were looking for safety; switched to small company growth when big company growth caught on; and when all kinds of growth got overpriced, he took to underpriced basics such as oil and timber. Like that other sage of Baltimore, the feisty editor-writer Henry L. Mencken, Price was an original.

Starting with a three-man shop in 1937, Price kept his strategy simple: Look for companies in "new and fertile fields," buy them in an early stage of growth, stick with them as long as earnings are demonstrably on the rise, and sell when the growth cycle begins to mature.

Price's theory, at bottom, is still the philosopher's stone. His long success helped create a school of thousands of mutual funds and investment advisers—followers who believe that exponential long-term earnings growth is the one sure way to outsized market gains.

As David Testa notes, Price had found ways to master major changes in market direction. Most money managers in the 1930s were in shock over the combined impact of a bear market and the Great Depression. The old idea that Golconda lay in buying blue chips and simply tucking them into the strongbox had died of a thousand cuts. In a deflationary spiral, when high current income and safety were the rule, few were willing to hazard that corporate earnings would ever retrace the palmy levels of the 1920s.

Price offered a beguiling option. Yes, many of the old war horses like American Tobacco no longer had legs, he said, but plenty of other vibrant possibilities had gotten lost in the general disenchantment. Look at Monsanto. The $4.40 a share it earned in 1937 was more than double the $2 a share of boom year 1929, and there were solid reasons for thinking the company would remain on the upgrade.

In a series of articles in *Barrons*, Price postulated that corporations—like humans—have a distinct three-phase life cycle—"growth, maturity, and decadence." "Risks," argued Price, "increase when maturity is reached." The trick to maximizing profits and minimizing risk lay in "growth stocks" of the sort Price had been tinkering with since 1934.

Price's goals were modest enough in an investment world sick of get-rich-quick hyperbole: A 100-percent gain in earnings over 10 years suited him just fine. Along with a bump in capital, you could also look to a rising curve of dividends.

The weight of Price's seemingly simplistic approach is underscored by the wreckage of yet another get-rich-quick market. Wall Street is littered with dozens of now flattened non-dividend-paying dot-coms that went through the roof of "pro forma" reported earnings that were in fact losses. The important thing to remember is that through good markets and bad, Price's approach worked.

The experimental portfolio Price unveiled in *Barrons* ("an actual fund, not theoretical," he insisted) from 1935 through 1938 showed a capital gain of 76 percent compared with 49 percent for the Dow Jones Industrial averages. Dividend income was up a striking 130 percent versus only 12 percent for the averages.

Price's main income producers included Coca-Cola, IBM, and Procter & Gamble—low yielding outfits even today whose continuing growth translates into cumulatively fattening dividend checks. Price scratched some of the better yielding stocks of the day—tobaccos, for example, as slipping into maturity. By 1972, $100 in Price's model growth portfolio had increased to $7,400; the income from cash dividends from $3.30 to $92.

What made IBM a better buy than the equally well-established American Tobacco? Price theorized that consistently higher earnings at each new peak in the business cycle was one of the tell tales. You had to check for new highs at the peaks to make sure you were looking at sustained underlying growth, and not a mere cyclical recovery. Growth stocks would almost certainly suffer along with everything else in a market decline, but as long as the earnings trajectory held, lower prices just made growth a better buy.

It wasn't easy to determine when a company was about to tilt out of its growth phase into maturity and decay, said Price. You had to watch trends in sales, profit margins, and returns on invested capital, any of which could be affected by X-factors like new competition, patent expirations, management changes, or adverse legislation.

To see how some of these negatives could choke growth, you had to look no further than the power and light companies, Price wrote in *Barrons*. Their earnings climbed right through the 1929 Crash only to run headlong into the pieties of the New Deal. A change in the regulatory climate bit deeply into profit margins—and stock prices.

Thus, in the search for "new and fertile fields," it was important to bypass industries in which government spoke in a loud voice—rails and communications, for example. In this *Barron's* piece in 1939, Price presciently saw air conditioning, aviation, plastics, and television as good places to start the hunt. Divisions of old industries focussing on new products (office equipment from typewriters to business machines, for example) showed promise. So did specialty producers pushing into expanding markets (Coca-Cola and Minnesota Mining & Manufacturing, for example). Searching today, Price would probably be canvassing cutting-edge but profitable software possibilities such as Adobe Systems and Xilinx.

Unfortunately for them, as David Testa notes, most competing money managers did not get Price's message. In a diary he kept for four decades, Price wrote that he was banking heavily on his *Barrons* article to bring in business. "We don't have enough money to pay the rent and the advertisement appearing in the *Sun* last month," he wrote. "It's not a very comfortable feeling to have paid out all you have borrowed and still have insufficient capital to pay salaries and bills each month. If this [the *Barrons* piece] doesn't put us on the road to success, I don't know what will."

That's Price, still struggling to get his fledgling advisory firm into the black two years after setting up shop at age 39 as an investment counselor in Wall Street's darkest days. "I may be a darn fool for taking this unnecessary risk, but I'm going to have the satisfaction of knowing that I tried," his diary says. "If I fail, I will have no regrets." Not till a decade later did T. Rowe Price Associates show a profit.

The first couple of years were especially rocky. Like Ben Graham, Price was crafting a new strategy for a devastated market. Price's take on growth seemed to carry a lot more risk than Graham's play on cheap assets, and it was consequently a much harder sell. Price made a couple of bad market calls, excoriating himself for "stubbornness" in bucking a sharp downturn in 1938. "I hereby resolve that in the future . . . I will not buy until it is established that the downward trend has been reversed," he wrote.

Looking for new ways to bring in business, Price mused that it might be a good idea to put in "a special powder room for the ladies, with such facilities as a telephone, writing desks, etc." "While lady clients are often difficult to handle," he reasoned, "there are certain advantages to be gained by catering to this class of business. A large percentage of accumulated wealth in stocks and bonds is held by women."

Price confessed he did not have the temperament "to spend the major part of (his) time listening and talking to fussy old ladies." It would pay, though, to do "the little things which create goodwill, which are keenly appreciated by the ladies, and which most other business organizations would not consider necessary."

In fact, without considerable help from one wealthy lady—his wife Eleanor, a daughter of William D. Gerzy, a nationally known designer of urban electric power grids—T. Rowe Price Associates might not have made it through the early years.

Just before Christmas 1941, for example, finances were at a "distressing crisis." The firm's checking account showed a balance of exactly $11.07. Price had to plead with the bank to get his notes extended. He and his partners, meeting for lunch, could barely muster a total of $2 among them. Price's secretary, Marie Walper, had not been paid for a month, but gamely "offered to lend her Christmas club money to help out in an emergency."

Price worried a lot. A kind of Splengerian gloom permeates much of the diaries and almost all of his professional writings. He frets about the impact of long hours on his health, and professes from the warp of his "life cycle" theory that "after one reaches 40, he does slow down both mentally and physically." Price is so "mentally exhausted" after completing all but the finishing paragraph of a brochure titled "Change—The Investor's Only Certainty" that he asks a friend to write a "decent conclusion" for him.

This promotion piece, floated at the beginning of President Franklin Roosevelt's second term in 1937, is Price's big picture look at how the tax and regulatory policies of the New Deal were reshaping investment potentials. "The government," wrote Price, "by increasing taxes on the wealthy, is taking away from the Haves and giving to the Have Nots in one form or another—relief, bonuses, public works projects, agricultural payments, etc." Price reassuringly notes this was not an attempt to overthrow capitalism, but "part of a process of great change in the kind of capitalism." Labor "will receive a larger percentage of corporate income, increasing regulation will stunt profits in such basic industries as public utilities." Price's conclusion: Buckle your seat belts against raging inflation.

The fear of toxic inflation is a specter that haunts Price right through the dozen interviews and/or columns that ran in *Forbes* in the late 1970s. Ultimately, it is at the heart of his growth stock theory. The only way to beat inflation was to get out in front of it. There are times when the doom theme seems almost indistinguishable from the sales spiel. This son of a country doctor conjures up the malady, and then pulls the cure out of his pocket. How to come out on top: Invest in "new and rapidly growing industries, employing relatively few people and less subject to governmental interference." That's all gospel now, but a break with convention when Price enunciated it.

So, scratch the dour Price and you find an optimist. And never more so than when he hung up his shingle as an independent investment adviser. He took some odd turns getting there. Some colleagues think Price was ticketed to Swarthmore College in 1915 with the idea he would soon take over his doctor father's general practice in the farm community of Glydon, Maryland.

Price loaded up on chemistry credits, but finessed medicine for a job at the laboratory bench of the Fort Pitt Stamping & Enameling Company. It didn't last very long. Price, years later, allowed that he was "green and inexperienced" and had taken the job because he "liked the young Princeton graduate who hired me." Fort Pitt was not in great shape. There was a strike and the company went bust—an experience that stuck deep in Price's investment consciousness. Low labor costs and good labor relations were two of the items Price learned to look for when he was scouting a buy.

His sense of the need for both intensified when he was laid off in a companywide cutback after two years as a chemist at DuPont. Though still interested in the technology, Price's enthusiasm had begun to drift. "I found that I was spending my evenings reading financial magazines instead of learning more about the chemical industry," he recalled.

Price's personnel file shows he spent the next two years at two small brokerage firms—less than happy with the job of selling securities. He made some money playing the market, vacationed in Europe, and came back to find that the first firm had been shut down as a bucket shop— yet another step in the making of T. Rowe Price, securities analyst.

"I considered this experience costly but helpful, Price recalled acidly. "Two out of the first three firms with which I had been associated failed—one because of lack of experience, the other because of dishonesty. This taught me to be more critical and skeptical." An assessment of management quality—extracted from interviews with chief executives—went to the top of Price's analytical checklist.

Price was certain now that the investment research side of Wall Street was where he wanted to be. It took five years of dues paying as a broker at the Baltimore firm of Mackubin, Goodrich & Company before he got there.

As the firm's newly breveted head of investment management, the ever-contentious Price had his own ideas about how things should be run. Further, he was having his own personal problems with a killer market in 1931 that had just dropped to new lows. Price's boss, John Legg (the firm was a predecessor of the existing Legg, Mason & Company) urged Price to take his losses and get out of the market. "I cannot write a sell ticket on stocks after the decline they have had. My hand would become paralyzed," Price noted in his diary. He hustled up more margin rather than take an $11,000 loss that would strip him of collateral and leave him with an outstanding loan that would take years to repay "a few dollars at a time." "I am going to hang on," vowed Price.

He griped that the research he was asked to do ended all too frequently being harnessed to stock issues Mackubin was trying to sell.

Price bridled at what he saw as a conflict between big producers' sales commissions and their clients' best interests. "The stocks and bonds which produced the biggest commissions for salesmen were often the least desirable for the client," goes one fretful diary entry.

Fighting to build an independent research group, Price was definitely not regarded as a team player. He was chastised for blowing up at an executive committee meeting, and variously described as being "unpleasant and unapproachable." "All in all," grumbled the nonconforming Price, "It seems that I am guilty of many misdeeds."

Worse yet, Price's investment management group was clearly not going to become a profit center any time soon. The "too idealistic, too impatient" Price just couldn't sell the idea that investment advice should be unbundled from the commission business and offered to clients on a fee basis. His growth stock theory was also plowing sterile ground in the Mackubin executive suite.

Price was 39. Time to go.

Price brought with him from Mackubin the indomitable Miss Walper and two other associates who shared his view that there was more to growth stocks than theory. The two: Charles Shaeffer, a bright, genial Harvard Business School grad who sparkled with the sales presence Price so conspicuously lacked; and Walter Kidd, a ferret of an analyst whose job it was to test the details of Price's larger conceptions.

Price often worked from the top down, drawn to promising industries like chemicals or aviation by the voracious range of reading that soothed his insomniac hours. He often invested across the board at first, buying as many as a half dozen companies in an industry in small lots, and then winnowing as he and Kidd picked the best of the crop.

On at least one occasion, Price was incensed to learn that Kidd had beaten him to a punch. Price had been bullish on aviation for more than a half dozen years, seeing growth of major proportions ahead. He did well with the likes of Douglas Aircraft and then sold out, convinced by Kidd that the stocks had become overpriced. Aviation issues dipped and then soared, leaving Price "angry with myself for not having the courage of my convictions." "Kidd tells me that while I was away he bought Glenn Martin in the low thirties," reads the diary entry for February 24, 1939. "I have continuously talked to him since last fall about the purchase of Glenn Martin and asked his views as to when to buy. The stock sold at 39 today."

As David Testa describes a collaboration that lasted for some three decades, "Mr. Price would get these ideas and send Walter Kidd halfway around the U.S., by train, with his trunk, to check them out."

Price's legman clocked plenty of mileage. Kidd once calculated that he'd made 893 visits to 187 firms during his tenure as Price's research director. There were a lot of peripatetic payoffs. While calling on computer manufacturer Minneapolis Honeywell in 1939, bought the year before at around $3.80 a share, a friend suggested that Kidd also go see the folks at Minnesota Mining & Manufacturing across town. Kidd flagged a taxi, got a look at the firm's work with adhesives and told Price the stock was a steal at $1 a share.

Charles Shaeffer was also on the road, trying to sell institutional investors on the virtues of growth stocks and at the same time prospecting for good buys. One of them turned out to be IBM. Price, always drawn to new technology, decided in 1940 to dip into slim resources for an IBM office system he hoped would save the firm $500 a year. Thus cued, Shaeffer talked his way into a promised "half hour" with IBM founder Thomas Watson, Sr. He got to spend most of the day with Watson and brought home another early portfolio win.

Price aimed to get at least three out of every four buys right. One miscalculation sealed his caveats about the workings of big government. Pursuing a favorite theme—growth spun off from old industries—Price put in a buy on International Nickel. Steel, he figured, even with rearmament orders pouring in, was over the hill as a growth candidate. But the industry's demand for alloys like nickel and molybdenum was heating up. Price's premise was right, but so were his forebodings about the dead hand of regulation. Federal price controls materialized soon after he bought the stock and put a lid on the rise in Inco profits he had looked for.

On the whole, T. Rowe Price & Associates was doing well by its clients, but there just weren't enough of them. Salaries were still going unpaid, and Price compensated his colleagues for their sweat equity by peeling off pieces of a still profitless partnership. "I let my associates write their own tickets and in every case offered more than they asked for," notes the diary entry for January 11, 1941. "I would like them to have every advantage that is possible, under the circumstances, believing that in future years they will prove their appreciation."

The World War II years brought not very much more recognition to Price's growth stock theory, and only modest growth to the firm. One of

Price's most notable purchases in the period may have been a 77-acre farm that he acquired some miles outside Baltimore. Price saw land as yet another buffer against inflation, of course, but associates joked that it was actually a hedge against the possibility of the Japanese winning the war.

"Everybody figured there would be no need for investment advisers and we could all go out and grow vegetables on Mr. Price's farm. "laughs one associate. This was something of an in joke on Price. He grew roses (often wearing one in his lapel), but for all his interest in technology, was a dub when it came to the practicalities of working the farm. It became something of a late Friday afternoon hangout for the partners—a place to do a couple of beers, talk strategy, and work at cutting locust fence posts. Charles Shaeffer, who grew up poor on a farm in Lancaster, Pennsylvania, shakes his head at the memory and smiles. "Rowe never could get the rhythm of the two-man crosscut saw," he says.

This recollection from one of Price's few close friends is yet another index to the angularity of the personality. Shaeffer was Mr.Outside to Price's Mr. Inside for 40 years and succeeded him as president in 1963.

Shaeffer says Price played some social golf and tennis mainly "because he thought it was good business for the firm." Price worked best alone. "He'd get an idea, he'd say 'I want to think about this' and close the door," concurs chairman George Roche.

What was the source of the stock-picking genius that flourished behind those closed doors? Go figure why Sammy Sosa hits all those home runs. A mix of preternatural skill and slavish work habits seem to be at least part of the answer. Price's perceptions were so sharply attuned that they sometimes seemed totally intuitive.

Take his hit on Magnavox, an early starter in the quality color TV market. Price woke at 2:00 A.M., two days before the president of the company was to make a pitch to security analysts, with a "premonition" he should buy the stock. On the phone at the first crack of business, he put in orders for his wife, the firm's trading account, and himself.

Next night, in the hours before dawn, "Magnavox was one of the chief thoughts again," and Price put a number of clients into the stock. He went to the security analysts meeting as scheduled, left before the Magnavox president finished his talk, and bought more stock—"for Eleanor, the firm, and me, and recommended it to others."

"God help me if I am wrong," Price told his diary, "but I still have a strong conviction that this company has sound management and that over a period of years, it would prove to be an outstanding 'growth' stock."

Magnavox went on to have a good run. The purchase was a perfect example of how Price was often driven by the white heat of his ideas, shooting first at some dimly sensed potential, and then filling in the details.

It also shows how Price often bought first for his family accounts before putting clients into a stock, apparently wanting to scope the target before advising them to pull the trigger. It's always a good sign when a money manager eats his own cooking, but Price would never have been able to trade in that unbuttoned way in today's ethos. "The SEC would call it front running and throw him in the slammer," laughs chairman George Roche.

One administrative problem Price took behind the closed door was the question of how to bundle dozens of the small trust accounts that clients had been pressing him to open for children and grandchildren. Price was managing around $40 million in 1950 (up 38 percent from $28 million in 1945) and eager to put even marginal-seeming accounts on the books. Too small to be handled individually, these were rolled up into a totally new business—the T. Rowe Price Growth Stock Fund.

The new outlet was unique in that it opened Price's growth stock strategy for the first time to investors of modest means; unusual (for the time) in that it was a "no load" fund. There were no sales commissions, with a one percent redemption fee (payable to the fund) to encourage long-term holding. Price's distaste for the commission business, of course, was one of the elements that drew him to fee-based counseling. And in any event, he had neither the capital nor the distribution channels it would take to put a major marketing effort behind the fund.

Here was Price once again going against the trend in a revolutionary way. The great truth of the day was that "mutual funds are not bought, they're sold." In fact, as Price was about to prove, the reverse was true. Investors needed no intermediary hands to find their way to consistent performance. Other major fund groups soon hopped aboard the "no load" bandwagon, happy to wash their hands of the gathering scandal in high-pressure mutual fund sales. Among the legion of salesman cold calling prospects (at commissions that ate up eight percent or more of capital) were plenty of former "tin men" who had cut their eyeteeth educating the hapless on the virtues of aluminum siding and phony oil leases.

There were other "growth" funds in the field, basically looking to growth of capital rather than to growth stocks in Price's single-minded sense of the term. The fund was run as an extension of the individual portfolios in-house, and Price was happy with the result. Assets climbed to over $1.2 million by the end of the first year, creating another modest layer of management fees that helped to build what Price called "the most successful year in my business career." His gross income for 1952, including dividends: a modest $23,000.

The Growth Stock Fund was something of a by-blow, serendipitous, but there was Price the innovator again, way out in front of a major marketing change. The Growth Stock Fund was an early model of the 3,000 or so mutual funds now pursuing the same objective with similar tactics. It took a while, but mutual fund assets surpassed the individual counseling side of T. Rowe Price Associates for the first time in 1984.

The fund's growing success did little to allay Price's worry over the inflationary pressures that were building with the Korean War. His outlook became ever more Darwinian. He explicitly added to his criteria the idea that to pass muster growth stock earnings had to significantly outpace the cost of living, rather than simply demonstrate some unspecified rate of "long-term secular growth." Generally, Price had targeted average earnings gains of about 10 percent a year, but now that might no longer be enough. The life cycle from growth to maturity, catalyzed by the advance of technology, was speeding up at an exponential rate. "Changes in the fortunes of whole industries as well as individual companies will take place more rapidly than ever before," wrote Price.

Companies shy of quality-management and dedicated research would inexorably slip more quickly into decline; new opportunities would have to be spotted early. One object lesson: the divergent fortunes of Air Reduction (ultimately merged into another company) and American Cyanamid. Price dropped Air Reduction from his growth lists in favor of Cyanamid as an all-too-familiar trend played out. Sharp competition cut into Air Reduction's most profitable lines of industrial gases and earnings began to slide as lackluster research failed to produce more promising alternatives. American Cyanamid's short-term earnings, on the other hand, were sacrificed to aggressive research spending and then doubled as heavy investment in pharmaceuticals paid off. The result: a double in Cyanamid's market value and a 50 percent decline in Air Reduction's.

It's the classic syndrome of growth slipping into maturity. One parallel today would be Xerox; its new product potential bedeviled by poor execution and a negative product mix.

Pension fund money—a new force in the stock market—began to roll in, attracted in part by the highly promotable record being run up by the growth fund. It was on its way to becoming the industry's biggest and best performing no-load fund, racking up an average gain of almost 40 percent a year in its first 10 years.

Price had audited performance statements ready to hand on all his prior portfolio returns, but none of them was as convincing to potential clients as the open and verifiable results the fund was required to file with the Securities & Exchange Commission. Growing press coverage of the results made Price a star, reinforcing the realization that creation of the fund had been one of his greatest growth coups.

It was positioned to benefit from a bull market that, with a few bumps in the road, ran for almost a decade. Stocks that Price had caught in their infancy began surging into brawling adolescence. By 1955, a $10,000 initial investment in the Growth Stock Fund had zipped to $27,300. Price tried to stay abreast of his own firm's growth by switching his three-man partnership to a corporation and adding staff, but he was still personally supervising more than 40 percent of the $150 million in assets on the books.

"A great weakness," this hands-on obsessive complains in his diary. "Price should transfer a substantial number of accounts to other people."

Stocks were getting "too high, too fast," he felt. When a break did come along in 1957, the sharpest in two years, Price was characteristically relieved, "although on paper we are all very much poorer." This was yet another case of Price wanting to be right, rather than make money. Price had been expecting a sell-off for nearly two years and "needed to be right or have my clients lose confidence." He guessed that the drop would be blamed, among other things, on the "excessive optimism" of investors "bidding up growth stocks as a hedge against inflation."

Investors bounded out of the decline bidding more eagerly than ever for such Price favorites as Avon Products and 3M, and—yes, even for his nocturnal hunch—Magnavox. The 14,300 shares of the TV-maker on Growth Stock books had more than doubled to some $540,000. By the end of 1959, a $10,000 initial investment in the fund was worth $45,200. Price once again retreated behind the closed door. How to get his clients into the growth cycle much earlier, and at a lot lower multiples? To stay ahead of the looming menace of inflation, you had to run faster than ever.

Price was thinking of a new category killer—emerging growth stocks "hundreds of companies in such 'new and fertile fields' as missiles, rocket propulsion, electronics, nuclear energy, and flight control systems."

Especially, he was thinking of companies too young, too small, too risky, and too far down the food chain to excite the interest of rabid institutional investors. By Price's lights, they were driving establishment growth stocks to nosebleed levels. "Growth stocks got ridiculously high," he later told *Forbes*. "I decided the thing to do was to go into little companies that would become growth stocks, little companies in the early stages of growth."

Price had actually been mulling such a strategy since 1935, when he unsuccessfully tried to persuade his heel-dragging bosses at Mackubin, Goodrich & Company to let him run a "tightly speculative fund invested in the younger industries, such as aviation, air conditioning, alloy metals, etc."

The time had come to put this brainchild in motion. The result was the New Horizons Fund—a creation that once again put the protean Price out in front of a major change in market direction. Getting out front called for subtle changes in tactics. Many young companies just hadn't been around long enough to put together the long-term earnings history Price had insisted on in the past. Nor by force-feeding growth with retained earnings, were they likely to give off the rising stream of dividend income that Price had also counted on. The trading strategy was different, too. The market in small capitalization stocks was thin. They had to be nibbled at in small quantities on the buy side and were far more volatile than stocks further on in the growth cycle.

Price figured he could lower the risk profile by blending small growth with a mix of possibilities—older companies rejuvenated by new management or new profits, or relatively unknown family-owned businesses on a growth roll coming public.

At 62, Price himself was on a growth roll, glorying in new challenges. "He just loved New Horizons," recalls Curran (Cub) Harvey. "He'd begun to lose interest in the Growth Stock Fund." Harvey, hired out of the aerospace business as an analyst for New Horizons, later went on to become its president. Anxious to get the new fund up and running, Price "nearly went crazy" when its registration got hung up on a bureaucratic snag at the Securities & Exchange Commission. The point at issue, prompted by a lower court decision, was Jesuitical: Would use of the

T. Rowe Price name on the New Horizons Fund confuse investors who might think they were buying into the less volatile Growth Fund? Price, recalls Harvey, finally resolved the impasse by storming into SEC chairman Donald Cook's office and settling it mano-a-mano. The new fund, laughs Harvey, made its debut as the Rowe Price New Horizons Fund—"without the T up front."

Price wasn't confused. He was furious. The delay had cost him six months, and multiples had run up on almost a dozen stocks on his buy list. True to his word, though, he put the biggest chunks of his portfolio in "new and fertile" fields: electronics (16 percent), controls and instruments (10 percent), and missiles and space (10 percent). Among the openers destined to make New Horizons a lot of money in the years ahead: Xerox, the analytical instruments producer Perkin-Elmer, and broadcaster MetroMedia.

Xerox was not an entirely new choice. Still in an early growth stage, the company had been in the Growth Stock Fund for a number of years. Its appearance in the new fund emphasized what initially had been one of Price's key investment points: Stick with a stock for as long as it continues to meet its earnings bogey. It was a point on which market mania would soon elicit from the wily Price a major change in tactics.

For ballast, Price slipped into New Horizons a cluster of aerospace companies (Lockheed, North American Aviation) that were also on the Growth Stock hold list. They qualified as older companies with a galaxy of new space-age products making their way to the launch pad.

The mix did well enough in New Horizons' first year—up 17 percent—but Price was unhappy about lagging the market (up 27 percent), and went ballistic himself in 1962, when the fund got creamed. Net asset value was off 29 percent (from $12.76 to $9.06 a share). A clutch of Price's small technology stocks showed losses of 50 percent or more as an overpriced market dumped them and fled to the sanctuary of blue chips. Price burned when the lunch crowd at the Merchants Club began razzing him about the "Blue Horizon Fund" and the "Horizontal Fund."

"Boy, it was tough," recalls Curran Harvey. "I was just the notetaker at the Friday lunch meetings, but I remember walking into the Club and this guy with a booming voice shouting 'Hey, Tom, is that young man there to help you out with that fund?'"

Laughter at the Merchants Club; gall to the competitive Price. He had warned from Day One that his small caps would often run counter to the market. He ate crow at the Club for two long years. His turn came in 1964 when New Horizons was up 43 percent (versus 9 percent for the S & P 500) as tech stocks like Alpine Geophysical (up 270 percent) and Sanders Associates (up 140 percent) tore through the roof. Earnings in the New Horizons portfolio had been compounding at better than 18 percent a year and the market was only now just catching up. Gaining a startling 87 percent in 1967, New Horizons handily beat the averages for three years running, and by 1970 had posted the best 10 year record in the industry. Thanks partly to the recognition its success stirred, T. Rowe Price Associates now had more than $1 billion under management—a long way from the days when only Marie Walper's Christmas club stood between the firm and disaster.

Was Price happy? Hell, no. He was worried. In a move with little precedent, he temporarily closed New Horizons entirely to new investments, and then reopened it only to shareholders already on the books. The decision cost the firm management fees on new money that was rolling in at the rate of about $10 million a month. The closing had a nice old-fashioned aura of rectitude about it. Better to forgo profits than to put shareholders at high risk by chasing overheated stocks selling well over Price's buy limits.

Price had begun to get leery at the runaway market in growth stocks as early as 1964. In the past, he had not worried much about rising prices as long as earnings were growing at a good clip. Now he'd begun to talk about "high" price earnings ratios; the need to look at "intrinsic investment values," a term he rarely used before; and the prudence of taking money off the table if earnings get "dangerously overvalued."

Ironically, Price was warning against excesses that had grown out of three decades of his own work. Price gloried in success, but was too wise a bird to believe in miracles. When prices got decoupled from demonstrated earning power, there was trouble ahead.

That hard-earned conviction put Price at total odds with the new breed of growth stock managers elevated to star power early in the Soaring Sixties—an era eerily reminiscent of the Nifty Nineties. The new breed "performance" cult gave lip service to fundamentals, but basically ignored them. The credo centered on maximizing profits by quick turnover on high volume in such quintessential growth stocks as IBM, Xerox, and Polaroid.

A lot of this was drivel, not to be heard again until the "New Paradigm" markets of the 1990s. "Creative management," pontificated one of the so-called gunslingers of the day, capitalized on "the proper timing of security transactions to take advantage of a stock's time in the sun.",

Forget about old fogey notions like risk levels and impaired capital. Manic trading pushed multiples to as much as 50 times earnings, discounting "not just the future, but the hereafter" in the words of one traditionalist. The go-go doctrine was a perversion of growth stock theory as Price saw it, and its impact on some of his own young people worried him deeply.

Bad enough that a wildly speculative market was riding for a fall. But it wasn't just the market. The craziness on Wall Street, Price thought, was merely a symptom of the deep underlying malaise that he'd long been certain would turn the economy into a basketcase.

The specter of runaway inflation had been dogging Price for years, of course, and he responded by building the safe house of growth stocks. Even that sanctuary's days were numbered now, with what the escalating cost of the ill-thought-of war in Vietnam, seething unrest in the streets over civil rights, and the overburden of heavily increased social spending. Debt was climbing, the trade balance was deteriorating, and so was the dollar. Foreign tariff barriers were rising and so were restrictions on American investing abroad.

To Price, the consequences were inevitable: "A bear market of indeterminate extent and duration, a business depression of possibly greater severity than any since the end of World War II." The Great Boom was ending and growth stocks were no longer the answer. "We are facing a new era in domestic and international affairs, calling for a change in our investment policy," wrote Price.

Price renouncing growth stocks? Turning on a theory he was often thought to have invented, one that brought him national recognition and made him the wealthy steward of more than $1 billion in assets? It was as if the Pope had denied the divinity of Christ. What was eating Price?

He had been ill—rushed to intensive care, and then out of commission for two months because of a grave intestinal disorder. There had been increasing managerial friction: the tart-tongued Price losing control of an organization long too big to be dominated by an autocratic founder. And there was the inevitable generation gap, too—a 68-year-old Price totally out of patience with young analysts who, as chairman George Roche recalls, "thought stocks would always go only one way—up."

On the surface, it sounds like a bad replay of a standard B-School case study: Crusty old founder, brilliant in his day, tired and ill, loses touch with the New Paradigm. A familiar tale, except this wasn't just any old founder—it was Thomas Rowe Price, with a vision that once again put him way out in front of both his colleagues—and yes, another dramatic change in market direction.

As usual, Price was quick to act on his vision. He sold control of T. Rowe Price Associates to a group of insiders headed by old friend (and president) Charles Shaeffer under a long-agreed-upon formula based on retained earnings. The deal brought Price a modest cash buyout of $792,000—not a lot of money for a brand name and brain power that put the firm on the map.

Price didn't care about money; he cared about being right. This was by no means his swan song. He stayed on as president of both the Growth Stock Fund and New Horizons—a corporate facesaver that eased the potential impact on sales of his startling no confidence turn on growth stocks.

Significantly, Price kept his ownership in the separate corporation—Rowe Price Management—that held the advisory contract on the New Horizons Fund. It became the launch vehicle for his answer to the inflationary panic he saw ahead—a fund heavily weighted to natural resources that would grow in value as inflation eroded the purchasing power of the dollar.

Price played with variations on a name. The Salvage & Recovery Fund? The Inflation Fund? Whatever the name, the ever-competitive Price relished the idea of going head-to-head with his own "young men." They would pay for flouting his investment policy and ignoring fundamentals like buy limits and intrinsic value. "The young men here will learn there's another way to look at investments than through earnings growth," Price told Forbes. "They have to learn how to predict trends in value."

Price put $10,000 of his own money into a demonstration portfolio that did well, but it was almost three years before his colleagues agreed to let Price take his "New Era" fund public. As Charles Shaeffer told Forbes: "You don't take Rowe's predictions lightly, but you don't have to buy them, either." Price's abrupt turnabout on the firm's growth stock identity had jammed his associates into a deep dilemma. They'd gone into hock to buy him out, and worried that showcasing Price's newest baby would siphon off assets from the standard growth product line.

The New Era Fund finally got out the door, only to make its debut in the teeth of a recession—not great for Price's prognostications, or the launch of anti-inflation cure-all.

Price had been dead-right about one thing, though. The stock market, just as he had called it, went to hell in a handbasket. The Growth Stock Fund's increasingly mediocre performance slipped to a minus 8 percent and New Horizons ran two negative years, back to back. Price raged that at "each meeting it becomes more obvious that the young group is not going to pay much attention to the investment strategy which I have advocated so long."

Price was right—again—but he was tiring of the struggle. "Teenagers, college students, and young people in business are set upon overthrowing the old regime," reads his diary. "They have little or no respect for age and experience, and have learned little from history."

The New Era Fund was a disappointment, too. Price as promised, put together a package of inflation-resistant real estate, forest products, and energy stocks. He even salted it with a few growth stocks. On the basis of his towering reputation, the fund sold well. It did not perform well. Up an average of 3.3 percent in the three years Price ran it, New Era did better than the market as a whole, but it did not outrun inflation. As Charles Shaeffer later conceded, "It would have been better to have started New Era (earlier), when Price wanted to."

By spring 1971, Price had had it. He quit New Era and severed the last of his ties to the firm he'd created 34 years before. Characteristically, he did not go gentle into that good night. "I still have confidence in my conviction...that we are headed for very serious troubles before we can have a renewed period of prosperity," he wrote.

Right again! Sharp recession was in the wind. So was a blood-bath stock market. In the 1973–1974 crash, both the Growth Stock Fund and New Horizons took a terrible pasting. Over the two years, Growth Stock was off 25 percent and 33 percent; New Horizons 42 percent and 38 percent, respectively.

The carnage was far worse among the more hyper go-go funds. The deluge swept away much of the sure-thing delusion that had hijacked Price's growth stock theory. Investors fled into a long morning after.

The Growth Stock Fund's assets peaked at $1.4 billion in 1972 and didn't get back to that level for 17 long years.

New Horizons fared better. Even so, it was a half-dozen years before its assets climbed back to the 1972 peak. Private advisory accounts were jumping ship, too, and there was a real crisis of confidence at T. Rowe Price Associates. Should the firm stick with the growth stock trademark? The answer was yes, but to diversify into a much broader line of income and stock funds.

Price had called the turn, all right. High multiple growth stocks as a group dragged the market into the worst sell-off since the crash of 1929. The disaster he saw coming was a phenomenon that began to build again the nineties—a lemming—like a rush of institutional money into an increasingly narrow range of high-tech names.

The pressure on prices was (and has been) extraordinary. At their 1972 peak, the likes of Coca-Cola, IBM, and Procter & Gamble were selling at an average of 43 times earnings—more than double the market as measured by the Standard & Poor's 500 stock index. The dividend yield, at 1.1 percent was less than half the market. Sound familiar? Of course, but few were looking at the market of the late 1990s with anything like Price's prescience, or even a sense of history. Price's point was for the ages: Crazily extrapolated earnings growth focused on "one decision" stocks is folly in search of an accident.

Would future earnings growth justify buying these "one decision" stocks at any price? If you do overpay, will time bail you out? It will if you like odds of three to one—against. Wharton School professor Jeremy Siegel found that over the next quarter century fewer than one out of every three of the Nifties bought at the 1972 peak would have earned their keep. For every stock like Coca-Cola, which could have been bought for almost twice its 1972 P/E of 46 and still have matched the market in total return, there were three fumbles like Polaroid. At peak, the company sold at close to 100 times earnings. It then shuffled through a rocky earnings history that at best should have commanded no more than 16 times earnings. At this writing the stock is selling at close to an all-time low.

Still backtracking, Siegel figured that a buy of the whole Nifty Fifty at the 1972 peak would have brought an annualized return of 12.7 percent. Return for the market as a whole: 12.9 percent.

What's the logic of taking on the high risk and volatility of growth stocks for a lower payoff than one that could have been had from the rocking chair serenity of an index mutual fund?

There is money to be made in growth stocks, but few of them are forever. That point was central to T. Rowe Price's theory. Buy early in the growth cycle, before institutional interest in an issue begins to build and keep close tabs on earnings quality. That's what Price preached, and it's what he practiced for decades until institutional mania so drastically changed the rules of the game.

So, long term, following his own advice, how well did Price do? His return from the business—as distinguished from the stock market— would have been a lot better if he'd stayed through the Crash he so accurately predicted. Even secretary Marie Walper—she of the Christmas club backup—ultimately took a lot more out of the firm than did her old boss. That cut no ice with him. He may have been early in his predictions, but he'd been right—by God—and he never let his old colleagues forget it.

Some of Price's zingers were transmitted through the dozen interviews and/or columns that appeared in *Forbes* between 1971 and his death in 1983 at age 85.

By 1974, the "New Error Fund" (as the wags at the Merchants Club dubbed it) was outperforming not only the market, but the growth funds as well. Price's personal portfolio, a parallel to New Era in which he'd invested half his buyout money was doing even better. "If my fund gets too far behind his accounts," Howard (Pete) Colhoun, Price's successor at New Era told *Forbes*, we hear about it. Once a quarter, he makes a critique of our portfolio and you can leave the room quite upset."

On his own, Price started nibbling at some of the old burned-out growth stocks that had begun to look cheap (Disney and Black & Decker among others). He sent on to *Forbes* his list of 20 "Growth Stocks of the Future" (Viacom, for one). Bedridden and seriously ill, Price wouldn't quit. His last piece in *Forbes* ("Stocks for the Mid-Eighties") ran just 10 months before he died, and his old pals at Rowe Price Associates were among the first to learn that he'd just made a killing in gold.

Tom Bailey, ever-challenging accepted wisdom, learned to leave no research stone unturned, even in executive parking lots. It shows in the way his Janus Funds have expanded by taking on the risks of high multiple growth stocks.

CHAPTER 4

—•— ⥥ —•—

Extending the Growth Culture
Tom Bailey

In 1984, WHEN THE deficit-ridden Kansas City Southern Railway laid out $25 million for an 83 percent stake in Janus Capital Corporation, the New Economy had not yet been invented. Diversification was nice, went the word on Wall Street, but what exactly did a venerable old hauler of coal and wheat know about sophisticated soft goods like mutual funds?

Not an awful lot, but enough to realize that management of the $400 million assets open-end Janus Fund was best left in the hands of its founder, the then 47-year-old Thomas H. Bailey. Bailey had been running money for more than two decades, picking up on early growth trends like bowling and discount department stores.

He brought to research the same doggedness he displayed in school years on the hockey rink. His watchwords: "Every stock blows up sometime. You can't take anything for granted." It was a mindset Bailey shared with the progenitor of growth stock theory, T. Rowe Price—a theory Bailey, over the next couple of decades, was to raise to new levels. Unlike Price, Bailey had no Man Friday to pack a steamer trunk and do his leg work for him, so he spent a lot of time on the road himself grilling management on earnings prospects and the basics of the business. Getting behind the income statements wasn't enough. Bailey talked to salesmen, customers, and competitors. He even checked out the executive parking lots. A lot of fancy, high-priced iron might show that the brass was not as hungry as Bailey himself. A Ferrari or a Bentley in the lot was a cue to take a good look at overhead expenses. By Bailey's lights, the nexus was simple: Tough-minded research meant investment performance; investment performance brought in more net assets to manage.

That proved to be such a winning formula that the KCS parent, Kansas City Southern Industries, soon became the caboose, and Janus the locomotive. From the KCS deal to 1997, Janus Fund assets alone grew almost five times to $19.3 billion, and from 1997 to more than $46 billion. Janus subsequently hived off at least 14 other brand-name funds, with total assets that peaked at more than $300 billion and then slipped to around $200 million. Most of the slippage was due to sharply declining market prices rather than wholesale shareholder liquidations.

Even top-notch research can take you only so far along the line of probability. Like almost everyone else, Janus got savaged in the blood-bath engulfing high-tech growth stocks. Volatile issues like Cisco Systems and Sun Microsystems had practically become a Janus trademark. Bailey has paid the price—temporarily, he hopes—for sticking with them. Typical of aggressive growth managers, he booked outsize gains while the market was soaring only to fall faster when it tanked. Long-term share-holders who'd hung in with Bailey for three years or so, however, were still ahead of the game. In the case of his two oldest and biggest domestic funds—the big company-oriented Janus and Janus 20—they were looking at average total returns of twice the market.

No one, least of all the pragmatic Tom Bailey, thought gains of that magnitude sustainable through every phase of the market. That was scant consolation to unwary investors who jumped in at the peak of the tech mania, but they can't say they weren't warned.

Bailey hedged against the turn when he began shutting down eight of his most popular funds to new investors well before the market hit the wall. The shutdown cost Janus billions in what would have been easily harvested assets and was unprecedented in magnitude. Bailey was unmistakably signaling that too much money was chasing too few stocks. Shades of growth guru T. Rowe Price and his prescient call on the great break of 1972–1974! The same old signs of excess were flashing, but few were picking them up. Wasn't this the New Paradigm?

Déjà vu all over again.

Targeting the long haul, Bailey made it clear he was not going to trim his aggressive style to what he saw as a short-term change in the weather. Janus would go right on doing what it had been doing—pur-suing the typically higher multiple "best business and financial models we can find." "Over a long period of time," insisted Bailey, "You're gonna make a ton of money."

As one of the U.S. top growth managers, Janus itself meets every test of the classic growth stock definition. Among the earmarks: consistently expanding earnings; whacking operating profit margins of better than 45 percent; no debt; a growing share of a growing market (at the expense of entrenched leaders like the Fidelity and Vanguard groups); and proven top-flight management in the person of Bailey. Bailey cannot be weighted too heavily in this equation. Now 64, he is one of those rare founders who has created a culture in which young people thrive, and who knows when to keep his hands off.

The question here is whether Janus—like all growth stocks ultimately—has reached apogee with only wobble ahead. Can it continue to prosper in a radically deflated market? What makes Janus tick? Better to ask what makes Bailey tick. Chatting over a latte in one of his favorite getaway corners recently—the coffee shop of The Tattered Cover Bookstore next door to Janus' Denver headquarters—Bailey is decidedly casual. He is in the standard Janus undress: open-necked shirt and odd slacks. Fit from decades of skiing Aspen and working his ranch there, Bailey talks of a "gradual gravitation" to stocks.

Although his mother owned "very minor" amounts of General Motors and AT&T, both parents "had come out of the Depression" and stocks were "not the stuff of dinner-table conversation." Born in Pittsburgh, Bailey grew up in Leamington, Ontario, where his father helped manage a tomato farm for RJ Heinz & Company. Bailey did his undergraduate work at Michigan State, where his main enthusiasms were "girls, sports, and skylarking." Bailey finished an MBA in finance in 1962 at the University of Western Ontario, and in the spirit of the times, headed for Denver and the Rockies. "I liked to ski Aspen, and was at peace in the mountains," recalls Bailey.

Bailey also cottoned to the Wall Street lore he picked up at grad school. "Classes were small and I had some great professors," he recalls. He talks about how he began to trade odd lots—"five shares of this, or fifteen shares of that"—while working at a stopgap job selling mimeograph machines. He did not buy on whim, "doing the numbers" with a slide rule. "It was the kind of thing that all the geeks at school would run around with sticking out of their shirt pockets," laughs Bailey. The mimeograph machines he was selling were old timey, too, "the kind that made your hands dirty when you worked with them." They sold briskly, though, briskly enough to leave Bailey with plenty of leisure so that it was "easy to be free by noon, and you could spend the rest of the day lying around the pool with airline stewardesses."

Crunching numbers and following trends like the play in bowling stocks brought purpose to the day. "I realized that if I wanted to learn the brokerage business, I'd have to work on Wall Street," says Bailey. He had already absorbed some important business lessons. They had to do with Bailey's aversion to structure, authority, and management by-the-book—attitudes that have played a major part in the shaping of Janus' freeform culture. Bailey's easy conversational tones sharpen as he recalls how Xerox made the mistake of turning the screws on its salesmen. "A couple of guys," said Bailey, "had the Boulder territory, and were doing well. So what does Xerox do? It quartered the territory, and then cut it in eighths."

"I saw what that did to those guys," continues Bailey. "It demoralized them. The theory was that you can't have salesmen making more money than the president. I couldn't see why not. These guys were at the frontline, while the president was isolated from reality. In outfits where they do things by the book, the big bucks are made by the suits."

Bailey does not have the pinstripe mentality. Commiserating with the Xerox salesmen brought nascent insights into the workings of research and incentive that are very much part of the Janus style. First, if you're trying to size up a business, and want the real skinny, talk to the working stiffs and competitors on the frontlines. Further, to get top performance, you need to offer high incentives.

Bailey's first step to Wall Street—and ultimately to Janus—was the New York outpost of Boettcher and Company, an old-line Denver regional brokerage firm. Dipping into Wall Street argot for an easy mark, Bailey describes himself as a "mullet," the bait fish replacement New York manager Fred Larkin needed to speed his own return to Denver. Larkin subsequently left the business and gained solid recognition as a photographer. Bailey recalls Larkin as unstintingly generous in teaching him the ropes. "If anyone ever had any influence on me, it was certainly Fred Larkin," says Bailey.

The influence was a lasting one. Bailey himself has similarly mentored Janus chief financial officer James Craig, leading him through something very like his own apprenticeship. It was a demanding one.

Bailey recalls that Larkin had him look "at a lot of companies and exposed me to a lot of people. I enjoyed selling, absolutely. The whole organization was about selling, and you had to do it. But I was more interested in the why," recalls Bailey.

Bailey isn't exactly sure why the research side of the business appealed most. "It wasn't rocket science," he says. "All it took was a sense of curiosity and some competitive fire." In the high-momentum markets of the 1960s—not unlike those of the 1990s—basic analysis took a backseat to hype. Under the Larkin tutelage, Bailey did traditional grunt work. He learned to figure out why the gross margins on a department store in Kansas City might be twice those in one in New York City, and still not be a great buy. "In those days, all you had to do was study the prospectus and the footnotes," says Bailey, "and you had a competitive advantage." "These days," he continues, "computers do the modeling and everybody is looking for an edge. I never had the pressure these kids have today. I'm not sure I'd get hired today."

Bailey liked the work. Surprisingly, he liked New York, too. It wasn't the Rockies, but Bailey remembers his old neighborhood in the East 70s with affection. "Right behind the Mad Hatter," he prompts, summoning up a popular neighborhood joint of the time. Bailey married and was happy except for one thing. He was desperate to take the step up from research to actually running money. In the evolution of growth stock investing, it was another turn of mind that Bailey shared with T. Rowe Price. Both served demanding apprenticeships in research, seasoning while itching to make the move up. Both responded with virtuosity to major changes in the direction of the market, and adjusted style accordingly. Bailey got his first chance to build a portfolio in 1967 when a group of a half dozen friends put together $150,000.

Taking the job freelance was definitely against the rules at Boettcher, making Bailey a stealth manager. He'd scoot from his office on the 25th floor to call in his trades to Loeb, Rhoades and Company from the pay phone on the ground floor, and did the bookkeeping at home at night. For 18 months or so, Bailey was quite pleased with himself. "In that market, everything went up, and I thought I was a genius. I pretty quickly learned differently." Bailey's ultimate objective was clear enough. He recalls seeing a magazine story on Fred Alger, then a gunslinger, now the considerably more conservative president of Alger Management Company. "Occupation: Portfolio Manager; 1967 Annual

Income: $1.1 Million," blared the cover. "I went home and told my wife, Jeanne, that's what I wanted to do."

It took a while to get there. Back in Denver, by early 1970, Bailey was the top name in a struggling three-man private money management firm. One of his fledgling clients was the $600,000 Rawhide Fund. Bailey bought out the management contract for $50,000 when the fund's original sponsors and its entire sales force ran for cover in a sharp market break.

Deciding that his status as a greenhorn with no long-term experience running money would make it difficult to reenergize a sales force, Bailey revamped the fund as a no-load. Out of her interest in mythology, his wife, Jeanne (the couple divorced in 1990), christened the fund Janus for the Roman god of new beginnings. Bailey was off as a one-man research team—a conservative one, with sometimes as much as 80 percent of his assets in cash. Working on his own gave Bailey a keen sense of responsibility. "You," he says, underscoring the pronoun, "are buying the stock. You've got to do the numbers yourself."

Bailey is describing another piece of personal experience that has become part of the Janus culture—large measures of autonomy for portfolio managers, combined with strict accountability. It was a personal code that helped Bailey grow through the 1970s, a period of "massive change, including the high cost of paying for the Vietnam War, inflation, and price controls." "I love change," continues Bailey. "You have to keep reinventing yourself."

Bailey saw reinvention at work in the retail business, and picked up early on the trend of discount chain stores like Levitz Furniture, Pay-Less Cashway, and House of Fabrics. Going through personal effects a while ago, Bailey came up with the audiotape of his first appearance on *Wall Street Week*. "While some of the stocks I mentioned were horrible," he recalls, "There was Wal-Mart." It was typical conservative Bailey strategy: Buy a group of stocks early in a trend and hope to catch the winners of the inevitable shake out.

With growth stocks, explains Bailey, you always have to look five to ten years out. "You know that many of these companies are going to be merged out. They'll be gone." Bailey has casualties like the once-promising Levitz Furniture in mind. "Change is the one constant, the unexpected, and I love it," he says.

Bailey's adaptability is one of the keys to his success. Although Janus is now practically a synonym for the likes of network hardware producer Cisco and mobilephone innovator Nokia, Bailey takes a lot of kidding about a study he did a number of years ago lambasting high-tech stocks. "If you can't wear it and you can't eat it, don't buy it" was his advice.

Bailey admits to having missed some bets along the way. He lost money in the 1973–1974 crash that brought about the downfall of "Nifty Fifty" one-decision stocks like Xerox and Polaroid. That debacle set off a bear market that really didn't lift for a decade. Bailey's consistent long-term results kept him afloat: up 15 percent in 1970; 40 percent in 1971; 35 percent in 1972. He beat the averages in 10 of the 16 years that he ran the Janus Fund.

One of the most difficult choices he had to make along the way was not a market call, but a highly emotional business call. It involved the sale of a major equity stake in Janus to Kansas City Southern. The sale grew partly out of the family needs of partner William Mangus who died of kidney failure, leaving three young daughters. The estate needed liquidity. Bailey didn't have the cash it would take to buy out the partnership interest, or the capital it would take to expand what was still a one-fund operation.

The sale to the railroad holding company, two-thirds for $11 million in 1984, and another 16 percent for a bit more later, seemed to be the answer. Bailey kept control of the Janus board, with a huge grant of autonomy over the company's money management operations. "KCSI guys can't get in the front door without an invitation," he says. Relations began to chill when KCSI moved to spin off Janus Capital in company with a couple of far less successful other investment management firms acquired after Janus.

For much of its life, the KCSI deal worked well enough. Bailey came out of it with about $4 million dollars net and more important still, with a chance to get his ducks in a row. "Without the sale, Janus would never have grown as it did. The deal made me let go of my old attitudes and taught me to think big," says Bailey. Janus, despite its consistent performance, was still small potatoes compared with industry leaders like Fidelity and Vanguard. If Bailey was going to start thinking big, it was time to add to the product line and establish a brand name.

Janus Fund, Bailey's baby, had prospered by concentrating on large, well-established companies. There was room under the tent for two new contenders: a more concentrated aggressive version of the flagship Janus Fund and a small company fund. The initiative required more talent than even Bailey could muster on his own. He began tutoring a new hire, young James Porter Craig, III, in the fine art of legwork, much as he had been. The Decatur, Alabama-born Craig, 27, had been working as an analyst for the Trust Company of the West. The graduate degree in finance he had picked up at the Wharton School hadn't prepared Craig for quite so demanding a life on the road. Visits to as many as 13 companies in four days, half of them with Bailey, weren't unusual. Pico Products, Hazeltine Electronics, Information Displays. As Thomas Easton reported in *Forbes*, most of the companies they hit are long forgotten. Not so the discipline Bailey was inculcating. "If you keep asking the right questions, you can learn any business," insists Bailey.

It took three years of seasoning for Craig to win his spurs. Bailey took hands off and the Janus Fund became Craig's baby. Around the same time, still on a talent hunt, Bailey paid a high compliment to his old million-dollar-a-year role model, Fred Alger. He poached portfolio manager Tom Marsico, then 31, back to his old stomping grounds in Denver. As one portfolio manager notes, Bailey likes to lead "with a velvet touch," but when the chips are down he is quick to act.

The newly launched Janus Value Fund was floundering. Marsico, with two years at Janus under his belt, was assigned to redesign it. The portfolio was stripped to concentrate on a more limited number of stocks and renamed the Janus 20. Now, with better than $30 billion in assets, it is second in size only to the Janus Fund. The new team—Craig at Janus and Marsico at Janus 20—quickly created a buzz. With returns approaching 50 percent at Janus and better than 50 percent at the more aggressively styled Janus 20 in 1989 and 1991, billions in new assets rolled in. Equally significant, both funds held up well in 1990, a bad year for most competing funds. Craig and Marsico weren't operating with mirrors. Both were pursuing growth at a reasonable price. The basic rule of thumb was conservative: Look for solid financials generally, but be particularly cautious about paying up for price multiples that exceeded earnings growth.

Their performance and Bailey's willingness to give Craig and Marsico a lot of running room made it easy to attract new talent. Thanks in part to Marsico's old connections, Bailey recruited three more aspirants from Fred Alger's bench, all of them in their twenties. The accent is definitely on youth, provoking the old Wall Street wheeze that the only way out-of-synch old-timers can make money in runaway high-tech markets like those of recent years is to "go get a kid." The subtext, of course, is that kids fearlessly going for broke on the upside, will founder on a downside they have never the hard luck to experience.

Hence Bailey's apprenticeship approach. The career path typically goes from analyst to assistant portfolio manager to portfolio manager with mentoring all the way. Bailey, who quit running money to concentrate on management in 1986, still interviews every new hire on the research side. The preference is not for cookie-cutter MBAs, but for "eclectic minds quick to grasp new ideas." "We like people who think wide," says Bailey. Thus, the research lineup is a mix of backgrounds. Laurence Chang, for example, comanager of Janus Overseas Fund, majored in philosophy and religion at Dartmouth. Claire Young, manager of Janus Olympus, studied electrical engineering. Scott Schoezel, the newly breveted manager of Janus Fund, spent almost a decade in commercial real estate before signing on with Bailey. Warren Lammert, manager of Janus Mercury, dropped out of the firm for a couple of years to complete a master's degree at the London School of Economics.

In keeping with Bailey's early insight into Xerox mishandling of its salesmen, incentive pay is tied to performance—bonuses for analysts who come up with viable ideas, and grants of scarce Janus stock for portfolio managers. Bottom-up research and legwork are still as much a part of the drill as they were when Bailey was putting Jim Craig through the hoops. Thus, analyst Matt Ankrum, checking out Metromedia Cyber Company recently, found himself taking a count of the number of competitor's fiber optic conduits under the streets of Manhattan. At the same time, Bob Jackson, an ophthalmologist by training, was picking apart clinical results on what a pharmaceutical company was touting as a major new drug.

Deep research is labor-intensive, which is one of the reasons why Janus expense ratios haven't come down as quickly in proportion to asset growth as they might. Still, there is no denying the payoff on the performance side. "With growth stocks," said research director Jim Craig, "you need the critical information early, before everyone else starts to pile into a stock."

As exhibit A, Craig cited the digging of Ron Sachs, now manager of Janus Orion. As an analyst several years ago, Sachs came away far more impressed with America Online's business strategy than Craig. "He came up with earnings estimates so much higher than anybody else, you either had to believe Ron, or think he was nuts," recalled Craig. "He beat the hell out of every portfolio manager to overcome the universal skepticism on AOL, mine being the greatest. He succeeded and I tripled my money." AOL, along with merger partner Time Warner, soon became one of Janus' top holdings.

Bailey works hard to encourage that kind of collegiality. Analysts and portfolio managers wander around the fifth floor of Janus' unassuming brick and glass headquarters, swapping chat and intelligence the way reporters used to schmooze around old-time city rooms. The culture is very tight. The senior portfolio managers are still mainly in their 30s. All have come up through the system. Friends recruited friends. Some are related by marriage. The group sees a lot of one another both in and outside of the office, sometimes rooting rinkside with Bailey for the Colorado Avalanche. *Forbes* editor Tom Easton put his finger on the linkage: "Helen Young Hayes and Warren Lammert knew Jim Goff, who knew David Corkins, who married Lammert's sister. And then Hayes' sister Claire arrived and worked with Marsico, etc., etc., etc."

Bailey, for all his laid back manner, demands a lot. "I want my guys to hit a winner every day," he says. In the same breath, Bailey notes that "I really can't explain how I feel about these guys. The pressure is enormous and their work is awesome."

Major defections from Janus are rare. The most conspicuous of them was the departure of Tom Marsico in 1997. He left under somewhat contentious circumstances to set up his own Denver-based shop, Marsico Capital Management. A 50 percent interest sold last year to the Bank of America for $950 million. Marsico's biggest pool of assets, not surprisingly, is a focus fund not unlike the Janus 20 Fund he ran so successfully for Bailey. Bright and articulate, Marsico had got adoring press in his decade at Janus, and was put up front as a brand-name poster boy, sporting returns that often ran to double digits. When he left, it was as if the celebrated Peter Lynch had walked out of Fidelity Management in a huff.

Even today there is speculation about the reasons for Marsico splitting. Did he fail in an abortive power play to buy back Janus from KCSI independently of Bailey? Was he piqued because the putative succession to Tom Bailey was clearly in the hands of fellow portfolio manager (and vice chairman) James Porter Craig? Bailey's curt all-purpose explanation: "philosophical differences."

Thanks to the incredibly strong personal bond at the heart of the Janus culture, none of Marsico's proteges left with him—an uncommon occurrence in such star turn exits. There was predictable hand-wringing in the press that money would follow Marsico out of Janus 20, leaving Bailey victim to the marketing strategy that put Marsico out front. Marsico's mug promptly disappeared from such prominent fixtures as the double-page spread in the Janus annual report and the cult of personality was purged. Press releases quickly began to talk up Janus research as a "team effort."

Marsico's departure could be written off as a teapot tempest except for one thing: the markedly more aggressive and riskier portfolio strategy that kicked in after he left. Looked at only in terms of top-line percentage returns, the Janus Fund and Janus 20 were world beaters. But the market was going great guns, too. The two big Janus funds were slipping both in peer-group rankings and the regularity with which they were beating the bogey of the Standard & Poor's 500 stock average. The glory days of the late 1980s and early 1990s were slipping away.

That didn't sit well with the perfectionist in Tom Bailey. "It hurt all of us," he said. "I don't want any portfolio manager at Janus to think I'm doing okay.' I want people to do really well. If they're hurting, I want them to help one another out."

The self-help took the form of what Bailey calls "open debate" on why Janus was doing less than past personal bests. There were good reasons for worry. The prospect of increased competition from the breakaway Marsico was the least of them. Unimpeachable top-notch performance was critical to strengthen Bailey's hand in dealing with the KCSI management. It was showing increasing determination to spin off Janus with its lesser mutual fund holdings in a way that could dilute the equity of both Bailey and his portfolio managers, prospectively costing them millions. Staff holdings of Janus Capital stock, awarded on performance and valued at close to $300 million, are an essential element of the group's unique culture. In the end, the stand-off was settled. The spin-off went through, but Bailey's autonomy was guaranteed, and Janus benefitted by getting access to the capital it needs to build a major Internet presence.

Yet another imperative pushing for a lift in performance was the paradox of how to deal with the penalties of success. So much new money was pouring in that the funds were becoming increasingly difficult to manage. Size is a mixed blessing in the fund business. It generates more management fees, but compromises the ability to take sizable positions that will have a measurable impact on performance. Big money demands high liquidity—issues with enough floating shares available to minimize the price impact of major buys and sells. The universe is a limited one. Driven by the huge sums increasingly devil-may-care investors were shoveling into the market, money managers crowded into many of the same high-tech names. As liquidity tightened, price swings widened, multiples tore through the roof, and so did risk levels. Chief investment officer Jim Craig was getting gun-shy.

Janus and Janus 20 were typically run at lower risk levels than more aggressive counterparts such as the Kansas City-based PBHG Large Cap 20 and Large Cap Growth Funds. Jim Craig, as mentor and chief investment officer, had held consistently to a conservative "growth at a reasonable price" doctrine. The research, as always, was bottom up—insistence on strong fundamentals. The emphasis on valuations was also iron-clad: Buy only when the price-earnings multiple was lower than the next year's projected earnings growth; sell when multiples exceed earnings growth. Thus, a stock growing at 30 percent a year and selling for 15 times earnings was a real buy and at 30 times earning and 15 percent growth, an obvious sell.

Rising valuations aside, Craig was deeply skeptical of the technology stocks that had been catching fire. As he told *Kiplinger's Personal Finance Magazine* as early as 1993, "I'm thoroughly convinced there's no franchise to these businesses. Product cycles are so fast that it's difficult for them to make money." "There's no barrier to new competitors," continued Craig. "A couple of engineers in their garage can make a super-computer. Even IBM has finally fallen. They all will."

The volatility of a few bad buys deepened Craig's skepticism. He was getting ready to sell a slug of Electronic Data Services only to see it drop 20 percent in a single day on a bum earnings report before he could kick the stuff out the door.

So, Craig kept his core holdings close to what he calls "steady Eddies"—conservative picks like Colgate Palmolive, Coca-Cola, and Computer Sciences. Though he thought of himself as "the world's worst technology investor," Craig didn't shy entirely from the field. The difficulty was that too many tech stocks went zipping through his price earnings-growth limits at high velocity. Clinging to bedrock discipline meant that Craig all too often was selling too soon. Exhibit A: Pfizer. "In 1996," recalled Craig, "I sold about 30 percent of our position in Pfizer when the price got to be 23 times our estimate for 1998 earnings." The stock was soon trading at more than twice that multiple. Object lesson: "I had to say to myself that I was naive and foolish to sell Pfizer when I did."

There were many such sales as a manic market pushed on to levels Craig thought unsustainable. "I sold Cisco Systems when it reached a valuation level I thought was too high," recalls Craig, only to buy it back a year later, "up another 40–50 percent." "The same thing happened to Microsoft," he adds.

With a turnover of well over 100 percent, hard-put to find quality growth at the right price, Craig was running performance-deadening cash positions that sometimes got as high as 20 percent of assets. Looking for the market to snap, Craig was also heavily diversified, carrying well over 100 stocks. "I was always guarding the downside," he said.

Time for some soul searching. Thanks to the wide grant of autonomy Bailey has instilled in the Janus culture, at least two other managers were approaching the market with a more aggressive tilt than Craig. Scott Schoezel, for one. Seconded out of Janus Olympus to replace the departed Marsico, Schoezel gave Janus 20 a thorough housecleaning. He cut the number of stocks in the portfolio for a sharper focus, dumped a number of cyclical stocks that had been in the fund for ballast, and brought in such new economy names as AOL.

Other more conservative managers began drifting in the same direction. In the end, so did Craig. He decided that he was trying to run big money the way he had run small money. "I was too reactive," he says, "too cautious to realize that Janus was in the midst of an unbelievable, unpredictable, inexplicable bull market where the rules and regulations regarding valuation parameters were being busted left and right."

Tech stocks Craig had viewed as struggling for franchise values a few years earlier were suddenly a lot easier to identify. Companies like Intel, Microsoft, AOL, and Cisco had all crushed their competitors to emerge as top dogs. Craig stopped looking at price multiples as a major determinant, and focused more on cash flow and return on equity. "If they're increasing," he says, "I'm not that concerned about the P/E relative to the growth rate. I've recognized that valuable companies making themselves more valuable deserve a premium."

In short, GARP (Growth At A Reasonable Price) was out. A once useful analytical tool was downplayed in an investment environment demanding immediate results—or else. Craig had decided to ride the tiger.

It was a radical change. In the new philosophy, paying 200 times earnings for a company like AOL would not be too much. As Janus Mercury manager Warren Lammert told *Forbes*, "Companies can grow into a valuation if they deliver on earnings. The reverse isn't true. Reasonable price won't protect you from nonperformance."

Focus was very much part of the new look. Craig more than halved the number of stocks in his portfolio from 140 to 65, allowing that "diversification led to mediocrity." Tech names such as Cadence Design Systems, Maxim Integrated Products, and Texas Instruments quickly mounted to 25 percent of Janus Fund assets; the top ten stocks to some 40 percent of assets.

Craig had to resolve a personal dilemma. He conceded that he didn't sleep as well under the new dispensation. But he was also troubled by the "missed opportunities" that went with his more conservative bent. In fact, Craig himself was being market-driven. A rising share of Janus' new business was coming from super market sellers like Charles Schwab and Company, driven by financial advisors whose necks were also on the performance line. "I had to change my style," says Craig. "We were being paid to be active."

The change in style quickly percolated through the rest of the funds. Even the conservatively run Equity-Income Fund was soon showing chunks of Microsoft and Cisco Systems. The generally good performance elicited a wariness from some fund analysts. "I was skeptical hearing about these changes, thinking it was late in the game to decide to go with the flow a little more," said Christine Benz of Morning-star, Incorporated, the Chicago-based fund rating outfit.

The shift brought higher risk and volatility, but once committed, Craig lost no time putting Janus on the board. Early one bright April afternoon in 1999, for example, eyeing a sagging market 45 minutes before the close, Craig plunged about $1 billion into the likes of Time Warner, Sun Microsystems, Tyco International, and Wal-Mart. And he had certainly taken to hanging on to winners. The high turnover prompted by his earlier caution dropped by more than half from 130 percent to 60 percent of the Janus Fund Portfolio.

The pay-off was immediate. In the two years following the strategy lift, Janus and Janus 20 handily beat the market and most competitors by double digits. As a group in 1999, Janus 19 equity funds according to Morning Star, generated an average return of 76 percent—almost twice as much as the second best complex, the AIM family of funds. As ever, new cash followed performance. Assets swelled 130 percent to $249 billion, making Janus the United States' fifth largest fund manager. Three years earlier, the group ran twelfth, with assets of $68 billion.

Tom Bailey tended to emphasize performance rather than the asset growth that was compounding Janus advisory profits. "This is not about asset growth," he told reporters. "If it was about asset growth, we wouldn't have closed half the funds." "If it was about asset growth," continued Bailey, "we'd be opening five funds a year, and I'd be hiring portfolio managers all over the place. That's not what we're about. We're about trying to get to that area roughly around first quartile performance, and add value to shareholders. That's the sole focus of this firm."

Still, Bailey's unquenchable competitive fire was compounding the higher risk levels he had taken on in the switch from the old standard of growth at a reasonable price.

As a business decision, the shift in emphasis could not be faulted. Bailey and Craig had got the temper of the times right. Sharper performance brought in so much more new money that Janus vaulted to a remarkable number three (behind Fidelity and Vanguard) among direct sellers of funds. Soon, 28¢ out of every dollar invested in mutual funds was being ticketed to Janus, and the group was so swamped that eight of the biggest funds were closed to new money.

The risks of *not* cranking up the strategy could be seen in the slowed headway of the T. Rowe Price group, the gilt-edged pioneer name of growth stock funds. As wary of runaway valuations as the converted Jim Craig had been earlier, the Price funds stuck to the traditional strategy of growth at a reasonable price. Performance slipped, redemptions rose, and the management company's own stock price fell to the point where Price began to be mentioned as a takeover candidate. It was an ironic riff on founder T. Rowe Price's urging colleagues to get out of growth stocks before the 1973–1974 crash.

The costs of not following the old man's advice—a decade of stagnation—were burned in management memory. Looking back on the experience, T. Rowe Price chairman George Roche recently noted that tech stocks are just not going to slip this latest sell-off and "go up to new highs." "You are going to require a period to repair it," he said.

Bailey had been hurt in 1973–1974, too, but was not haunted by history. By the end of fiscal 1999, big winners like Sun Microsystems, Cisco, and Nokia were beginning to pop up in almost all of the Janus major funds.

Comcast, Sun, and Cisco alone, for example, accounted for about 15 percent of Janus Fund's $35.8 billion in assets. The latter two stocks made up 12 percent of Janus 20's $28.7 billion in assets. More broadly, there were 17 overlaps among the 10 top holdings of Janus Fund, Janus 20, Worldwide, and Mercury. Most prominent among the common holdings: AOL Time Warner, Cisco, AOL, Nokia, Sprint, EMC, and AT&T Liberty. Even the conservatively run Balanced Fund was holding goodly chunks of cable outfits like Comcast and Viacom.

The concentration was an inevitable result of Janus' decision to go where the growth was, but the overlapping big bets on so many volatile high-tech names worried some analysts. Morningstar's Christine Benz, for one, argued that the core holdings tended to make "the funds act a lot alike," so that owning more than one of them could increase risk rather than provide the higher level of diversification conservative investors might be looking for.

Predictably, when tech stocks got clocked big time, concentration in them left Bailey particularly vulnerable. Most of the Janus Funds fell faster than the market as a whole. Top holdings like AOL Time Warner and Cisco Systems were off 50 percent or more. Janus 20, in a whirlwind 60 days, lost 20 percent of its value.

It's not as if the Janus portfolio managers were caught flat-footed. A half dozen had moved defensively into cash positions as uncharacteristically high as 17 percent of assets.

Though some of the managers agreed on many of the major hold-ings spread across the funds, you can see their autonomy at work in a comparison of Bailey's two biggies, Janus 20 and Janus. Janus 20's Scott Schoezel, for example, for three years hands running, had been warn-ing investors that "outsize returns were not sustainable." He was among those who upped his cash position, but otherwise made few concessions to the prospect of a major sell-off. He even eased low-risk standards like Fannie Mae and Wal-Mart out of the portfolio in favor of more adven-turous names like Network Solutions and Aether Systems, soon ham-mered to well under their highs.

Janus Fund's Blaine Rollins, on the other hand, took on a more con-servative coloration. He unloaded a big stake of cell phone companies, and jacked up his holdings of defensive stocks like United Parcel. Rollins also took on ballast (along with a half dozen colleagues) with a big slug of low multiple Boeing Company.

The range of strategic shifts showed that adversity had not chilled the Bailey doctrine of letting a thousand flowers bloom among his port-folio managers. Some seemed to be edging out of tech to a broader reach of core holdings in pharmaceutical and energy stocks. Others remained convinced that a lot of still-promising tech stocks had been thrown out with the bath water. They unswervingly continued buying into suddenly unhot stocks like radio broadcast behemoth Clear Channels Communications and cable big Comcast Corporation. Multiples on many such stocks had dropped so far so fast that Janus could almost argue it was once again edging into the comfort zone of growth at a rea-sonable price.

Still, even with a lot of water wrung out of them, fading favorites did not look all that cheap at 50 times earnings. As that famous tech skep-tic Warren Buffett told Berkshire Hathaway shareholders, "There is nothing obvious to us that the sector is a good buy or undervalued."

Janus, in keeping with its aggressive style, continued to do some buying in the teeth of unhappy earnings surprises, but was cautious about what it took on. Seeming bargain prices were not necessarily cheap. The trick was to distinguish the impact of panicky selling from changes in underlying basics. Contrarians with iron nerves might have thought Cisco a terrific buy at 18 (down from a high of 82), but Bailey's managers chopped total holdings of the company by more than a third—from 180 million shares (2.5 percent of outstanding) to just under 100 million shares. Big chunks of semi-conductor producer Texas Instruments, fiber optics supplier JDS Uniphase and other denuded favorites also went out the window. "I've lowered exposure where I didn't see (earnings) visibility and was concerned about fundamentals," Janus Mercury's Warren Lammert told Morningstar senior analyst Kunal Kapoor.

Some of the seeming inviolates, it now developed, were no more immune to down turns in the economy than less glamorous peers. Unsettled by the $50 billion chunk a fast-declining market gouged out of asset values, worried investors at one point were cashing in Janus shares at the rate of a billion dollars a day.

Sticking to its guns, Janus was taking long bets on the quality of its own research. In general, Bailey was holding and/or adding to a core of familiar tech names—Nokia, GE, Comcast, AOL Time Warner—that had done so well on the upside. Some were now down 60 percent or more from their highs, dizzying descents that in Warren Lammert's view discounted a lot of bad news. The now winnowed group might ship still more water short term, went the rationale, but the long-term payoff was still there. "I have tried to maintain a core of holdings in technology that I think will be marketshare winners as we go through a very difficult economic environment," said Warren Lammert.

A few other canny institutional investors were also hoovering up quantities of what they regarded as merely interrupted growth at distress prices. Yes, multiples were down, but still very high by historical standards. Janus hadn't done any better at predicting the killer reversal in high-tech capital spending than the Great Panjandrum himself, Federal Reserve Board chairman Alan Greenspan. "The slow down has been much sharper than I expected, as have the price declines in the technology group," said Warren Lammert.

So, was Tom Bailey's much vaunted research living up to its press clippings? The jury is still out on that question and will be for some time to come. Within the limits of his larger strategy, you have to give Bailey a qualified yes. The heavily concentrated Janus 20, for example, was among the worst hit. But by closing it (and seven other stable mates), Bailey was, in effect, limiting risk. Shutting the till saved many investors from socking away more new money at the wrong time.

The logic of Janus tight stock selection, good for extraordinary gains in 1998 and 1999, drove it into huge positions that could not be unwound overnight. Thus Janus 20, like Bailey's other most assertive offerings, has to be seen as mainly a one-track animal. The nature of the beast is to run well ahead of the pack in rising markets; well behind in sell-offs. Investors who neglect to diversify against that phenomenon are not getting the message. Except for people willing to shoot crap against the market, growth stocks are definitely not a short-term play. The key question is whether Janus has gotten the long-term right. If it hasn't, Bailey will pay the price for his doggedness.

He's got one thing working for him. In the main, shareholders are hanging tough. A comparatively low level of redemptions suggested investors were betting they would come out all right in the end. The past offered some comfort, maybe even for those who got in at the top. In rolling three-year periods over two decades, Janus had generally out-performed the market.

Comfort, but no guarantees. Over most of that period, Bailey had played a much more conservative hand. The flagship Janus Fund, for example, was far more diversified and growth at a reasonable price (rather than momentum-driven buying) was the rule. The souped-up funds of today are a totally different breed. Will they do as well in the future as in the past? Probably not—certainly not until the next new wave of growth gathers force in what seems to be a repetitive pattern of discovery, rising stock mania, and ultimate crash. In the 1960s, as *Forbes* has noted, the catalyst was the mainframe computer; in the 1970s, the minicomputer; in the 1980s, the PC; in the 1990s, the Internet. Is Janus research still sharp enough to beat the crowd to the next big thing?

Janus is no longer quite the same organization. Jim Craig, intense and haggard at age 44, has gone to run his family foundation. He cashed in his Janus stock for $78 million, and was extraordinarily candid on how the quest for high performance had become a synonym for burnout. "There is a limit to the time you can endure one stress followed by another," Craig told reporters. "You have one big year, you wake up the next morning. It's another year and you've got to do it all over again."

Craig's mentoring would be missed, and his departure left Tom Bailey without an anointed successor. Bailey reassured his troops that he planned to stay in control for a long time to come. Still, sale of half of his remaining Janus stock for "estate reasons" (and $610 million) offered an easy inference that Bailey was easing out at what he saw as a market top. Would some of his talented young managers follow suit? Where is Janus heading?

More reassuring than the portent of purely statistical past perform-ance was a continuing show of self-questioning and fierce internal debate. They demonstrate that Janus' biggest asset—its culture—is still alive and well. Some managers felt free enough to concede that they had gone overboard on tech stocks. "I think we were caught up in over-enthusiasm for everything in technology," said Warren Lammert. "We got a little carried away and valuation insensitive in some of the tech-nology and telecom names," added Janus World Wide co-manager Laurence Chang. Bailey himself conceded there was some risk that Janus analysts, committed to getting close to the companies they fol-lowed, might begin seeing things through management eyes. "We rec-ognize that danger and are trying to do something about it," he said.

Thus, Janus managers are not coming on as high-tech hotshots, glorying in past successes. Persevere in hard times, counsels Bailey. "We're going to go on doing exactly what we're doing today," he says. "Doing work on the companies, the competitors, and the suppliers because in the end, what you're buying is a business, living breathing things run by people."

There have been mistakes—a real shocker in the case of Web MD Corporation, a highly touted health portal linking doctors, patients, and insurance companies that unaccountedly imploded. Trapped in the debris with a private purchase of almost a billion dollars in difficult-to-sell restricted Web MD shares were three Janus funds (Global Life Sciences, Global Technology, and Janus 20). As the Web's troubles deepened, Janus' billion-dollar holding withered to a fair market value of just under $125 million. This huge bath underscored the dangers of concentrating big holdings across several funds. Janus had also been stung by comparatively illiquid holdings in a half dozen or so IPOs. They were great on the upside; deadly on the downside.

So, why didn't Tom Bailey take a leaf from old, T. Rowe Price's book and preserve his gains by shifting to a more conservative stance? Would Janus have done better if it had diversified more broadly and retreated to its more traditional strategy of growth at a reasonable price? Short term, yes. Janus 20, for example, sold off far more sharply than the more cautious Rowe Price Growth Stock Fund. Some of Bailey's glory day gains were wiped out, but over the last five years (at this writing)

Janus 20 still trumps the average Rowe Price return to shareholders by more than 25 percent. Risk does have its rewards." We're paid to manage growth," says Bailey. "We aren't market timers."

Still, the magnitude of Janus lost values is a sharp reminder that risk and volatility are the price of admission to aggressive growth investing. Growth is a revolving door. Over the last three decades, according to value-oriented Sanford Bernstein and Company, the average high-tech stock had only one chance in three of maintaining growth status for five years; only one chance in nine of doing so for ten years.

Does that mean that the conservative investors should stick with value—that it's safer to waltz with Ben Graham and Marty Whitman than to swing with T. Rowe Price and Tom Bailey? Nope, it just means that both schools take on different coloration in different phases of the market. It's no blinding epiphany to say that both are best bought cheap; or that you can never go broke taking profits off the table. How to measure cheap? Buy Marty Whitman or Tom Bailey when they are clearly out of phase. Homework helps. Even such rudimentary precautions as tracking earnings multiples and return on equity help to keep the malarial pull of irrational exuberance at bay. Janus may be the god of new beginnings, but he's been looking both ways for a long, long time.

Rotund and affable, Anthony "Tino" DeAngelis cut quite a figure in commodity markets. It took creditors a long time to realize he was doing it on OPM—Other People's Money—and a ton of phony paper.

CHAPTER 5

Swindle of the Century
Anthony DeAngelis

I N REACH AND CONSEQUENCES, it was the swindle of the century. The
first faint intimation of havoc came in a sparse two-line statement
from the New York Stock Exchange.

Gathering momentum like an avalanche, the con would cost panicky investors millions in market losses; bust two old-line brokerage
firms and a clutch of commodity exporters; and relieve some of the United
States' smartest financial names, in current terms, of an embarassing
$2.5 billion.

Unfolding, as yet unrecognized, was a morality play full of enduring
lessons for investors. Among them: markets almost always overreact
and panics are almost always a buy; almost all major fraud feeds on
phony assets; accountants and securities analysts almost never get it
straight; greed is almost always a more disorienting drive than sex or the
political itch.

The Exchange itself had no sense of the carnage to come behind the
simple statement that it was auditing two member firms because a big
commodities customer had run into "serious financial difficulties."

Neither the firms nor the customer was identified. For the moment
it seemed only that the Exchange was dealing with an unusual but not
alarming set of circumstances.

The customer unaccountably had failed to come up to scratch on
margin—money borrowed against commodity futures he was trading in
big volume through the firms. They, in turn, had borrowed heavily from
the banks on their own to cover for him and had slipped slightly below
the minimum capital they were required to keep on hand.

Taking a quick pass at the numbers, the Exchange did not see a serious enough impairment to suspend the two well-established firms, Ira Haupt & Company and J. R. Williston & Beane.

Beyond the seeming calm at the Stock Exchange, there was yet another hint of calamity. For the second successive day, soybean oil futures on the Chicago Board of Trade and cottonseed oil contracts on the New York Produce Exchange were being routed in unprecedented volume by speculators betting on a major drop in prices.

Across the Hudson River in Newark, New Jersey, there was yet another unrecognized portent. Allied Crude Vegetable Oil Refining Company, the biggest vendor of commodity oils in the U. S. Food For Peace program was filing a bankruptcy petition showing some $200 million in liabilities.

In nearby Bayonne, New Jersey, yet another mysterious strand was being teased into place. Hurriedly assigned surveyors prowled in confusion the surreal limits of the sprawling storage tank farm that was Allied Crude's headquarters. The commodity oils that Allied processed and held for sale to big export customers like Bunge Corporation were stored in dozens of 42-foot-high cylindrical tanks linked by a Tinker Toy tangle of connecting pipes and valves.

Wayward clouds of steam from the tanks heating units drifted erratically around the surveyors and oil-saturated mud sucked at their boots as they searched for the 160 million pounds of soybean oil Bunge Corporation had asked them to make sure was in place.

Stored in four specifically designated tanks, the stuff was worth about $15 million. Bunge had been stuck with some bounced checks. Worried about the solidity of Allied Crude's finances, the exporter wanted to make doubly sure that its oil was on tap.

Making their way through a maze of undifferentiated tanks, the surveyors first reported that all was well. Ordered to take a second look, they came back with hardly credible intelligence. The calibrations now showed that only one of the Bunge tanks was full to its floating top with what appeared to be soybean oil. Two were empty and one was half full.

Pandemonium!

Where was the missing oil? Could 160 million pounds of it, in the space of four short hours, somehow been siphoned into the interconnected tanks on the now suspect Allied Crude's backlot? To move that much oil in that little time was a physical impossibility.

The uproar spread from the Bunge surveyors to employees of American Express Warehousing, a subsidiary of the American Express Company. Its task, as independent custodian of the farm, was to measure and certify the amount of oil Allied had sequestered in its own and customers' tanks.

The certification was crucial. Allied, backed by the blue-chip name, financed its own business by borrowing against warehouse receipts issued by the Amexco subsidiary. The paper was collateralized by the oil Allied held in its tanks—a long-established practice in the commodities trade. With American Express on the job as a third-party cop, the banks and exporters that had been routinely lending Allied in the tens of millions on warehouse paper had nothing to worry about. Or did they? Where was the missing Bunge oil?

What missing oil? rasped the Amexco custodians. They had released it to Allied two days ago on signed Bunge orders.

Into the midst of this peevish dialogue at the tank farm plunged bankruptcy court-appointed attorneys also in search of oil. It was their job to nail down Allied Crude assets of any kind, and pay off creditors whose own lawyers over the next several days began to show up outside the tank farm like suppliant depositors in a 1930s bank run.

Kept at bay by security guards the bankruptcy attorneys had posted, the creditors' representatives swapped indignities about the paucity of information with newsmen who had also begun to show up in force.

Yet another posse of lawyers was milling about in the Haupt conference room in New York. They were trying to learn why a series of Haupt checks, mounting in the millions, had bounced—dead on arrival—in the cashiers' cages of such top banks as Chase Manhattan and Morgan Guaranty. Except for the prospect that thousands of innocent investors might get hurt if Haupt or Williston went bust, the imbroglio was beginning to take on the dimensions of farce.

Lawyers were running around everywhere like a bunch of Keystone Kops in pinstripes. As one frustrated attorney in the clamoring mob in the Haupt conference room put it, "The most difficult thing is to find anyone who knows what the problem is."

The Produce Exchange, panicked by runaway selling, offered no better insight than anyone else in the commodity trade. It peremptorily decided to shut down trading for a day. It ordered the liquidation of cottonseed oil contracts at settlement prices that added heavily to the brokerage firms' woes.

Every one had a piece of the puzzle; no one could put it together. Bunge, in hot pursuit of its missing oil, charged American Express with abdicating its custodial obligations. The missing oil, the exporter contended in a New Jersey state court, had been released to Allied on forged orders and surreptiously pumped into adjoining tanks. Bunge wasn't talking missing oil; it was talking stolen oil.

Were the warehouse subsidiary's troubles serious enough to endanger its blue-chip parent? Howard Clark, the can-do president of American Express, was off on a field trip to Bayonne. After climbing to the summit of several 42-foot-high tanks and peering through hatch covers, he talked to newsmen. He assured them that the mystery of the missing oil would soon be resolved. Of course, hedged Clark, "There's quite a lot of confusion out there, as you can imagine."

Some of the confusion was already reflected in the price of American Express stock. There was no telling what kind of liabilities the warehouse subsidiary was facing, with every likelihood the parent would have to pick up the tab. This became all too clear when American Express Warehousing filed a bankruptcy petition showing liabilities of $144 million against assets of only $363,683.

Adding to the confusion was American Express' reverence for tradition. Rather than take on the Teflon protection of the corporate form, American chose to cling to the joint stock company charter under which it had been formed 115 years before. Tradition has its price. Anachronistically, if American Express couldn't meet its obligations, shareholders would have to assume them. The possibility was theoretical, remote as Ultima Thule. The travel business was booming, but institutional shareholders—worried about their own potential exposure—began to sell the stock down from 65 to a low of 35. It was one more worrisome sign of the panicky herd instinct creeping into the market.

Thanks partly to Clark's field trip, the confusion at Haupt was deepening into despair. American Express, sensing deep trouble, disavowed the $18.5 million in warehouse receipts the brokerage firm was holding against loans to Allied Crude as out and out forgeries. Forgeries? Who was the forger?

Stock Exchange auditors, beginning to sense the full dimensions of the brokerage firms' troubles, suspended both Haupt and Williston for being unable to meet current obligations. It was only the second time in its long history that the Exchange had shut down a member firm for insolvency. The sense of crisis sharpened as investors who attempted to close out accounts were turned away and some banks refused to honor Haupt checks. To some, it smelled of 1929, but the circumstances could not have been more different. Profits were up, interest rates stable, and the economy moving, but psychology once again trumped reason. Ancient flawed memories of The Great Crash brought heavy selling into the market, even as the Big Board managed to get Williston & Beane back into business with a bridge loan of less than a million.

The Exchange then turned to the far more intractable issue of a rescue plan for Haupt. The Exchange was fearful that the heavy press notice stirred by the plight of Haupt's locked-in customers would continue to hang over the market and trigger a run on other member firms.

Haupt's condition was far worse than originally thought. It had gone to the banks to cover Allied Crude's unmet margin calls, and owed more than a dozen of them well over $35 million. It was on the hook for who knew how much more in apparently phony warehouse receipts. Then there was the $100 million or so in securities Haupt clients had bought on margin. These, too, in the ordinary course of business, had been pledged with banks.

The Haupt partners, young men predominantly in their 30s, their personal resources at risk, had long since run out of credit. There was no standby mechanism the Exchange could call up to get the firm out of hock. Any one of the Haupt bank creditors could push the firm into bankruptcy. This very real threat could tie up Haupt's clients for years, and make hash of the Big Board's costly promotional efforts to bring "Wall Street to Main Street."

The much-feared possibility of a run on Wall Street was hardening into reality at the Bayonne tank farm. Rumors that the amount of collateralized oil in storage fell many millions short of the warehouse receipts outstanding were sweeping the trade. Traffic jammed the narrow approach roads to the farm as representatives of creditors as far afield as Rotterdam and Zurich were in search of not just vegetable oils, but such other pledged oddments as tallow and fish oil.

The lenders fared no better in getting their assets released than the beleaguered investors at Haupt. Nathan Ravin, the short, snappish chief of the bankruptcy court-appointed lawyers, was badgered by so many conflicting claims that he got a writ banning withdrawals of any kind from the farm. Nothing was going out pending yet another survey of the tanks and the warehouse receipts behind them.

The reports were not encouraging. At least two of Bunge's supposedly segregated tanks were now found to contain not soybean oil, but gasoline. Others were loaded with sludge and sea water. More confounding still, missing oil seemed to correlate with a whole series of tanks that could not be found in the confines of one of Allied's related entities, Harbor Tank Storage Company. It, too, had generated a spate of warehouse receipts. A partner in one export house, a major customer of Allied Crude, summed up the air of consternation at Bayonne.

"I couldn't believe that anyone in his right mind was giving out certificates that have no merchandise behind them," he told the *Wall Street Journal*. "I expect that as little as I expect you to take a revolver and shoot me because you don't like the color of my suit. That's exactly the same thing."

It wasn't just missing oil and missing tanks. There was quite a lot of cash missing, too, as a read of Allied Crude's bank accounts showed. Shortages of one kind or other might mean that Wall Street and as many as 50 banks were out as much as $200 million. For perspective on the shock waves following that discovery, consider the incredulity sweeping the market over recent federal charges that the former chairman and former vice chairman of Cendant Corporation had brought some $500 million in bogus reported earnings to a merger with the motel and auto rental concern. While all others around him were losing their heads, Allied Crude lead bankruptcy attorney Nathan Ravin kept his. He called in the FBI. Then real panic struck. It was November 22, 1963.

BULLETIN

Dallas, Nov. 22 (AP)—*President Kennedy was shot today just as his motorcade left downtown Dallas. Mrs. Kennedy jumped up and grabbed Mr. Kennedy. She cried, "Oh, no!" The motorcade sped on.*

The bulletin moved over the AP wires just before 12:30 P.M. Suddenly, switchboards everywhere were jammed. Husbands called wives, wives called friends. Church pews filled. A stunned nation crowded in knots around transistor radios, bunched in front of tavern TVs, fearing the worst.

Rumors raced through the streets: Johnson was dead, too. Shot. No, he'd had a heart attack. U.S. military units around the world were put on instant alert. Half the Strategic Air Command bomber force idled on runways. Some 600 other aircraft were already in the air, homing on preassigned targets.

At 1:33 P.M. the grim news became official: "President John Kennedy died at approximately 1:00 P.M. Central Standard time today here in Dallas. He died of a gunshot wound in the brain."

Vice President Johnson was sworn as President in the gold upholstered conference room of Air Force One, taking his oath on the small leather bound bible John Kennedy kept in his aft bedroom.

At the Stock Exchange, officials had scheduled another go round with Haupt's partners. Its problems were summarily pigeonholed as panic over the Kennedy assassination swept the floor. Record sales, all of them on down ticks, swamped the tape. Fully one-third of the 6.6 million shares that changed hands were thrown at the market in the seven minutes before the Exchange halted trading at 2:07 P.M., some 83 minutes before the regular close at 3:30 P.M. The last trade did not clear the tape until 2:49 P.M. Panic fed on panic as reported prices lagged far behind what was actually happening on the floor. The Dow Jones averages gave up 21 points, for the time a very big move that wiped out more than $11 billion in market values and set off a blizzard of margin calls.

The SEC faulted floor traders and specialists for not doing a better job keeping price spreads under control, but the real demon was the one that haunts every bad moment in the market place, the herd instinct. "People in markets often behave like crowds at a theater fire—all running toward the same exit," says *Forbes* columnist David Dreman.

Myopia rules as investors get "immersed in the details of the situation" and lose a sense of proportion. Often, they get blindsided by a series of events. The sharp market break of May 1962 (but not the equally sharp recovery) was still in memory. And the impact of the Haupt suspension still had not been absorbed when word of the Kennedy assassination struck.

No question that markets tend to overreact to bad news. True catastrophes (1929 and 1973–1974) are rare and bear markets typically bucket back to new highs within a year or so.

In the Kennedy-soybean oil sell off, high flying "Nifty Fifty" stocks such as Xerox (off 73 points from its high in a week of troubles) and Polaroid (off 40 from the high) got hammered on heavy volume, just as the likes of Microsoft and Lucent got their lumps in the great technology sell-off of the last two years.

What's the lesson that runs from the Allied Crude swindle market to today? Fear drives all such surges. Behavioral psychologists talk of "thought contagion," a herd instinct that propels selling (or buying) frenzies simply because others are doing so. Call it the Hula Hoop or Tulip Bulb phenomenon. The tendency is exacerbated these days by delusion spread through the instant communication of the Internet.

Pros are no more immune to these emotional pulls than the newest hot-shot day trader. Ralph Wanger, president of the multi-billion Acorn Investment Trust, recalls his own emotional state when the market fell off the cliff on October 19, 1987. "I was shaken," says Wanger. "What we had made in a year we lost in a week." Wanger sold some stocks at the best prices he could get, bought others dirt cheap, and on the whole now believes that he would have been just as well-off staying pat.

If you are holding some really long gains, it's probably prudent to take some money off the table from time to time, rather than get caught in the sort of stampede that drove hot tech stocks into the stratosphere and then into the cellar.

A time of seemingly acute trouble is not a time to sell. It's often a time to buy. If the market is climbing a wall of worry—inflation, declining profits, a war scare—wait to see what happens. Better to make a rational decision than to be swept along with the crowd. Many who sold into the Kennedy-salad oil swindle break paid a sizable premium to get back into the market.

One exemplar of the virtues of having the cool to exploit bad news: Warren Buffett. Scoping American Express through the clutter of the swindle, he saw a first-class franchise with all growth engines intact—and cheap. Bucking conventional analysis, wrong as usual at a crucial turn in the market, Buffett put $13 million into American Express—some 40 percent of his partnership assets—and picked up 5 percent of American Express at a low of $35 a share. Over the next two years, the stock tripled and Buffett walked away with a $20 million profit.

The turnaround in the market generally, as it usually does, came from a return to basics. The economy was strong and Lyndon Johnson had the nation's confidence. There was also a big push from the good news that the Exchange over the weekend had worked out a plan to free up the Haupt accounts and make sure that customers would not be out of pocket. The key was an unparalleled assessment against other member firms.

The Haupt rescue did nothing to resolve the unknowns that set it in motion. Missing oil, missing storage tanks, missing money. Also conspicuously missing was the one person who might have all of the pieces to the puzzle up his sleeve—Anthony DeAngelis, president and chief shareholder of Allied Crude.

DeAngelis, 50, was nowhere to be found at the tank farm. Even his lawyer hadn't seen DeAngelis since the company's hastily prepared bankruptcy petition had first been rejected and then presented with less skimpy financials a day later. The court-appointed attorneys charged with unraveling Allied's affairs staked out both the suite DeAngelis regularly occupied in a midtown Manhattan hotel and his estranged wife's home in suburban New Jersey with no success. In the inevitable tabloidese, DeAngelis had become a "mystery man." What did he have to hide?

High School dropout and one of an immigrant rail worker's five children, DeAngelis was very much the self-made man. In a few short years, he had become Mr. Vegetable Oil, making big money out of a strategy that put Allied Crude at the hub of a thriving export trade.

He was prospering with a major assist from the heavily subsidized U.S. Food For Peace program—American idealism wrapped around a hardheaded commercial core. Supervised by the Agriculture Department, the program provided edible oils and other commodities on the cheap to hungry nations abroad. The humanitarian aim of feeding a less favored world not coincidentally helped to keep domestic farm prices high (and farm state legislators happy) by shunting surpluses off market.

DeAngelis, whose early ventures had been in the meat and tallow trade, saw an opportunity in a middleman's role—buy soybean oil and cottonseed oil from crushers in the Midwest, refine the product in the East, sell to exporters at water's edge. Logistically, the Bayonne tank farm fit DeAngelis' specifications like a glove. It had good rail, barge, and deep-water connections, and the bulk space he needed to hold processed oil for such well-established exporters as Bunge Corporation and Continental Grain Company.

Starting with $500,000 in capital, DeAngelis whipped the tank farm, long a petroleum storage area, into shape. In a major coup, he persuaded American Express Warehousing to take over as custodian. The connection enabled DeAngelis to bootstrap his thin financials by borrowing against inventory certified by Amexco and its eminently negotiable warehouse receipts. In the same way, he took on additional loans at premium rates from his pleased export clients to build the newest and most efficient refinery in the trade.

Soon DeAngelis himself was barnstorming foreign markets, drumming up orders that pushed Allied Crude's revenues and those of half a dozen satellites to some $200 million a year.

By the early 1960s, Anthony DeAngelis was supplying some 75 percent of the edible oils being ticketed abroad—quite a distinction for the short (five feet five inches), rotund (well over 200 pounds) figure who'd started out as a butcher boy in the Bronx. DeAngelis had a rag-to-riches story to tell. Why was he hiding out? Why had Allied Crude so suddenly gone down the tubes?

Newsmen fired those questions at DeAngelis as he finally surfaced in response to a subpoena eight harrowing days after he put Allied Crude into bankruptcy. The bankruptcy court, painted the usual institutional bile green, was jammed with creditors' lawyers. Jockeying for seats, briefcases and yellow legal pads much in evidence, they craned toward the door for their first view of DeAngelis as he sparred with the press in the corridor and obligingly posed for photographers. The "mystery man" was very much the archetypal small businessman—white shirt, dark tie, ballpoint pens sticking out of his breast pocket like the barrels of a carburetor.

DeAngelis had not come alone. Convoying him through the crowd of newsmen was the well-connected criminal lawyer Walter D. Van Riper, a former judge and State Attorney General. Elegant in bold stripes, sonorous, a lawyer of the old school, Van Riper begged bankruptcy referee William H. Tallyn to know that DeAngelis retained him only an hour before. Van Riper needed several days to confer with his new client—a reasonable request because DeAngelis "might incriminate himself—I don't know that he would—if he testified at this time."

Tallyn ritualistically ordered DeAngelis to testify. DeAngelis eased his bulk into the witness chair, and went through a mantra rare for a civil bankruptcy court proceeding:

Q: What is your official position with Allied Crude Vegetable Oil Refining?

A: I respectfully decline to answer because to do so would tend to incriminate me.

Elucidating the now obvious, Van Riper intoned that DeAngelis, "for now," will refuse to answer all further questions. That brought the day to a standstill. The bankruptcy referee had no power to force DeAngelis to testify. Only a federal judge could rule on Fifth Amendment issues. Still a mystery man—black-rimmed spectacles framing iron gray hair—DeAngelis posed for a couple more photographs, and was wafted off in his waiting Cadillac. The salad oil debacle had taken an abrupt adversarial turn that intensified the journalistic dig into DeAngelis' past. What did lay hidden behind the cover of the Fifth Amendment?

The beginnings were prosaic enough. Starting out as an apprentice butcher, DeAngelis (known by the diminutive "Tino" to family and friends) sharpened his skills at the City Provision Company, a major hog cutter in the Bronx. In later years, DeAngelis talked of his "exceptional ability in knowing how to process hogs."

In 1938, the 23-year-old DeAngelis set out on his own, putting $2,000 in savings into an outfit called M & D Hog Cutters. Never bashful about his business acumen, DeAngelis liked to recall that he helped pioneer a major change in the way the business worked.

Porkers that used to be shipped live from the Midwest to the East were instead slaughtered in the farm belt and shipped as slabs for further reduction by packers like M & D.

Whatever the paternity, the change brought major efficiencies to the trade. It may have been a model for the logistics later brought to bear on

Allied Crude—move partly processed commodities from the Midwest to New York for further upgrading and sale in Eastern markets.

By all accounts, DeAngelis was an important enough supplier of meat to the government in World War II to have been exempt from military service. Married now, with a son, DeAngelis prospered, boasting in later years that he had managed to sock away $1 million for the family "in case anything happened."

Post war, DeAngelis began looking to the foreign markets he later tapped with Allied Crude. One of his first such ventures was a syndicate formed to sell $1 million worth of lard to the Yugoslav government. Tino himself negotiated the deal, and put his customary charitable spin on it. The people DeAngelis had seen queuing outside food shops "were so badly off—some with burlap on their feet"—that he generously gave the Yugoslavs a full year to pay. He was stung by ingratitude—a suit charging that the newly formed DeAngelis Packing Company had shipped substandard stuff. DeAngelis settled the claim for $100,000.

Newsmen probing the silent DeAngelis' background found that paying to make business scrapes go away was a way of life with him.

When the German government complained about substandard lard, Tino settled that one, too. There was the Agriculture Department complaint that DeAngelis had fobbed off some two million pounds of uninspected meat on the federal school lunch program—and short weighted it to boot. Also in the Agriculture Department dossier were a series of other administrative complaints: shipping illegal vegetable oil; rancid vegetable oil, vegetable oil in leaky containeers. All were settled.

More serious still was a wrangle with the Securities Exchange Commission. The SEC charged that DeAngelis had understated losses in a publicly owned meatpacker he took over. Creditors subsequently forced the firm, the Adolph Gobel Company, into bankruptcy. Yet another SEC charge grew out of the Gobel case. The allegation was that DeAngelis had talked a witness into recanting damaging testimony that Tino had been borrowing money against phantom lard inventories.

The engineering of phony assets had been very much in the news. Texan Billie Sol Estes, churchgoer and family man, had just taken farmers across the Southwest for $150 million by persuading them to invest in liquid fertilizer tanks.

The smooth talking Estes conjured up an impressive facade on paper, but the fertilizer tanks behind the facade existed only in his fevered imagination and that of his beguiled marks. The fertilizer was an illusion, too.

Out of the slammer six years later, Estes went right back to his old trade, this time borowing against the collateral of phantom oil field cleaning equipment.

Estes was part of a solid phantomist tradition in American business, going back to the turn of the century and the long-running star turn of Philip Musica. The protean Musica was at that point in his career a wig-maker. Operating out of New York, he euchered a score of banks out of a million, using doctored invoices collateralized by the long human hair he was supposedly importing from his native Italy.

Caught, Musica emerged from jail with a new persona. As Frank Costa, producer of hair tonic, he was entitled at the height of Prohibition to 5,000 gallons of pure alcohol a month. The bootlegger Costa then morphed into F. Donald Coster, respected physician, president, and major shareholder of the 93-year-old drug wholesaler, McKesson & Robbins.

McKesson prospered handsomely through the Crash of 1929 and most of the depression. In 1937, the edifice of imaginate acquisitions, phony invoices, and fake audit collapsed under its own dead weight. More than $20 million worth of drug inventories proved to be fictitious, as did the warehouses in which they were stored.

Does the shade of F. Donald Coster still haunt McKesson? In 1999, the company acquired the health care information provider, HBO & Company, in a $12 billion stock deal. It then discovered that HBO had systematically been booking software sales that hadn't actually been completed—an accounting impropriety that forced McKesson to restate earnings. Investors responded by knocking some $9 billion off McKesson's market value. Coster at least, had the decency to commit suicide when he was caught, while one of the major considerations in the HBO acquisition was the accelerated vesting of McKesson management stock options.

Going forward in the history of scam, there were the phony insurance policies of Equity Funding Corporation and the phony job contracts of Barry Minkow's ZZZZ Best—all swallowed whole by fevered investors and bankers. In the early stages, the suspicion that Tino DeAngelis might be hanging paper, too, was little heard.

There was, after all, the probity of American Express behind those warehouse receipts, and the näive trust in the sanctity of audits that continues to bedevil securities analysts and investors today. Companies working overtime to make their numbers routinely inflate revenues early by kicking inventory out the door, or hype earnings by cutting rerserves for inventory obsolescence—all under the rubric of Standard Accounting Procedures. Qualitatively, how does that differ from fudging on warehouse receipts? In the commodity trade as elsewhere, aggressive accounting was a given.

Much of the background on DeAngelis was spelled out in routine credit reports, but none of the questions raised hurt him in the trade. Business is business. DeAngelis was selling oil at sharply competitive prices. With only rare protest, he paid high interest rates on the increasing amount of borrowed money piggybacking into Allied Crude on warehouse receipts.

Though very much the rising tycoon, Tino was not for the high life. "I've had only one ambition in life, success," he said in his grandiloquent way. "Even as a kid, work came first. I partook very little of the gay life." On rare occasions DeAngelis could be spotted in an out-of-the-way saloon in Greenwich Village, quietly watching television with his companion, Lillian Pascarelli, the smartly turned out divorceé who was on the Allied Crude payroll as a "social hostess."

DeAngelis had anted the $40,000 down payment on the roomy Pascarelli home in suburban Tenafly, New Jersey, a few miles from the George Washington Bridge, on the pleasingly green reverse slope of the Palisades.

Tino's estranged wife lived in Tenafly, too, not far from the others in Tino's set. They included Leo Bracconeri, Tino's brother-in-law and Allied's plant manager; Ben Rotello, Allied's controller; and George Bitter, one of Allied's chief commodity traders. Foreign buyers were sometimes entertained at the Pascarelli home, and in summer the Allied Crude crowd enjoyed one another's company at backyard barbecues.

DeAngelis' suburban cronies were the nucleus of a tight-knit group of 20 or so that kept the Bayonne plant humming. There were a number of DeAngelis cousins on the payroll, all in a family circle where Tino often rewarded good work with handsome cash bonuses and the occasional gift of a Cadillac.

DeAngelis good works were many. He'd been an enthusiastic cyclist in his youth. In more rotund later years, Tino boasted that "bicycle racing developed me physically. I possess exceptional strength in my hands and legs."

DeAngelis showed his gratitude to the sport by donating bicycles and the gold DeAngelis cup to local racing clubs.

The DeAngelis philanthropy wasn't limited to sport. There were the chimes he gave to a Jersey City church, donations to the building drives of Greenville Hospital in Jersey City (Tino was on the board), and a Jewish home for the Aged.

DeAngelis was famous for carrying around wads of cash and peeling off big bills whenever he was touched by a hard-luck story: $500 for an old rail worker friend who was having a hard time meeting a son's college bills; florist bills in the thousands "all year round to different people that would die, and to funerals or this or that."

Also, there were peace offerings to the odd foreign customers who might show up at the Bayonne office, complaining of leaking salad oil drums; and medical expenses picked up for a seriously ill Agriculture Department inspector who had been assigned to the Bayonne plant.

Many of the DeAngelis benefactions seemed to come from checks drawn against Allied Crude's petty cash account. Since something like $450,000 had gone through the account in the months before Allied lurched into bankruptcy, the court-appointed attorneys were hot to learn where it had all gone. How much of it had stuck to DeAngelis and his pals?

They were equally curious about the $63,500 DeAngelis had withdrawn against cash in much the same period from a personal bank account. For a guy drawing $100,000 a year in salary, DeAngelis seemed to have an inordinate amount of cash tucked away in unbusiness-like noninterest-bearing checking accounts.

Still pending was the question of whether DeAngelis could be prodded into talking about such things. In a quickie second appearance in bankruptcy court, DeAngelis again took the Fifth. Attorney Walter Van Riper argued his client had no alternative, considering the volume of press coverage "alleging gross improprieties on his part."

Hailed before a federal judge on a contempt charge, DeAngelis altered his strategy. He agreed to answer more than 40 of the 60 questions he had finessed in bankruptcy court, with the proviso that the federal court would rule question-by-question on any other queries he chose not to answer.

Back to the bankruptcy court, then, where DeAngelis continued to obfuscate, well aware that he was now also the target of a federal grand jury investigation.

Two days before Christmas, the grand jury charged DeAngelis with 18 counts of moving $39.4 million in forged warehouse receipts in interstate commerce. Theoretical maximum penalty: 180 years in jail and a $180,000 fine.

Courthouse buffs were betting that more indictments were in the works. Smaller fish, given promises of immunity, might well be pressured into giving up the kingfish himself. The government case, largely circumstantial, could use some reinforcement.

However noncommunicative in court, DeAngelis was now on a first name basis with the gaggle of reporters following in his wake. "Powerful forces have teamed with the federal government to put the little fellow out of business," Tino told at one impromptu press conference. All he had tried to do was expand the export trade so soybean growers "could get another 25¢ a bushel and the powerful interests didn't like it."

Like the chimes of the Jersey City church and the Jewish Home for the Aged, the farmers of the Midwest were suddenly part of the DeAngelis benefice. Tino's canonical mood was shattered by the equally sudden invocation of an obscure scrap of New Jersey law. Rarely invoked, it provides that defendants in a civil suit can be made to post bonds equal to the damages sought, or go to jail.

This arcane threat of debtors prison was draped over the now visibly troubled DeAngelis by Joseph M. Nolan, bankruptcy trustee for yet another of the Bayonne causalities, Harbor Tank Storage Company.

The dimmest bulb in any of the local gin mills would have instantly made Nolan as some kind Fed—dark suit, white shirt, dark tie, face as Irish as the name—and assertive. The one-time treasury agent's brief, filed in a state court in Jersey City, succeeded in getting what none of the

hundreds of other lawyers working on the cases had seemed possible—
a warrant for DeAngelis' arrest.

Nolan's complaint: DeAngelis had hatched a "devious, complicated,
and sinister plan" that resulted in Harbor Tank Storage floating $46.5
million in phony warehouse receipts. DeAngelis had been aided by a
crony, Joseph Lomuscio, the Harbor Tank Storage custodian.

Nolan's position: The two, under this quirk in the state law, could
either stump up $46.5 million in bail or go to jail. Caught off guard,
Walter Van Riper resisted as best he could. Why any bail at all?
DeAngelis had no more chance of running from a civil judgment than
the vice president of the United States. "He'd be known wherever he
was, and be found wherever he was," argued Van Riper.

It was getting on dinner time of a Friday evening when Judge
Robert A. Matthews called a temporary halt. He rescheduled the hearing for Monday morning and set interim bail of $150,000 for DeAngelis
($100,000 for Lomuscio). Then came the real sting: Both men would
have to testify before the judge would fix permanent bail.

The ruling threatened to put a crimp in Tino's Fifth Amendment
defense, and to throw embarrassing light on the state of his finances. If
Tino could afford the $6,000 a weekend worth bail would cost, he
would be playing into the general suspicion that plenty of coconuts
were stashed away some place. For the moment, Tino had run out of
options. He chose to weekend in the Hudson County jail.

DeAngelis came back into court Monday morning with his customary air of aggrieved innocence and a list. Ticking off the numbers with
one of his ever handy pens, DeAngelis testified that he was $27 million
in hock. Most of the liabilities were personal guarantees against Allied
Crude debt. On the asset side, he could count only $140,000—mainly
in loans due from Allied Crude's in-group. All told, DeAngelis poor-
mouthed his liquid assets to less than $5,000, including "maybe six or
seven suits."

This woebegone tale was catnip to the waiting Nolan, who had been
feeding on DeAngelis personal bank statements. What about the $8,800
check drawn to Thomas Clarkin, one of Allied's messengers?

Tino rambled on with a story of yet another benefaction. Clarkin, he
testified, was a long-time Allied employee, working two jobs to buy a

home. Tino was touched by Clarkin's industriousness. "To the best of my knowledge, I gave him funds to put a down payment on or buy a home. I believe I gave it to him, not expecting to get it back."

An incredulous Nolan pursued DeAngelis when he subsequently changed his testimony to say the $8,800 had, in fact, been paid back. Yes, there was also a $3,000 check made out to his codefendant Joseph Lomuscio, but DeAngelis couldn't remember why.

The level of transparency got no better when Nolan brought up the $63,500 that had come out of DeAngelis' account in checks payable to cash. The questions cracked like pistol fire: Why didn't you pay these people by check? Why would you take out $10,000 in cash and pay these obligations? You gave people cash, didn't you? And you can't remember who you gave its to?

Tino was definitely having memory problems. Nolan might just as well have been punching smoke. If he only had possession of his records, now "in the possession of Allied," DeAngelis would be only too happy to help.

Then Tino went on the offensive. He succeeded in getting an order that enabled him to reassign his assets from the custody of the bankruptcy court to Judge Matthews' Superior Court. That satisfied the judge. The bail Joseph Nolan was demanding had been mooted because "Mr. DeAngelis has in effect pauperized himself."

Aced out of his own ingenious ploy, Nolan fumed. He was now convinced more than ever that "when I named DeAngelis a swindler, I was right." DeAngelis, magnanimous in victory, allowed that he had "no ill feelings to Mr. Nolan," but certainly did "want to protest his calling me a liar." DeAngelis' skill in playing one court jurisdiction against another in his one-upmanship with Nolan explained why pieces of the salad oil puzzle were still all over the floor a full three months after the swindle broke over Wall Street.

With several different sets of investigators tripping over one another in the effort to crack the mystery of missing assets, the initiative was still very much with DeAngelis. He showed that when he let the Allied bankruptcy trustee in on a little secret. There was, Tino just remembered, some $500,000 of Allied Crude money tucked away in a numbered account in the Union Bank of Switzerland. In the rush to get the Allied bankruptcy petition filed, said Tino, he'd forgotten totally about the cache in Geneva.

Never mind that the account broke down into better than $200,000 in Tino's name, with the rest credited individually in smaller amounts to three of his top lieutenants. The money, an accumulation of kickbacks on exports billed to the Spanish government, DeAngelis said, has always been considered to belong to Allied.

The voluntary disclosure of the Swiss accounts, however tardy, was yet another sign of his good faith, argued DeAngelis. "No one ever got a single penny. I would never allow anyone to take a penny," he said grandly.

Cynics—the still fuming Joseph Nolan, for one—sniffed at this surprise repatriation as yet another DeAngelis ploy. Was he looking down the road to what its impact might be in extenuation of the criminal rap sure to come?

If so, he was at considerable risk. His ledger on the account was full of erasures. The money showed up nowhere in Allied's main accounts. It had never been reported in Allied's income tax returns, and the way cash moved in and out of the account made it look very much like a private piggy bank.

Nolan was about to make that very point before Judge Matthews. He demanded that DeAngelis be cited for criminal contempt. It was an open and shut case, he argued. Less than a month ago in this very court DeAngelis had denied under oath having a foreign bank account. And now this $500,000 providentially arrived in bankruptcy court from Geneva. What more needed to be said?

DeAngelis pleaded that life was too short for him ever to lie. He'd told the truth—literally. It wasn't his account. Never had been. The money belonged to Allied.

Judge Matthews wasn't buying. "My conclusion is that when asked about his personal assets, DeAngelis lied to this court," said the judge, and sentenced Tino to four months in jail. Out on $10,000 bail, DeAngelis appealed—and won. There was "no incontrovertible evidence" DeAngelis lied, ruled a three-judge appellate bench. Further, since he'd helped expedite repatriation of the money, DeAngelis could not be charged with obstructing justice.

DeAngelis was leading a charmed life. In the months they'd been working on the case, all the investigators had so far been able to pin on DeAngelis were suspicions of a highly creative accounting approach to petty cash. Quite a lot of petty cash, but there had been no showing that much of it stuck to DeAngelis.

More vexing still, there was no definitive explanation of the two critical elements—missing oil and supposedly forged warehouse receipts. The federal grand jury had come down with a second indictment, but with no proof showing other than an assertion that DeAngelis had circulated $100 million in phony American Express Warehouse receipts.

Not to be upstaged by federal prosecutors in a case that was drawing national attention, local law enforcement jumped into the act with a laundry list of conspiracy charges. "I plead absolutely not guilty," the imperturbable DeAngelis told reporters. "Do me a favor—put in 'absolutely.'"

The new federal charges ensured one thing: Tino's memory was not going to get any better. Now under injunction to answer all "reasonable questions" about the Allied bankruptcy, he was more evasive than ever.

DeAngelis was particularly incensed about parts of his private life that were being spattered on the record. Put on the stand in bankruptcy court, the twice-divorced Lillian Pascarelli, Allied Crude's "social hostess," testified that she was on the payroll at $25,000 a year. There was also a subvention of $100 a week from an Allied affiliate—hardly enough to support a life style that included $70,000 worth of insurance on furs and jewelry. Among the baubles were a $9,000 diamond ring and a $10,500 platinum necklace. Attesting to frugality, Pascarelli told the court that her mink and sable coats had been picked up on the cheap—the sable "because the lady who originally ordered it didn't want it."

Pascarelli said she did a lot of entertaining for Allied. She sometimes put up the wives of important foreign customers for months at a time, a duty that presumably explained the $40,000 down payment DeAngelis had made on her suburban New Jersey home. DeAngelis sometimes handed her as much as $15,000 in cash for household expenses.

Then there was the foreign travel—months at the Castellana Hilton in Madrid while Tino sold the Spanish market. Her job was not just a sometime thing, Pascarelli wanted the court to know. Her mother had loaned DeAngelis $2,500 when he started out in business. The proviso was that he had to take care of Lillian for the rest of her life.

The tabloids had a lot of fun with Pascarelli's job description, but missed the significance of the long stays in Madrid. Tino was busily cultivating pals in the Ministry of Supply, and finally came up with a real showstopper—a huge contract for 275 million pounds of soybean oil worth around $36.5 million.

This was big money for Allied. DeAngelis did not have in storage anything like the amount of oil he needed to cover the contract. In standard business practice, he went into the futures market to nail down his supply.

Then came the body blow. The Spaniards abruptly cancelled, with no explanation. DeAngelis knew why. His American competitors, the Midwest crushers, had got to Opus Dei, the conservative Catholic faction with a lot of clout in the upper reaches of government.

DeAngelis gave the bankruptcy court a long tale of how he had been jobbed. Here he was "a man who had come up the hard way, without any lobby, without any politics, without any help." The crushers wanted him out of the way so they could grab the businesses for themselves.

Conniving through the shadowy mechanism of Opus Dei, they succeeded in pushing Allied out of the running. Blustering, DeAngelis told the court that if "somebody sabotages you, you either have one thing to do or the other"—fight, or throw in the towel.

Instead of unwinding his commitments in the futures market at some reasonably sustainable loss, DeAngelis elected to fight. He hung onto his contracts, running the risk that he might have to swallow delivery on as much as $20 million worth of soybean oil, with no big buyers in sight.

The Agriculture Department, though, was forecasting record export demand. DeAngelis' own sources, "the greatest system of information in the world," concurred. DeAngelis took the gamble. He bought ever more deeply into the futures market.

Much of the trading was funneled through dummy accounts, many of them opened in the names of Tino's tank farm operatives. One member of the network was a poultryman whose account was run under the name of his chicken farm. The terms were standard—an even split on profits; Allied Crude to swallow the losses.

The sweetheart deals were a sign of how hard DeAngelis had to work to keep prices up. The Agriculture Department export estimates he had been banking on proved grossly optimistic. DeAngelis kept rolling over futures at increasing losses, gambling that a couple of big deals would come along to bail him out.

It certainly looked as though they were out there somewhere. DeAngelis figured that even the Agriculture Department could not be wrong two years in a row. His own sources were reporting major stirrings for well over 500 million pounds of oil in Indonesia, Pakistan, and eastern Europe.

Allied was now generating as much as 90 percent of the cottonseed oil buying on the Produce Exchange, and probably 50 percent of the volume in soybean oil on the much broader Board of Trade. The scale of Tino's action drew only modest regulatory response. The Board of Trade slapped him on the wrist with a 30-day suspension for fictitious trades, and the Agriculture Department made a warning pass at some of his dummy accounts.

DeAngelis' buying was reaching manic proportions, but who was going to quarrel with prosperity? DeAngelis was booking more than $100,000 a month in commissions with Produce Exchange brokers alone. Market manipulation? No way. It didn't take a genius to see that export markets were going to boom again.

The brokerage looked especially good to the young, aggressive partners—new names—who had just come into Ira Haupt & Company. Older heads at the firm first vetoed DeAngelis as a client because of his checkered past.

What was the risk, came the expansionist argument. There was the double incentive of a growing stream of commissions, plus interest on the loans backed by gilt-edge American Express warehouse receipts. Why leave all the gravy to the competition? DeAngelis swept away the last of the reservations at Haupt by leading a tour of the Bayonne plant. It was the most efficient processor in the business, he bragged, run 24 hours around the clock, with only seven or eight men per shift.

Haupt did not learn that many of these $400-a-week shift workers were the dummy names fronting for some of the trading accounts the firm was so eager to land.

The accountants certainly hadn't been able to find anything out of line at Bayonne. An audit report to American Express found the "usual segregation of functional responsibilities between operating and accounting departments intact." "Sound accounting practices are being followed," the report continued. "The system of internal controls is satisfactory."

What straight arrow of a Haskins & Sells accountant could dream that DeAngelis, short of cash, might simply lift a couple of warehouse receipt pads from an unlocked drawer, practice the signatures of Amexco custodians, and buck the paper on to lenders with never a hitch?

Howard Clark's instincts were a lot sharper than the accountants. American Express was not prepared to share with Haupt or anyone else the intelligence it had picked up about the trading pool being run out of Bayonne. Amexco was shocked to learn that its chief custodian at the warehouse subsidiary—literally the keeper of the keys and warehouse receipts—was one of the dozens of traders DeAngelis was guaranteeing against losses. He'd also become a shareholder in a DeAngelis satellite.

The connection seemed to compromise the integrity of the place at a time when the volume of warehouse receipts outstanding was exploding. They had gone up $20 million in the last month alone, raising the total to $85 million. The subsidiary was insured for only $30 million. There had been a number of whistle-blower phone calls that DeAngelis was borrowing against phony inventories. The calls had been pretty much explained away. Increasingly wary, American Express decided to put the warehouse subsidiary up for sale. No more new receipts would be issued, DeAngelis was told.

Some brokers were also beginning to take a harder look at the risk of carrying DeAngelis' huge position. There were more decisions either to cut back or make no more new loans.

The expansion-minded partners at Haupt saw only opportunity and eagerly took on a $30 million sheaf of warehouse receipts. They were immediately pledged with big-name lenders like the Continental Illinois National Bank & Trust Company. Haupt itself was now holding for DeAngelis futures contracts with a value of more than $100 million—a huge potential burden if the market broke.

A drop of just a penny a pound in soybean oil would mean margin calls of some $13 million. DeAngelis had one slim hope going for him: rumors that Russia was on the brink of a big buy. That prospect was scotched when the Senate put on hold a wheat deal with the Soviets. Selling rolled like gun smoke over the markets. Tino's instructions for his traders: Scalp early buys through Williston & Beane, where there was a good chance they wouldn't have to put up any margin (the firm's floor manager that day was a son-in-law of Lillian Pascarelli); hold the line for DeAngelis to jack up prices with a flurry of buy orders just before the close.

DeAngelis appeared to have plenty of firepower left—some $8 million in warehouse receipts written against oil Bunge Corporation had just released to Allied.

Tino never got a chance to put the big money in play. A Commodity Exchange Authority investigator walked unannounced into the Bayonne office, flashed his ID, and demanded to see the books. It was Friday, November 15, 1963, and the first intimations of DeAngelis' duplicity were about to break.

So much for Tino's last roll of the dice. All the efforts now would go into figuring how he did it. How did this moonfaced, rumpled, ex-butcher's helper with a penchant for fractured syntax manage to bamboozle some of the United States' biggest financial names for so long?

Tino himself still wasn't giving anything away in bankruptcy court. Questioned about an Allied inventory sheet showing there had been more than 800 million pounds of oil in American Express' now nearly empty tanks five months before, DeAngelis was at his orotund best:"You show me a piece of paper, but I know not from where it comes."

So where was the missing oil? Most of it had never been there in the first place, testimony extracted from the workforce in Bayonne was beginning to show. DeAngelis—solidly in the line of tradition with Estes and Musica—had become the biggest phantomist of them all. He began whistling up assets out of paper tentatively at first, whenever he was pinched for a little cash, than ever more massively as his frantic run at the futures markets spun wildly out of control. The design was simple: All he had to do was keep Amexco convinced he had more than enough oil to cover the receipts it was cranking out.

At the working level in Bayonne, where things counted, the environment could not have been more accommodating. Many of Amexco's assistant custodians were hired right off Tino's payroll when Amexco's warehouse company took over the Allied account. The head custodian was buddy-buddy with Michael DeAngelis, one of Tino's many cousins, and shared an office with him. The custodian's chief assistant was a brother-in-law of Tino's secretary, and so it went—one big happy family at work and play on both sides of the custodial fence.

On inventory Fridays, Allied and Amexco workers deployed in two-man teams. The Allied member called off liquid measurements from the top of the tanks; remarkably uninquisitive Amexco workers jotted down the numbers. "They never checked on any of us who was gauging," testified one Allied hand. If the Amexco teams knew they were taking down phony numbers, "they kept it to themselves."

For insurance against more industrious outside surveyors, sea water-loaded tanks were topped with a layer of oil. Other tanks were doctored with an oil-spiked core welded to the measuring hatch.

It wasn't just phantom oil. Testimony elicited by trustee Joseph Nolan revealed that Tino had even fitted out Harbor Tank Storage Company, controlled at the operations level by yet another accommodating loyalist, with a set of nonexisting tanks. Receipts written against phantom tanks proved to be as negotiable as the real thing.

Nolan, to his immense satisfaction, was developing in bankruptcy court damning stuff that went to the heart of the charges levied against DeAngelis in the Feds criminal case. In effect, DeAngelis was getting a preview of the chain of evidence the federal grand jury was pursuing in private.

Time for Tino to cut a deal before some of his hirelings did. He pleaded guilty to a conspiracy charge and bargained from eighteen to three the charges of circulating forged warehouse receipts he had been indicted on. The plea cut the maximum jail time he might face from 135 years to 35 years and a $35,000 fine.

DeAngelis came before Federal Judge Reynier D. Wortendyke for sentencing. Properly penitent, DeAngelis murmured that his only wish was to be able "to dedicate the rest of my life in an effort to repay the damage which has been done."

Relying on apparently benign presentencing reports, the 70-year-old jurist surprisingly broke into a riff on how DeAngelis personified the virtues of the free enterprise system. DeAngelis' early success, the judge said, "exemplified what can be achieved with a limited background through courage and vision," and demonstrated that "we have a work-able democracy." Though DeAngelis had jumped the rails, causing "ter-rific loss," the judge was convinced that he "had never started out or intentionally desired to deprive anyone of a dollar."

DeAngelis did have to be censured, though, and Wortendyke sen-tenced him provisionally to 10 years, pending deeper psychological study of his motives at the Lewisburg, Pennsylvania federal penitentiary.

Ten years—to say nothing of the praise for the drive and energy that went into pulling off one of the century's biggest commercial frauds—looked good to DeAngelis.

DeAngelis himself looked good when he came back for permanent sentencing 10 weeks later. He'd lost 35 pounds doing chores like mop-ping hospital floors at Lewisburg while the shrinks checked him out. His dark conservatively cut suit hung loosely over his still ample frame.

Expecting no more than the provisional 10 years he had been handed initially, DeAngelis was jolted when Wortendyke upped the ante to 20 years—10 years consecutively on two warehouse receipts charges, to run concurrently with the other two charges he had pleaded to. DeAngelis was dabbing his eyes with a handkerchief as two U.S. marshals whisked him past a group of reporters into a detention room.

Why the stiff double in the sentence? Had the shrinks brought to the judge's attention something darker in the DeAngelis psyche than mere entrepreneurial waywardness? In fact, a certain amount of judicial con-fusion had creeped into the proceedings. Under the little used law he had invoked, the judge had to sentence DeAngelis to a minimum of 10 years to get the psychological study he wanted done. Yes, he had unfortunately used the term "concurrent" in his initial discussion of the charges, thus creating the impresssion that DeAngelis was facing only a tenner. But 20 it was, making DeAngelis eligible for parole in six years and eight months. "I don't want DeAngelis loose on society in less than six years," Wortendyke told a reporter. "He might get into another scrape."

So the steel doors of Lewisburg closed on DeAngelis again, leaving in his wake at least 20 bankruptcies, many of them Allied affiliates, and a clamor of unanswered questions. One thing was now certain. Matched against outstanding warehouse receipts, the total shortage of oil at Bayonne amounted to around 1.8 billion pounds worth more than $175 million. Loose cash had sluiced through Allied's corporate account as if driven by a fire hose. In a little less than a year before Allied collapsed, some $505 million went into the account; $508 million came out. About $100 million sloshed through the account in the last 45 days before the collapse. Cash had been tracked in generous amounts to any number of DeAngelis associates: $14,000 in living expenses for Lillian Pascarelli the day of the bankruptcy; $65,000 tucked away in the bedroom closet of a key commodity trader.

Apart from the $500,000 repatriated from Switzerland, though, Allied's bankruptcy trustee could locate no other large sums. The speculation was that the wily DeAngelis had put a lot more money on ice somewhere—easy to speculate, but a truly romantic assumption. DeAngelis was for a time a marvel of a swindler, until his own excesses did him in. If he had kept the scam small, he might still be at it. But at bottom, he was just a lousy businessman, with a larcenous streak, driven by the chimera of success. He cheated to stay alive and keep up his front. The manic fling at the futures market ate him up, but the real problem lay with his basic business plan. It was flawed from the get-go.

The Midwest oil DeAngelis was processing could have been more economically barged to southern ports. Rail freight costs into Bayonne put DeAngelis at a heavy disadvantage.

So did the interest costs he paid to keep his chronically underfinanced effort afloat. DeAngelis was famous for paying top dollar for unrefined oil, and selling the processed stuff at discount, the better to preempt market share. The Bayonnne plant was a crony-ridden, unmanaged shambles, with DeAngelis paying double the going wage rate to sustain his role as the padrone of the group. One way or another, it was inevitable that Allied Crude would go bust.

If DeAngelis had salvaged a lot of loot from Allied Crude, it certainly did not show when he walked out of the gates after seven years in Lewisburg. Reunited with Lillian Pascarelli and other members of the old crowd, DeAngelis lost no time getting back into his first love, the pork business.

Presumably with the blessing of his probation officer, DeAngelis became the behind-the-scenes general manager of a cluster of pork processors and brokers fronted by his sister Angela. As with the Allied Crude model, Tino was a middleman. He bought pork on the hoof, cut it up, and sold it to wholesalers. As exposed to volatile commodity prices as ever, bloodied by razor-thin profit margins, DeAngelis soon reverted to type. He had trouble meeting his bills, and for four increasingly frantic years managed to fob off hectoring creditors with kited checks and phony letters of credit.

The federal indictment, when it came down, sounded all too familiar: DeAngelis had engineered a "scheme to defraud and to obtain money and property by means of false and fraudulent practices."

Prosecutors contended the scam had cost farmers and other suppliers some $13 million. The evidence suggested that at least $750,000 had been diverted to the DeAngelis crowd in "loans" through an Allied Crude-like network of affiliates.

Facing yet another 20-year sentence, DeAngelis copped a plea and was hustled off to the pen again, this time for three years.

Same old Tino: a lousy business kept alive by scam. Even while under indictment, DeAngelis was still hustling. Lillian Pascarelli, along with old Allied hand Leo Bracconeri, was charged with trying to hide from the Agriculture Department DeAngelis' presence as general manager in yet another new company they were about to loose on a credulous meat trade.

Fast forward to 1991, and the pretty little town of Ovid, in the Finger Lakes district of upstate New York. DeAngelis is out of jail and once again back in the pork business, operating through a cluster of names—Sandy Acre Foods, Incorporated, J.R. Quinn, Incorporated, and Transworld Meat Specialities, Incorporated.

He had been trading with his major supplier, a Canadian outfit, Fearman's Fresh Meats, under a $40,000 letter of credit guaranteed by a local bank.

DeAngelis paid down some bad debts, and when asked to put more cash up front, produced three letters of credit totaling $660,000. Fearman's accordingly shipped him 32 truckloads of product worth about $1 million before discovering it had been gulled. Trying to milk the float, DeAngelis hoped to sell the meat and pay down his debt before his Canadian supplier caught on.

No question. The letters had been forged. Tino DeAngelis, now 77, was once again in federal court pleading to a felony count of moving in interstate commerce "falsely made, forged, and counterfeited securities."

At an age when most contemporaries were given to snoozing under their steamer rugs after lunch, DeAngelis went off to do another 21 months in the slammer, thanking federal agents for treating him "like a gentleman."

The recidivism should have surprised no one who had ever heard of Philip Musica or Billie Sol Estes. DeAngelis was running true to type. The itch to succeed never lets up. DeAngelis wasn't much of a businessman, and in the end, not much of a swindler either.

In his haste for quick growth, Henry F. Silverman confused illusions and reality. Even he didn't catch the sleight of hand behind the accountants' numbers.

CHAPTER 6

Investor Beware
A Cautionary Tale

WHETHER YOU ARE a value investor in the Ben Graham/Marty Whitman mold or a growth investor in the T. Rowe Price/Tom Bailey ambit, trust your instincts. If the story behind a stock looks too good to be true, it probably is. Despite SEC watchdogs and the billions industry spends on outside accountants, somebody may be cooking the books. Exhibit A: the astounding case of HFS and CUC International.

It starts with two centimillionaires, and you'd be hard put to find two more disparate personalities than Henry R. Silverman and Walter A. Forbes. Silverman, 61, thinks of himself as a "neurotic workaholic," a "perfectionist with no tolerance for people who are not as stressed out as I am."

Forbes, on the other hand, comes on as a laid-back visionary, said to pad about the office in sneakers and jeans, snacking on saltines, often playing softball or flag football on weekends with his staff.

Forbes (no relation to the magazine clan) has described Silverman, in a burst of seemingly contradictory insight, as his "exact clone." For all their differences—hands-on numbers man versus the soft-hands delegator—this description could not be more apt. Both men got big rich playing the megamerger game. Looking at some of the recent road kill—garbage hauler Waste Management Company, for example—you can see that the much-trumpeted synergies of megamergers are often illusory.

They sure sell in the stock market, though. Digging deep into the financial engineering kit, Silverman and Forbes flashed reported earnings growth of better than 25 percent a year, mainly by acquisition, and generally to raves on Wall Street. The securities analyst cheering squad, coupled with the impact of aggressive merger accounting, helped to boost Silverman's and Forbes' multiples to as high as 50 times earnings. High multiples were a crucial part of the game. Thanks to the mysteries of purchase accounting, they enabled Silverman and Forbes to post reported earnings growth far in excess of real internal growth. In 1996, for example, Silverman's HFS told shareholders earnings were up 75 percent. If you x-ed out the acquisition for that year (and knew where to look in the footnotes), you could see that the real gain was closer to 20 percent. And much of the 20 percent, of course, in endless regress, was due to earlier acquisitions.

Thus, the single-minded Silverman, a tax lawyer by training, and Forbes, the soft-sell marketer, were brothers under the strategic skin. They raised to high art the quite legal technique of using the virtual currency of inflated stock to buy real assets. Inevitably, the art brought the two together in a megamerger, with still more hosannas from Wall Street. Against all predictions, the combination quickly disintegrated into one of the great financial disasters of the century, costing unwary investors billions.

It didn't have to happen. There were early warning signs that alert shareholders could have picked up. Some did. Most, victimized with a major assist by complacent accountants and securities analysts, took a shellacking. The story of Silverman and Forbes is worth looking at in detail. It is a cautionary tale and a survival guide in a time when reported earnings are almost never quite what they seem.

The early form looked good. Silverman was born to business. His father was Chief Executive Officer of James Talcott, Incorporated, a Manhattan-based commercial finance company. Silverman was raised in the upper reaches of suburban Westchester county. He often went on business trips with his father, and played "every sport with more enthusiasm than aptitude" at Hackley, an elite prep school in nearby Tarrytown. Silverman doesn't credit his success to the playing fields of Hackley. He once told *Lodger Magazine* that he has "friends who say winning is everything, but that's not me." Significantly, Silverman added that "competitiveness in business is a different issue."

Silverman went on to Williams College and earned a degree in American Civilization; then, in 1964 received a law degree at the University of Pennsylvania. Silverman practiced tax law for a while, but felt underemployed; the work was too "reactive." "I've always been more proactive," he says. Driven by the entrepreneurial itch, Silverman headed for Wall Street, financing a lot of real estate—mainly hotels—and learning the franchising trade.

By the early 1980s, Silverman was in a leveraged buyout partnership with Reliance Insurance Company and Drexel Burnham and Company, checking out leverage and cash flow propositions with two of the shrewdest names in the business—corporate raider Saul Steinberg and junk bond innovator Mike Milken. Buyouts are not for the long term. As Silverman told the *Lodger*, "You buy companies, fix them and sell them." "It was just like buying a used car," he went on. "You polished the car, changed the driver, and sold it," hoping "there's someone out there who thinks you've improved the value and will pay you more."

One of the six deals Silverman engineered in his six years as Chief Executive Office of Reliance Capital Corporation was the buyout in 1984 of Days Inn, a low-end southern motel chain for around $590 million. Polishing up the chain, Silverman pushed it from 200 units to 1,000 units, largely through franchising. He sold it five years later to a major franchisee for a $125 million profit. Two years later Days Inn, loaded with debt, flipped into bankruptcy. Moral: Look at heavy borrowings with a jaundiced eye.

Silverman has described himself as "very detail-oriented," and friends credit him with always doing his homework. Among other prospects, he had been keeping a weather eye on the bankrupt Days Inn. One of the first things Silverman did on moving from Reliance to the Blackstone Group, a prestigious buyout firm, was to persuade his partners that the motel chain was once again a steal. Silverman plucked Days Inn out of receivership for around $260 million.

The deal was naked, covering only the franchise. Silverman was going virtual, leaving the bricks and mortar and the risk of actually running the company to others. His strategy of providing a centralized reservation and marketing system against a slice of the revenues was tailored to the leveraged buyout ideal. The aim was to invest in high margin situations that require minimal capital expenditures and generate enough cash flow to quickly pay down acquisition debt. Days Inn, coupled nicely with the Howard Johnson and Ramada Inn chains already under the Blackstone house flag, bought from the ailing Prime Motor Inns for around $170 million. Blackstone, eager to turn over its capital, began to bail out of what had become Hospitality Franchise Systems in a 1992 stock offering at $16 a share. Two years later, presplit, Hospitality

Franchise was at $60. The guy at the front desk, with some four million shares in hand, was none other than Henry Silverman.

Friends say Silverman felt upstaged by some of the strong person-alities at Blackstone. He put in less than two years at the firm. Now he was out on his own, putting plenty of polish on still more hotel franchise acquisitions. The currency: some cash, usually borrowed, and lots of stock. By 1996, Silverman was fronting eight national hotel-motel chains. Recorded earnings had spurted from $21 million to $80 million, and Wall Street hailed Hospitality Franchise, now renamed HFS, as a great new growth story. Growth fueled the market price, which made acqui-sitions cheap; cheap acquisitions helped keep the growth rate up. So the strategy went, propelling Silverman down the diversification path into other fragmented brand-name franchise fields, like real estate bro-kerage and auto rentals. The focus was unchanged: Keep HFS a virtual company by acquiring only the franchise; spin off or sell hard assets that would swallow capital. The purchases, first of Century 21, and then Coldwell Banker, made Silverman a major player in the residential bro-kerage and relocation business.

The Coldwell Banker buy shows the kind of merger arithmetic that was making HFS the toast of Wall Street. The deal cost Silverman $640 million in cash plus about $100 million in assumed debt. As *Forbes* staffer Howard Rudnitsky reported, Silverman financed the purchase by selling stock at a whopping 50 times projected earnings, 23 times cash flow (earnings before interest, taxes, depreciation, and amortiza-tion). He bought Coldwell Banker for seven times cash flow.

On those numbers, equity that cost Silverman around four percent was going to earn some 14 percent. So long as Silverman's multiple pro-vided the currency to buy lower multiples, HFS was in clover. There was some internal growth, difficult to calculate, as the franchisors added thousands of new rooms. But the iron logic was that to keep get-ting bigger, Silverman had to keep buying.

Silverman is quite candid about his mistakes ("Some of my deals were wonderful, some horrible"). He rarely let the mistakes hang around long enough to smell up the income sheet. One example: the quick wave of the wand that erased an abortive throw at the casino gam-bling business. Silverman spun off the effort, National Gaming Company, with a modest writeoff of around $2 million. Just in time because a year later National Gaming reported a loss of $18 million, but with zero impact on the HFS books. Renamed National Lodging, the company bought interests in 112 Travelodge Hotels for $98 million. HFS guaranteed most of this borrowed money (for an annual $1.5 million fee, plus $2 million in advisory fees), but at the same time, stripped off the royalty generating franchise. Voila! With ingenuity and a deft accounting touch, Silverman transformed a loser into a money spinner.

It was vintage Silverman, enchanting analysts and big institutional investors like Fidelity and Massachusetts Financial that in toto held some 80 percent of HFS outstanding common. They had done well, and so had Silverman. In five short years, from an initial public offer to the end of 1997, HFS common was up some 2,000 percent. Silverman's own holdings, mainly extremely generous options, at the high were worth more than $2 billion. Then came the first signs of potential trouble ahead. Silverman's mix of hotel, auto rental, and real estate franchises, did not seem to be generating the synergies he hoped for. *Forbes* (the magazine) noted that merger accounting, however legitimate, had significantly inflated HFS reported earnings. Further, the revenue growth of Silverman's half million hotel rooms had slowed to below the industry average. For anyone willing to look, the basic arithmetic raised questions about the inflated multiple at which HFS was selling, the company's basic earning power, and the validity of Silverman's underlying business plan. To keep his machine running full tilt, Silverman had to go right on looking to new and bigger buys.

Silverman's "exact clone," Walter Forbes, Chairman of CUC International, was in much the same position. Forbes, a Harvard MBA (1968), in just under a quarter century, had nursed CUC from its larval stage into the United States' biggest purveyor of discount membership buying services with sales of $2.3 billion. Forbes had a vision: Conventional retailing was doomed by an archaic, cumbersome, high-cost distribution system. Why couldn't his Comp-U-Card of America play the middleman? By some electronic means could it connect consumers to manufacturers or wholesalers willing to sell direct on credit cards at a discount?

It is commonplace now, but Forbes began turning over the idea while he was still in B-School. In 1973, he and a half dozen other venture capitalists put it to the test. First results suggested that doom threatened not conventional retailers, but Forbes' visionary virtual retailer. "It was a silly investment at the time because there were no home computers," recalled

Forbes. Several years and $2 million later, Forbes' fellow investors threw in the sponge. Among other connections, they tried pedaling home shopping by TV and on the retail floor through kiosks flashing items that could be ordered electronically. Nothing clicked.

So in 1979, in classic entrepreneurial fashion, Forbes gave up his day job as a management consultant and took over the chronic money loser full time. As Suzanne Oliver noted in *Forbes* magazine, "His colleagues said he was nuts. Why throw time and good money after bad?" Back to the drawing board. Television didn't work, electronic kiosks didn't work either, but the plain-old low-tech telephone did. Members who joined up for an annual fee (typically $49–$59), catalog at the ready, could dial an 800-number from home and tell the operator what they wanted to buy. A computer sifted through thousands of items with bids from the manufacturers and wholesalers Forbes lined up. The latter, in exchange for volume, lowballed their prices. Forbes tacked on a seven percent surcharge to cover his costs. Buyers, in a no-sweat transaction that saved them from comparison-shopping at the malls, generally got better prices than they could at a discount store.

Forbes worked hard at selling his service as an add-on to banks, conventional retailers, oil companies, and other credit card imprints for a cut of the membership fees garnered from their lists. Because those same membership fees were his primary source of revenue, Forbes faced a major marketing cost. He had to continuously bombard credit card holders by direct mail to get any kind of growth.

There were some signs of success. In 1984, Comp-U-Card first broke into the black with a net of $1.5 million. After more than a decade of trying, Forbes seemed to be on his way to a storeless society. He took public what was to become CUC International with a $25 million offering in 1983. His strategy called for adding more discount services (dining and travel, for instance), building a broad base of membership that he could cross sell. Forbes' aim: To coax the card carrier who had just bought a washing machine through his "Shoppers Advantage Club" to line up a discount vacation through Travelers Advantage—hotels, airfare, car rentals—dining out the while, all at a discount, on Comp-U-Card's enhanced plastic. Forbes cross-selling effort resembled nothing so much as the links Henry Silverman was trying to cinch into place at HFS: The hotel franchises would tout guests into the recently purchased Avis auto rentals, and both companies would nudge househunters onto Century 21 real estate brokers.

One other element the two shared: a wildly enthusiastic following on Wall Street. Both were virtual entities—no inventory, with little use for hard assets, and every prospect of rich cash flow. CUC had the additional kicker of zipping into the Internet. Partly because of that promise, Forbes' fledgling had barely broken into the black before it was sporting multiples of 40 to 60 times earnings. Analysts at Morgan Stanley (Forbes' underwriter) were hailing CUC as a top-flight emerging growth company. Truism: Look with a jaundiced eye on research put out by vested interests such as a company's investment banker.

Institutional investors such as Massachusetts Financial were beginning to prick up their ears, too, as sales between 1985 and 1988 climbed from $87.5 million to $271.8 million. CUC was on its way to becoming the fifth largest holding of the 66 mutual funds specializing in small companies. The multiples generated by its demand (as they did with Henry Silverman) made CUC stock a super merger currency. So Walter Forbes had it right. He and Henry Silverman were strategic clones—merger equaled growth, equaled multiples, equaled merger, equaled . . . .

By the time CUC's sales approached $2 billion in 1996, Forbes had engineered at least 25 acquisitions. Purchase accounting made CUC's numbers somewhat opaque. Few Wall Street analysts made much of an effort to look behind them, but as early as 1991 *Forbes'* (the magazine) Michael Ozanian began to question the aggressive accounting that was helping to propel CUC's seeming straight-line growth. Cutting through the Wall Street complacency, Ozanian found a cluster of early warning signs:

* CUC was finding it increasingly difficult to line up new members;
* Nearly one-third of those who did sign up were canceling their memberships at the end of the first year;
* The idea of cross-selling members multiple services was not panning out;
* Cash flow was being squeezed by marketing expenses, a dynamic masked by the company's accounting massage.

An SEC challenge to CUC's accounting practices deepened the unease among some analysts, yet Wall Street continued to put CUC common right up there with glamour multiples like Home Shopping Network, QVC, and MCI. Those multiples kept Forbes in the acquisition game. Reported sales and earnings continued their almost metronomic growth and led inevitably to one triumphal possibility: What about a combination of two great virtual companies—CUC and HFS? Great financial engineers both, Walter Forbes and Henry Silverman needed one another. Synergies and cross-selling were the ticket.

One conspicuous failure showed how iffy it could be to push these much-dramatized synergies through the pipeline. In one such effort, Silverman picked up a minority interest in Amre, Incorporated, a roofing and siding installer that had long operated as a Sears, Roebuck vendor. Profits were thin and Sears wanted out. Silverman installed three of his own officers on the board (one as chairman) to get Amre back on track. The concept: Amre would now sell its services under the HFS Century 21 brand-name, with its franchised real estate brokers drumming up the leads.

In response to the Silverman touch, Amre common ran from 5 to around 16, at which point the company unloaded 1.1 million new shares on bemused investors. There were distinct signs that the brand transplant was not working (sales had dropped below the Sears level), but management soothingly allowed it was "optimistic about the company's ultimate profitability."

Too optimistic by far. There was a burst of insider selling (none from HFS) several months before Amre lurched into bankruptcy. Undaunted, Silverman announced he planned to build a whole new lineup of home improvement licensees. In the case of Amre, he proclaimed, "We were just not good passive investors."

Dubious synergies aside, there were other question marks dangling over the $11 billion HFS-CUC combination as the merger talks moved to fruition. Among them were the sharply distinct personalities of the principals—Forbes, the delegator, whose substantial outside interests ran to venture capital and golf course development versus the single-minded command and control of Silverman. As to the corporate cultures, Silverman's staffers (unlike Forbes') definitely did not show up in costume on Halloween and strew their offices with ersatz cobwebs.

The signals on leadership were also decidedly mixed. Who would run the show? From the effective date of the merger (December, 1997) to January 1, 2000, Silverman was to be president/CEO, with Forbes as chairman. After that date, the two would switch—Silverman to chairman; Forbes to CEO. The "merger of equals" spawned a superstructure that would not have been out of place in the upper reaches of the French bureaucracy. The table of organization carried eight vice-chairmen (four from either side) and 28 directors (14 from each side). A number of directors had close enough outside business ties with the new company to raise obvious questions about their independence. Few mainstream analysts even hinted at these glaring drawbacks.

Whatever long-term promise the merger held for shareholders, there were immediate benefits for the brass. Forbes' base pay, premerger, was a little over $780,000 with a bonus of the same amount. His new scale went to a base of $1.25 million. His new bonus: The lesser of 100 percent of base pay, or 0.75 percent (from the first dollar rather than some performance bogey) of earnings before taxes and other costs. The merger was conveniently construed as a change in control, so Forbes picked up an additional $7.3 million in retirement pay, the benefit of $538,000 a year in life insurance premiums, and exercisable options with a value of around $65 million.

Though the deal was billed as a merger of equals, it was clear that Silverman was more equal. His base pay: $1.5 million plus a bonus of the lesser of 150 percent of base pay, or 0.75 percent of earnings before taxes and other costs from the first dollar. And, in what may have been one of the biggest such awards ever (14.4 million shares), Silverman got vested calls on a market value of around $830 million. This cornucopia—bigger base pay, bigger bonuses, bigger option grants, and easy vesting—trickled down from Silverman and Forbes through the rest of senior management. Silverman and Forbes were patting themselves on the back for having found one another.

With the two companies now united as Cendant, Silverman barnstormed many of CUC's subsidiaries for a firsthand look. His auditors had been given only limited access to CUC's nonpublic files. CUC was worried about giving away competitive information if the merger did not gel. Silverman was pleased to learn that almost all his new business units were on target. He was edgy, though, about the amount of detail and timeliness with which CUC corporate results were reaching his desk. Silverman told Forbes he wanted division reporting switched from a two-step path through a CUC intermediary directly to one of his own people, chief accounting officer Scott Forbes (no relation to Walter).

Walter Forbes agreed, but asked to delay the change for a month until the close of the first quarter. An impatient Silverman agreed, but a week later abruptly changed his mind. He wanted CUC's reports forthwith. Scott Forbes met with E. Kirk Shelton, former CUC president and new Cendant vice chairman, to iron out the details. Four other CUC executives in the accounting loop sat in on the meeting.

Recollections of who said what to whom differ. Scott Forbes remembers that Shelton gave him a cash flow spreadsheet and asked him to help the CUC side to be "creative" for the new fiscal year in moving $165 million from merger reserves into income. The schedule Forbes was handed in fact shows that CUC was budgeting a total of $202 million in "revenue adjustments" for a couple of its divisions. The cash would come from reversing some of the $550 million the new company had charged against operations to cover such anticipated merger expenses as severance payments, litigation, plant closings, and other restructuring costs.

CUC seemed to be talking an aggressive push on audit standards, the so-called "big bath" accounting common enough in the great megamerger boom. Jamming what may turn out to be several years expenses into a "one-time charge" rather than stretching them out as the money is actually spent guarantees that future earnings will look better. In cases like CUC (and HFS), the compounding effect of multiyear mergers makes it difficult for outsiders to get a good picture of operating earnings. Overestimate the merger expenses, and you can then tap the excess to smooth out what might otherwise be a bumpy earnings curve. Scott Forbes did not like the tone of what he was hearing. True, Ernst & Young, the big five accounting firm that had been auditing CUC since the company went public in 1983, had signed off on the numbers. But the discussion with Shelton prompted the gnawing questions that Scott Forbes took to Silverman.

How much of CUC's rising sales and earnings had come from operations, and how much of it had been hyped with nonrecurring items HFS had somehow failed to catch? Told that $144 million of CUC's

1997 net income had come from nonoperating sources, Silverman hit the roof. He was doubly vexed to learn that his CUC "equals" needed to pull as much as $200 million out of reserves to meet the proposed operating budget for 1998.

By now, Silverman had heard enough. He flatly told Walter Forbes that he wanted vice-chairman Shelton and chief financial officer Cosmo Corigliano out of the company, pronto! The honeymoon was definitely over. The resignations were glossed over in a press release that gave not a hint of the turmoil behind the scenes.

It blandly announced the two were leaving "to pursue other interests" and even offered them a friendly little pat on the back, pointedly attributed to both Silverman and Walter Forbes: "We thank Kirk and Cosmo for their service. These types of management changes are inevitable when any two large companies merge." As to Cendant itself, "our fundamentals remain extremely strong. We continue to be excited about our business," the press release said.

Even as Silverman poured soothing syrup over Wall Street in a conference call, accounting chief Scott Forbes was getting an earful at Cendant's Parsippany, New Jersey, headquarters. Still bird-dogging accounting chicanery, he sat down with old CUC hand Casper Sabatino. Sabatino told a flabbergasted Forbes that in the first three quarters of 1997 he had made a series of "topside" adjustments to sales and expenses that inflated CUC's reported earnings by about $176 million. The manufactured numbers were injected into consolidated numbers at the corporate level, but not into any of the operating unit's books. Laying out the detail for Forbes and chief financial officer Michael Monaco, who joined the meeting late, Sabatino said that he had then dressed up fourth quarter earnings by $93 million from reserves "without factual substantiation or support."

Basically, confessed Sabatino, the numbers were pulled out of thin air by higher-ups such as the departed CFO Corigliano to meet the earnings targets promised Wall Street. Predictable earnings growth— no downside surprises thank you—is the key to the megamergers game and momentum investing. Forget about basics. As long as there appears to be earnings growth, no price is too high to pay.

What the whistle-blowing Scott Forbes and Monaco were hearing from Sabatino was an exercise in self-preservation. With Corigliano exiting, they did not want to take the rap for the book cooking he and senior vice president of finance Anne Pember had supposedly ordered. Other subalterns in the accounting loop at the division level had also been ordered to make "adjustments," either by helping with the booking of fictitious "topside" numbers, or with a grab on reserves. The topside adjustments typically spun on booking sales before they were actually made and understating or deferring expenses. It was a classic example of how easy it is for aggressive accounting to jump the tracks.

Monaco, as chief financial offficer was detailed to break the bad news to Henry Silverman. "Are you sitting down?" he asked.

The bad news quickly found its way into yet another press release—and less publicly to the SEC and the U.S. Attorney in Newark, New Jersey. The discovery of "potential" accounting irregularities at CUC might force Cendant to lop $100 to $115 million off the $872 million profit (before restructuring costs) it had reported for 1997. Earlier reported earnings on the CUC side might have to be restated as well.

"Cendant remains a strong and highly liquid company," the release continued and added point to the claim by noting three pending acquisitions involving almost $5 billion were still on the fire. Wall Street reacted savagely, whacking on extremely heavy volume almost 50 percent off the stock.

The first of more than 70 stockholder suits against Cendant, Silverman, and Forbes and, alleging major disclosure breaches of the securities laws, was already on its way up the courthouse steps. Among the complaints: that Forbes and Silverman had benefitted by selling between them a total of more than $70 million in Cendant stock in the months before word of the accounting debacle broke.

On the defensive, both Forbes and Silverman denied any prior knowledge of the doctored books.

"I am not taking it well," Silverman bitterly told the *Economist*. "I have visions of these people responsible at CUC laughing into their reflections in the morning mirror, saying '*Fortune* magazine called this man a genius.' Other than death or bankruptcy this is as bad as it gets." He tried to channel his rage into daily workouts in the gym or on the tennis court. Much of Silverman's rage was directed at his equal and clone, Walter A. Forbes. How could Forbes and Shelton—let alone the accountants at Ernst & Young—not have picked up the fraud? A trenchant question. Silverman felt he had been betrayed. So did Forbes. He wasn't told about the Sabatino whistle-blowing until five days after the event. "I should have known the second Henry Silverman knew," complained Forbes. Silverman retorted that Forbes had been kept in the dark because he (Silverman) "did not know who was complicit." It was in that poisoned atmosphere that Silverman began trying to elbow Forbes out of the company. The cumbersome governance structure Silverman had agreed to, though—a board divided equally between the two companies—tied his hands. Like many megamergers, Cendant was a house built on sand.

The impasse, reflected in Cendant's still sinking stock, was broken when forensic accountants at Arthur Anderson produced a preliminary report indicating the damages were far worse than the original estimates. An additional $200 million in "accounting errors"—accelerated revenues, deferred expenses—had been uncovered. CUC had been booking phony revenues for at least three years, and Cendant would have to cut its 1997 result by as much as $240 million—more than twice the first projections. The new numbers suggested that something like one-third of CUC's 1997 reported revenues were thin air.

Further, the auditors tweaked out some $2 million in questionable expenses Forbes had run up between 1995 and 1997. They included $1 million in undocumented cash advances and American Express charges, and almost $600,000 in private jet charges. The expense report Forbes signed for the plane charges noted that they were to be charged to the all-accommodating Cendant merger reserve. One easy inference was that the loose financial controls at CUC extended to the very top.

Forbes finally elected to jump before he was pushed. His resignation, he said, was "in the best interests of our shareholders and employees to resolve this uncertainty."

There were huge incentives for Forbes to bow out. Since he was resigning "without cause," Cendant had to stump up the severance stipulated in his employment contract. It was quite a package: $35 million in cash, some $22 million in fully vested options (on 1.3-million shares at $17, close to the then market), and a $2.1 million in escrowed life insurance premiums.

Forbes' golden handshake cost shareholders 3¢ per share, but an ebullient Silverman let them know the price was worth it. "Now we can focus all of our energies on rebuilding confidence in our company," he crowed. It had taken seven wildly contentious months but Henry Silverman was once again alone at the helm.

The full Arthur Anderson report was out now, and it demonstrated beyond all doubt that Henry Silverman had bought a pig in a poke. Between 1995 and 1997, "irregular" accounting had inflated CUC earnings before charges by $500 million; accounting "errors" had overstated earnings by another $200 million. Stripped of the fictions, CUC now looked like a slow to no-growth hulk.

Building on the original whistle-blowing charges, the report cited innumerable phony entries on revenues, expenses, and merger reserves by a score of people in an accounting loop traduced by orders from above. Their commands were handed down, the lower ranks contended, by executive vice president Cosmo Corigliano, CUC controller Anne Pember, and accounting chief Casper Sabatino. The final product was then sent to the board, the SEC, and the shareholders. The objective: to pump up quarterly earnings by "the amount needed to bring CUC's results into line with Wall Street earnings expectations." "If actual income in a particular quarter was 10¢ per share and consensus analysts' expectations were 18¢ a share," the report continued, "then adjustments of approximately 8¢ were made, without support, to increase earnings."

Ernst & Young had been auditing CUC for 15 years. Where were the accountants? At least four of CUC's top accounting people—including Corigliano and Pember—had worked at E & Y before joining CUC. So, they were certainly familiar with the firm's audit patterns. The Arthur Anderson report pieced together "a carefully planned exercise" in which operating, marketing, and administrative expense ratios were painstakingly kept consistent from quarter to quarter. One single bit of sleight of hand, for example, required 105 separate ledger entries, all back-dated to the preceding year to produce an ordered $40 million increase in quarterly income.

E & Y had signed off without qualification on CUC's books before the merger and like almost everyone else involved, became the target of several stockholders suits. Cendant also went on the attack. It charged that the accountants had "looked the other way" while the scheme rolled on, sometimes even tipping the direction its audits would take. "Rather than expose the fraud, Ernst & Young chose to facilitate it and continue to reap millions of dollars in fees," complained Cendant.

Ernst & Young, without admitting any wrongdoing, settled the Cendant stockholders suit for some $335 million, one of the largest such settlements ever.

The Arthur Anderson report cited several warning signs that E & Y might have picked up, but its main thrust was on the workings of Corigliano, Pember, and Sabatino. The report left hanging an obvious question: Why would the three have such an unfettered interest in running the risk of criminal charges in keeping CUC's earnings (and multiples) on the growth track?

Corigliano held options on more than 800,000 shares of CUC. He was making about $300,000 a year, including a $100,000 bonus, before he was fired, but did not seem to enjoy an exalted lifestyle. Home was a pleasant suburban enclave in Connecticut with a couple of Toyotas in the driveway. Was Corigliano the ringleader, subverting the entire accounting group on his own, or was he—like his underlings—just following orders?

The Arthur Anderson report stopped at Corigliano and his cronies. None of the 80 witnesses interviewed directly implicated Forbes or Shelton. The directors on Cendant's audit committee, in their report to the full board, went no further than the general statement that both men were "among those who must bear responsibility for what occurred." They failed "to create an environment in which it was clear that inaccurate financial reporting would not be tolerated," the committee went on. Senior management failed to put in financial controls "that might have enabled them to detect the irregularities in the absence of actual knowledge" of them.

For all the moiling and toiling, Arthur Anderson had not come up with a smoking gun on top management. Indirectly, the report reinforced what Forbes and Shelton had been insisting right along—notably that they had no part in what was now being billed as "the accounting swindle of the decade."

Forbes and Shelton though, were by no means out of woods. The Anderson investigation had pinned so much detail on Corigliano, Pember, Sabatino, and others in the accounting loop that U.S. Attorney Robert Cleary and the SEC had no trouble building a case. Corigliano quickly copped a plea in Newark, New Jersey Federal Court to one count of conspiracy to commit false statements and one count of wire fraud. Pember pleaded guilty to a single conspiracy count and Sabatino to one count of aiding and abetting wire fraud.

The pleas signaled that Corigliano and his two colleagues had pledged to give up whatever they knew about anyone else involved in the fraud. Corigliano, admitting to his own guilt to U.S. District Judge William H. Walls, said flatly that "my superiors were encouraging me." CUC's free and easy culture, continued Corigliano, "had been developed over many years" and "was ingrained by our superiors."

Reporters didn't need an organization chart to tell that Corigliano's only superiors were Walter Forbes and E. Kirk Shelton. U.S. Attorney Cleary pointedly told newsmen he would "follow the evidence wherever it takes us." Henry Silverman had no doubts about where the evidence would lead. "Obviously," he told reporters, "only a very few" knew about the fraud and "at the end were Shelton and Forbes."

It was no great surprise, then, when a sitting grand jury indicted Forbes and Shelton on conspiracy and wire fraud charges going back more than a decade. Both men denied any wrongdoing, but were also faced with an SEC civil suit demanding they "disgorge" profits on the CUC shares they sold while the supposed scheme was afoot.

What did Henry Silverman know and when did he know it? CUC's earlier accounting problems with the SEC were in the database for anyone willing to call them up. So were *Forbes* editor Michael Ozanian's pieces on CUC's aggressive accounting. One of Ozanian's sources was Manhattan-based investment advisor Robert Renck. Renck's challenge to the validity of CUC's reported earnings was based in part on correspondence between CUC and the SEC, harvested under a Freedom of Information Act filing.

Silverman could have done the same. So could Goldman, Sachs and Bear Stearns, the investment bankers that did the "due diligence" on the merger (at a combined cost of $45 million). Irate shareholders, who had swallowed billions of loss in market capitalization, were climbing all over Silverman for failure to pick up the scent.

There are hints, suggested the magazine *CFO*, that Silverman relied on the due diligence not to avoid risk, but to justify it. "You want to win, so you take some informed risks," Cendant vice-chairman Michael Monaco told *CFO*. Silverman was willing to take some risks, because he needed CUC to keep his own growth scenario going. Such calculated risks are typical of the megamerger boom. The mortality rate among combinations that look good on paper but can't cut it in the real world is very high. The temptation to push the accounting envelope to meet Wall Street's all-compelling expectations (ah, those options!) is often irresistible. Cendant is not an isolated instance. Cases of egregious accounting manipulation are multiplying. A sampling of the big names: W. R. Grace, Livent Corporation, Rite Aid, Safety-Kleen, Sunbeam Corporation, and Waste Management Company. There are even double-dippers. McKesson HBOC, for example, pumped up on con man Philip Musica's phoney inventories some 60 years ago, was recently flagged once again for falsely inflating sales.

Are executives so driven by the need to meet Wall Street numbers (ah, those options!) that they are willing to risk jail time? Typically, as appears to be the case in Cendant, the chicanery starts small, with the need to smooth out a bumpy quarter. What looks like a "temporary" problem is still unfixed, so you have to grab more revenue next quarter to keep the treadmill rolling. Expedience becomes a way of life. "People don't get into these things in sharp percussive steps," says one forensic accountant. "They kind of ooze into them and they wish to heck later on that they never had. These crises start off not with a meltdown but with a little smoke."

Where are the accountants as smoke billows into meltdown? It's a question the SEC has been raising for years, trying to inject clarity into grey judgmental areas that often leave too much room for loose interpretation. The culture of the accounting profession itself has undergone a major change. As what used to be the "Big Eight" coalesced into what is now the "Big Five," competition sharpened. One solution was to diversify out of the labor-intensive business of bookkeeping into the much higher margin line of "consulting" on items like management, technology, and recruiting. Consulting has boomed to the point where traditional audit fees now account for only 30 percent of Big Five revenues. Some of the cross-selling is done by regular line bean counters who have no wish to irritate the clients they are hoping to upgrade. Such potential conflicts raise real questions of independence. How tough will the accountants hang in areas of judgment against an executive determined to make his numbers, no matter what? Warren Buffett highlighted this dilemma in a letter to his Berkshire Hathaway shareholders. "The attitude of disrespect many executives have for accurate reporting is a business disgrace," said Buffett. "For their part," he continued, "auditors have done little on the positive side. Though auditors should regard the investing public as their client, they tend instead to kowtow to the managers who choose them and dole out their pay."

The SEC, stung by the doubts over the quality of the numbers on which investors are basing their decisions, has tried to get accountants out of the consulting business. Some firms have already done so, others are duking it out. Here again, the SEC has a couple of high-profile cases to buttress its point. One of them is the Merry-Go-Round Enterprises suit that Ernst & Young settled for a bell ringing $185 million. Stockholders and creditors charged the firm's consulting arm with duplicity. Hired (at fees totaling $4.5 million) to devise a turnaround plan for the struggling retailer, E & Y took nearly a year to come up with $11 million in cuts for a company losing more than $180 million a year. Creditors argued that the obvious strategy was to close unprofitable outlets. E & Y (denying liability) was allegedly slow to suggest this approach because it was also doing consulting work for developers who would have lost money on some of the stores likely to be closed. E & Y never disclosed this link, shareholders contended, and the conflict of interest was the root cause of Merry-Go-Round's bankruptcy.

What's to be learned from the Cendant debacle? Are some of today's hot stocks just smoke and mirrors like CUC? Are some apparent value stocks actually lousy value because the assets are overstated? You can almost bet on it. Not so easy, though, is detection.

Picking up internal fraud is beyond the reach of the armchair analyst. But as investment advisor Robert Renck showed in his early contrary opinions on CUC, early recognition of the illusions of aggressive accounting is a primary line of defense. His digging showed that Walter Forbes was hyping his cash flow by low-balling the reserves he should have been setting up for rising membership cancellations. Pulling on that thread, Renck was among the few Wall Streeters to conclude that Forbes' reported earnings were all smoke and mirrors.

Aggressive accounting, totally out of control at CUC, is usually legal enough because of the many grey areas pasted over the supposed Bible of Generally Accepted Accounting Principles. Like the Holy Bible, GAAP is subject to broad interpretation. Hence the abuse of the merger reserves that were recycled into earnings at CUC.

Manipulating merger reserves is a common enough practice. How to detect it? Check the footnotes in the annual report. They should spell out the size of the reserve, how it is being spent (severance pay, for example), and how much (if any) is filtering back into earnings. Reserves don't last forever. If they account for half of the $1 a share profit a company is reporting, for example, and the stock is selling at $20, it's trading not at a notional 20 times earnings but at 40 times earnings. Is the stock really worth that much?

Yet another front-loaded charge that distorts true earnings is the broadening trend for an acquiring company to take as big a write-off as possible on its new partner's research and development "in process."

The theory is that none of this R&D, underway but not yet at a commercial stage, may never pan out. The incentive to chalk up as many billions as possible to R&D is that they can be written off at once, making later earnings (presumably enhanced by maturing R&D) look good by comparison. The R&D write-off also tends to reduce the drag of "goodwill"—the premium the acquirer paid over book value. Since goodwill is depreciated and impacts earnings over many years, the aim is to keep it to a minimum. Every dollar lumped into R&D is one less dollar that gets shunted into goodwill. Once again, check the quarterlies and annual reports for a clearer picture of real earnings.

Yet another merger wrinkle to check out is pooling of interest accounting, which permits the partners to combine their assets at book value. Doing so eliminates the whole nasty question of depreciating goodwill and hypes earnings for years to come. The hurdles for doing pooling are high. Poolings are supposed to meet a dozen accounting criteria, but the number of such deals has been increasing almost geometrically since the start of the great bull market in 1990. One other pleasing effect of pooling: It makes it easier for management to bury the premium it paid for a combination that may not work out.

Some other soft spots to check include: cash flow versus reported earnings. Cash flow (revenue minus all costs) is probably the truest measure of how well a company is doing. If reported earnings are growing faster than cash flow, the incremental difference has to be coming from somewhere. Hope that the source is not "topside" adjustments like the flummery at CUC. As Robert A. Olstein, manager of the Financial Alert Fund notes, there are many ways to juice earnings, and it's just not bad guys like CUC who capitalize on them. Olstein has been tracking the quality of earnings for decades. His long-term performance shows it. As he told Gretchen Morgenson of the *New York Times*, "the best long-term performance is associated with making the fewest errors." Hence the need to look "around and between the numbers to see what a company's real or repetitive earnings are."

Two of the most common ploys Olstein cited are also a by-product of the great bull market. In one recent quarter, for example, Bank of America reported a gain of 8¢ a share on securities sales—six percent of the $1.33 a share total. Thanks to a then rising market, pension fund assets were also mounting. Investment gains that exceed the cash a company has to recycle to retirees are tucked into earnings. The surplus can be used only for pension payments, but it does help to put a nice, if only temporary, sheen on profits.

One of Olstein's prime examples is General Electric. A gain of almost 40 percent in its pension fund assets amounted to nine percent of G.E.'s pretax operating income. Without that fillip, the company's earnings for the year in question would have been 7.6 percent lower. Olstein's point with both Bank of America and G.E.: No sensible investor would think of stock market gains as lasting forever. They are nice to have, but should be valued at a much lower multiple than true operating profits.

Olstein also warns of the trend among high-tech companies to finance customer purchases of equipment. Doing so gives outfits like Cisco Systems and IBM a leg up in a competitive market, but it also loads them with potentially weak paper.

To see how a number of these quite legal adjuvants can come together and cosmeticize earnings, look no further than IBM. As recently as 1996, swelling pension fund assets accounted for a little under two percent of Big Blue's reported operating income. By 1999, a rip-roaring stock market (and conversion to a controversial new pension plan) had pushed the number to 6.7 percent of reported operating income. It takes some searching to dig this number out of a forest of footnotes, but it's vital to tracking the course of IBM's true earnings growth. To cite Robert Olstein again, "It's time to look at the true quality of earnings."

Another tell-tale sign: Although IBM's reported earnings had been rising at a good clip, sales had been climbing much more slowly, and gross profit margins have been shrinking. All of this puts IBM's vaunted turnaround in a less favorable light.

Another potential danger is stock buybacks. There's nothing wrong with buybacks per se. If a company's stock is cheap in the market, a buyback can be a good use of excess cash. But watch out for buybacks financed with debt; this is simply a way to goose earnings by substituting debt for equity and can leave a company ill-equipped to handle a downturn in its business or the economy. This is fairly easy to detect: Go back a few years in the corporate history. Is the equity portion of capital shrinking while the debt portion is rising—along with growing earnings? Be skeptical of the growth. You can find the relevant historical numbers in Value Line's excellent industry reports.

Also take a hard look at the impact of management stock options on reported earnings. Though widely touted as an incentive to keep management hustling, options are in fact a two-edged sword. Although truly a labor cost, they are not stated as an expense, but capitalized. Thus, options have the effect of understating costs and overstating earnings, often by 30 percent or more.

The dilutive effect comes from the increase in the number of shares outstanding—the divisor used to calculate profits per share. The arithmetic is inexorable. If the number of shares outstanding increases by 10 percent without a corresponding increase in earnings, you are looking at a dilution of 10 percent. A 20 percent increase in profits against that dilutive factor would net to an increase of only nine percent in earnings per share. The option effect has to be seen as a mortgage on the future. Assess it before you buy a stock with yet another foray into the footnotes of the annual report. Good luck. The rules are so ambiguous you can't be sure that any two companies value their options in the same way.

Options, not surprisingly, have been a major source of controversy at Cendant. So what about Henry Silverman and his discredited stock? As Silverman beavers away at repairing the damage, some of the skeptics are turning bullish on Cendant. "We don't need capital," Silverman recently told reporters. "We need credibility." Credibility, once shattered, is not easily rebuilt.

There is a moral here, more easily stated than applied: Don't—as so many investors and analysts do—take the reported numbers at face value. Do the homework it takes to get behind the numbers. And above all, remember this: If the "story" behind a stock seems too good to be true, it probably is.

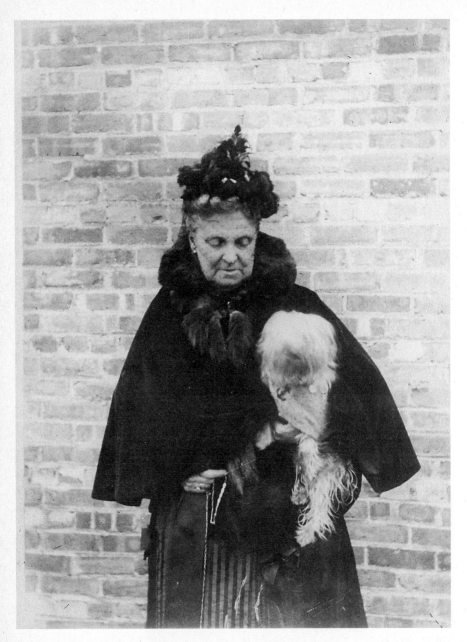

Hetty Green and friend. Shrewd stock picker and real estate mogul, Hetty Green was hated and feared by many, including her own family.

The Richest Woman in the World
Hetty Green

As THE STORY GOES, Addison Cammack came north from Kentucky after the Civil War to make it big on Wall Street. He was already pretty well-heeled, they said, with cash squeezed from such other speculative pursuits as cotton trading and blockade running. In short, a man who lived by his wits. But then, so did Hetty Green.

Cammack was well-connected. He was among the first to learn that the long prosperous Louisville & Nashville Railroad had hit a rough spot and was about to cut its dividend. Cammack did what any respectable New York Stock Exchange member of the 1880s would have done with inside information. He went heavily short on the L&N. Cammack was certain he could turn a fast profit from a major sell-off on this abrupt change in the L&N's fortunes.

Cammack's information was dead on. With the L&N down 30 points on the bad news, he looked to take his profit with a sub-cellar buy to cover the borrowed shares he had sold at much higher prices. To his pain, Cammack quickly discovered there was little stock to be had. Canny as he was, Cammack had fallen into the classic bear trap of his day, a corner. It had been engineered by someone with even better information than Cammack. Anticipating the bear raid, his adversary had bought up huge amounts of the stock on the way down and was now in a position to dictate the penalty Cammack would have to pay to get out of trouble. "I was in a slaughterhouse," Cammack told Wall Street journalist Harry Alloway. "Whichever way I looked, I spurted blood."

Cammack's dilemma was summed up in the old trader's jingle: "He who sells what isn't his'n, must buy it back or go to prison."

The desperate Cammack put out feelers and got some tenuous acknowledgment that there might be some stock for sale, but its owner wouldn't be able to see him for a couple of days. Left to twist in the wind, fearful of the extortionate price he would have to pay, Cammack was finally ushered into the presence of Hetty Howland Robinson Green. Hetty Green allowed that she had 40,000 shares of L&N she was willing to give up; it was just a matter of price. Demanding $10 a share above her own cost, Green tucked into her black reticule a check that gave her a $400,000 profit on the corner. Hetty Green, "The Witch of Wall Street," had struck again in one of the many ploys that made her the richest woman of her time.

Green was 82 when she died in 1916, leaving an estimated estate of $100,000,000—a sum that translates into some $2.5 billion today. Riches brought her power, but little respect. Green was branded a criminal for allegedly forging a signature that turned an aunt's will in her favor. Green was mocked for the often dirty and disheveled widow's weeds and veil she affected. She was reviled for miserliness so unyielding that her insistence on charity medical care literally cost her only son a leg. She was castigated for an intractable money hunger that didn't blink at such antisocial behavior as foreclosing on a delinquent church mortgage.

Some of Green's milder eccentricities—her reluctance to bathe regularly, her snacking on raw onions through the day—seem well-documented. Others are almost certainly hand-me-downs, embroidered in the telling over the years by hostile neighbors and newsmen pumping color into a Sunday feature. It's fair to say that Hetty Green was driven and calculating. She prospered in a predatory no-holds-barred environment, beating robber barons like Collis P. Huntington at their own game. In a time when women were thought to be congenitally incapable of handling money, tapped-out speculators like Addison Cammack played Green the supreme compliment. They spoke of her as having a "man's brain."

Often fearful of being murdered or kidnapped, Hetty Green carried with her a whiff of paranoia. But she was also something of a proto-feminist. Green split from her *bon vivant* husband of 15 years, taking their two children with her, when he insisted that her assets be held to collateralize several hundred thousand dollars of his own trading losses. He made the mistake of viewing Green's property as his own.

Pragmatic as ever, Green said she didn't "believe much in so-called women's rights," but added that "I wish women had more rights in business." " I find men will take advantage of women in business in ways they would not attempt with men," continued Green. "I have found this particularly so in the courts, where I have been fighting men all my life."

A ferocious litigant, Green loathed lawyers, including her own. They often had to sue her to get paid and she was quick with the lawyers' jokes of her day. "Why is a lawyer like a man who is restless in bed?" she once asked a clueless reporter. "Because both lie first on one side, then the other." She carried a revolver, Hetty deadpanned, "Mostly to protect myself against lawyers. I'm not much afraid of burglars or highwaymen."

Green was often trailed by reporters on street car and ferry en route from her sometime "$14 a month" flat in Hoboken, New Jersey, to her vault at the Chemical National Bank across the river in Lower Manhattan. Badgered for tips by the news hounds, this tart-tongued Quaker would tell them to "invest in another world." Hetty Green was big news in her day.

Except for a recent musical ("The Witch of Wall Street"), a Hofstra University off-off-Broadway production, and a museum Web site dedicated to her early days in New Bedford, Massachusetts (www.hetty-green.com), Hetty Green is little heard of today. That's too bad. Much of her basic investment strategy is still sound as a $20 gold piece and one can argue that her real legacy as a trailblazer is the growing cadre of women now making their own mark on Wall Street. Many of them, like Hetty, are value players, looking to buy quality assets on the cheap.

Green's interest in money and business started early. She was born Hetty Howland Robinson in one of New Bedford's most prosperous whaling families. Grandfather Gideon Howland and father Edward Mott Robinson ran Isaac Howland & Company, founded by her great-grandfather. The firm owned or had interests in a fleet of more than 30 ships.

Vessels under the Howland house flag, like the *William Hamilton*, put out to sea in the 1840s for voyages lasting as long as two years. With luck, they hove back in view of the mansions on the hill with a cargo of whalebone and oil that might be worth $100,000 or more. "What luck?" shouted excited owners as the vessels were warped in. "Clean or greasy?" They ran mostly greasy until the late 1850s, when cheap petroleum products began to displace whale oil in the lamps of America.

It was a boom time in New Bedford, good for the Howlands. Good, too, for the scores of newcomers pushing into town "all a-thirst for gain and glory in the fishery," as Herman Melville put it. Melville caught the polyglot hustle of the place. "Actual cannibals stood chatting at street corners; savages outright; many of whom yet carrying on their bones unholy flesh," he wrote. "It makes a stranger stare."

This world of spar, sail, and rancid-smelling oil casks was Hetty Howland Robinson's backyard. Her mother Abigail was a semi-invalid, passive, depressed. So Hetty was left to tag along after her father and grandfather, scrambling around decks, climbing in and out of holds, sitting around the cracker barrel in the Howland general store, listening and learning.

No one on the docks drove a harder bargain than Hetty's father, "Black Hawk" Robinson. His description in a Massachusetts rich list of the 1850s: "The very Napoleon of our little business community over-leaps all barriers in his love of moneymaking and that, he confesses, is the great object of his life." In later years, Hetty Green recalled "my father taught me never to owe anyone anything, not even a kindness."

It was a rough-and-tumble upbringing. While other young women of her class were bound to the embroidery hoop and the pianoforte, Hetty Green compensated for her grandfather's failing eyesight by reading him the financial news and talking it over with him. Hetty later recalled the regimen taught her "what stocks and bonds were, how the markets fluctuated, and the meaning of bulls and bears." "By the time I was 15," remembered Green, "I knew more about these things than many a man that makes a living out of them."

Hetty's spinster maternal aunt, Sylvia Ann Howland, was unhappy with the way Hetty was growing up. She finally persuaded Black Hawk that Hetty should be packed off to a finishing school in Boston, run by a cadet branch of the very Brahmin Lowells and Cabots. Three years later, at 19, Hetty came back to a formal coming-out party in New Bedford and was then dispatched to a winter season in New York under the watchful eyes of her socially prominent cousins, the Grinnells.

There was a whirl of dances and parties and elegant houses whose servants would have scorned the low-rent, down-at-the-heels spaces Hetty Green subsequently chose to occupy. Hetty talked of having a "mighty gay time in New York," but was soon back in New Bedford, "tired of the round of parties and balls long before the winter was over."

She returned much to the distress of her mother and Aunt Sylvia, who had hoped Hetty would find some eligible bachelor in the glitterati of New York.

Hetty came back with no rings on her fingers but richer than when she had left. Black Hawk had given her a $1,200 draft on his New York bankers to put together an appropriately fashionable wardrobe. Hetty instead slipped $1,000 of the allowance into government bonds and frugally let her Grinnell cousins outfit her for the season. Hetty Howland Robinson was daddy's little girl.

She proved that not long after her mother, the ailing Abigail, died without a will in 1860. The mother had been left $40,000 in trust by her grandfather, Isaac Howland, with another $90,000 paid out "in her interest" directly to her husband, Black Hawk. The $40,000 (managed by someone other than Black Hawk) over the years had grown to around $140,000. Abigail was barely cold when Black Hawk moved to grab the $140,000, too. Egged on by Aunt Sylvia, who loathed Black Hawk, Hetty went to arbitration. She had no doubt that, as a Howland, the money was unquestionably hers. In the 1860s—father versus daughter—there was little uncertainty about the outcome. Black Hawk swept all, leaving on the table for Hetty only an $8,000 parcel of real estate her mother had owned.

Did life with a marginalized mother and forceful father nurture Hetty's drive to be her own woman? Boyden Sparkes and Samuel Taylor Moore, authors of the definitive *The Witch of Wall Street*, published in 1935, theorized Hetty decided early on that all the Howland money was hers, rightfully—outright, no trusts, no fee-gouging intermediaries. Hetty was in the right place at the right time. She was the only great-granddaughter of founder Isaac Howland Jr., the only granddaughter of Gideon Jr., and the only niece of Sylvia Ann Howland. As the only living person in the fourth generation of Howlands, she was the "heir at law" to all the others.

Foiled by her father in her attempt to pick off her mother's estate, Hetty campaigned to make sure that her Aunt Sylvia's cash would wind up in the right pocket—hers. She keyed her strategy to her aunt's antagonism to Black Hawk, Edward Mott Robinson. Hetty kept hammering at the thought that never another penny should go to her father. Howland money was for Howlands, and Howlands alone! Hetty began coaxing Sylvia Ann into writing reciprocal wills under which each would become the other's primary beneficiary. Both agreed not to make any changes without notice to the other.

Hetty was right on one point. Her father was rolling in Howland money, much of it the product of his tight-fisted management of the family business. Yet another of his business lessons Hetty followed for the rest of her days: Invest where the growth is. Black Hawk had cashed in his share of Isaac Howland Jr. and Company for around $5 million. The good years were going.

Decimated herds and the advent of kerosene oil were taking all the profit out of whaling. Hetty's father shrewdly reinvested his take in the fast-paced clipper ship trade and moved to New York. So did Hetty, where she nursed her supposedly despised father through his last days. Black Hawk died at age 65 on June 14, 1865. One of her father's executors later testified that Hetty had spent a lot of time pumping him about the contents of Black Hawk's will, asking him to urge Robinson "not to give too much to charity."

There were few surprises when Black Hawk's will was read after the funeral. Charity was stiffed. Robinson left a total of $5.6 million, including about $650,000 in stocks and bonds, along with interests in a flotilla of merchant ships like the *James Maury* and the *Hibernia*. Hetty was to get about $1-million outright ($910,000 in cash and title to a San Francisco warehouse). The balance was to be put in trust with a life income, the principal earmarked for offspring.

It was a heart-racing time for Hetty. The flowers on Black Hawk's grave had barely begun to fade when word came that Sylvia Ann Howland had outlasted Black Hawk by only a couple of weeks. The aunt died on July 2, 1865. She was 59 and had been for most of her latter years a bedridden invalid. Hetty, at age 30, was already a rich woman when she arrived in New Bedford for her aunt's funeral, the intent of the reciprocal wills of 1860 very much in mind. Howland money for the Howlands, meaning Hetty.

This time there were surprises, terrible surprises. With no notice to Hetty, a new will dated January 11, 1862, ticketed half of Sylvia Ann's $2 million to a cluster of bizarre beneficiaries: $100,000 to the New Bedford Council toward the piping of water into the city; $200,000 to a clamor of widows and spinsters; $100,000 for the public library (which the thrifty council pinched by zeroing out the library budget).

Hundreds of thousands more went to remote relatives, servants, and trustees, with an especially nice dollop of $100,000 to Dr. William L. Gordon. He had given up his practice to care exclusively for Sylvia Ann in her last years. The most unkind cut was the approximately $1 million reserved for "Hetty H. Robinson, the daughter of my sister Abby S. Robinson." Hetty got only a life income on the money, with the corpus to revert equally only to Howlands—all of them!

The injunction was almost biblical: "Upon the decease of the said Hetty H. Robinson, I direct and order trustees to pay over, distribute and divide the whole of said residuary estate among all the lineal descendants, then living, of my grandfather, Gideon Howland." Sylvia had kept her word all right—perversely, by Hetty's lights. Parceled out to children yet unborn, the estate would stay in the family, but Hetty's own kids (if any) would fare no better than perhaps hundreds of remote kin.

Stunned by the prospect that *her* money would become theirs, Hetty went into action. Who had sidetracked the so-carefully planned reciprocal wills? Hetty called on probate court judge Edward H. Bennett. She demanded that he look into the "influences" behind the switch. First of all, there was Dr. Gordon, who had given all his time to care for Sylvia Ann. Now profiting as both a trustee and a beneficiary, Gordon had kept Sylvia Ann heavily sedated, leaving her easy prey to suggestion. The judge should remove Gordon as a trustee, and take over the job himself—including the trustee fees, of course. "Money was no object," Hetty told the judge. When Bennett emphatically refused to discuss the case, Hetty hared off to his home "and left some money there for a present for my child," recounted the judge. Bennett promptly mailed the cash back, unaware of yet another of the lessons Hetty absorbed at the knees of her grandfather and father: Politicians are for hire.

Though she struck out with Judge Bennett, Hetty's not entirely debased sense of politicians was so acute that she both courted and savaged them. One example of the soft approach: She regularly shaded below market the rate on the millions in spare cash she recycled into New York City tax anticipation notes. The city controller pronounced her a "grand little woman." "We can always rely on her," he said. "If she has the money when we need it, we can always get it from her." The unspoken part of the contract was that Hetty would have no tax problems.

In her pass at Judge Bennett, Hetty outlined the hand she intended to play in her attack on Sylvia's last will. In a case the tenacious Hetty fought for almost a decade, she first contended that her aunt, totally infirm, was incapable of making a valid will. She had been shamelessly manipulated by caretakers, servants, trustees, and the other new beneficiaries surrounding her. When Judge Bennett rejected that argument, Hetty submitted a more sophisticated legal theory to the U.S. Circuit Court for the District of Massachusetts. The new complaint contended that the mutual wills making Hetty and Sylvia Ann one another's beneficiaries were in fact a contract that could not be revoked without due notice. Hetty had been given no such notice and the earlier will therefore stood, making all of Sylvia's money hers.

Hetty's obstinance did not make her popular among the scores of widows and orphans (and relatives) who would be dished if she won. Thus, when Hetty, five months after the aunt's death, produced a secret "second page" to the 1862 will, it was hooted down as an outright fraud. Hetty conceded that the appendage was in her handwriting, but testified that she had drafted it at her aunt's request and insisted that Sylvia had signed it in her presence.

The 1862 will, argued Hetty, so generous to Sylvia's caretakers, was in fact a ruse to keep them working for her. The appendage negated that will, leaving everything to Hetty. Though intended to be part of the will, the so-called "second page" was never recorded because to have done so while Sylvia was living would really have turned her minders against her.

In part, the document read, "I give this will to my niece to shew if there appears a will made without notifying her." "I implore the judge to decide in favor of this will," the second page continued, "as nothing would induce me to make a will unfavorable to my niece. But being ill and afraid (to refuse) if any of my caretakers insisting on my making a will, I give this will to appear against another will found after my death."

The rebuttal was simple enough: Hetty Green had forged her aunt's name to a totally contrived document. Learned handwriting experts summoned by both sides testified pro and con. Chief Justice-to-be Oliver Wendell Holmes was among the three Harvard luminaries appearing for the defense. The defense argued that the signatures on both pages of the will were far too similar to be anything but traced. The odds on their being identical, opined one math-oriented defense expert, were 2,666,000,000,000,000,000,000 times to one against.

The trial brought national headlines: "Rich Heiress Battles Aunt's Will/ Fraud and Perjury Charged." Hetty was contradicted at every turn by defense witnesses who in the main will were also beneficiaries. The defense hammered away so persistently at possible criminal charges that Hetty decorously faded from the jurisdiction. She was off to London, leaving the battle to her lawyers. Hetty had her opponents stymied. For as long as the war of attrition continued, the trustees were enjoined from putting so much as a nickel into the hot hands of the New Bedford beneficiaries.

Hetty did not leave town alone. Traveling with her was a newly acquired husband, Edward Henry Green. The two, an endearing "mama" and "papa" to each other, were respectively 32 and 46. They had been courting for a couple of years.

Thought to be a millionaire from two decades of trading commodities like tea and hemp in Manila, Green clearly was not one of those fortune-hunters Hetty had been warned about for years. Green was Vermont-born, of a long New England line. A friend of her father, he had been helpful in straightening out some of the details of Black Hawk's estate.

One anecdote has it that Hetty's heart was won by a mis-addressed valentine. As the *New York Times* reported, Green's "handsome person had already prepossessed" Hetty when he bought her a card romantically embellished "with a dove, several hearts, and a motto." It went into a wrong envelope, but with surprisingly good results. Instead of the valentine, Hetty got a bill and a check for a "very cheap set of clothes" that should have been addressed to Green's tailor. "It was said that she was won over by this evidence of economy," reported the *Times*. In fact, Edward Green liked to live large.

The marriage of the millions, sanctified at the fashionable home of Hetty's Grinnell relatives, was heavy society page stuff. The Howlands were of Mayflower stock and the Greens had made it from London to Boston in 1635. For all the tales of Hetty's penny-pinching, Mr. and Mrs. Green put up at the posh Langham Hotel in London, their names inscribed on a register that listed such other luminaries as Mark Twain and Andrew Carnegie.

Some commentators argue the frugal Hetty could endure living at the pricey Langham only because her husband was paying the bills. In fact, there were times when Hetty enjoyed comfort, moving from one of her many low-rent apartments to upscale boarding houses in Manhattan. For one glorious period, late in life, she startled everyone by taking a suite at the Plaza Hotel. Also somewhat in dispute is whether Edward H. Green was managing Hetty's money during the eight years they lived in London, or whether she herself was calling the shots. The husband was a director of three quite successful banks. Hetty later recalled starting two of them with "some men" and making "a good deal of money."

She was also long on U.S. Treasuries. They were trading at deep discounts, but a good speculation against the possibility that Congress would soon vote to once again back paper money, the much-despised "greenbacks," with gold. As treasuries shot to a premium, Hetty recalled pocketing more than $1.25 million in her first year in London alone. "$200,000 is the largest sum I ever made in a day, though I've cleared more than that on single deals," she once told the *Ladies Home Journal*. Truly a value player, Hetty always looked for a discount.

It wasn't all business. The Green's first heir, Edward Howland Robinson Green, was born in London on August 22, 1868. A sister, Hetty Sylvia Ann Howland Robinson Green, followed on January 7, 1871. Hetty insisted that naming her daughter after her Aunt Sylvia was one more proof that there had been no funny stuff in her production of the controversial second will.

"Do you suppose I would have named my daughter Sylvia Ann Howland if I had forged my aunt's name? I'd have had a living picture of forgery before me all those years," Hetty told the *New York World*. That case was now winding down and so, it appeared to the Greens, was the statute of limitations on possible forgery and perjury charges. Except for public calumny, Hetty could rest easy. Her case was dismissed in the Massachusetts court after five inconclusive years on a key legal point. The judge ruled there was not enough evidence to substantiate Hetty's claim of a contract with her aunt on the mutual wills. The decision mooted the question of advance notice. The issues of forgery and perjury were never reached.

Time to go home. The panic of 1873 had solidified into depression, the markets had collapsed, and Hetty Green had plenty of money to go shopping. She concentrated on hard assets with a growth kicker. "Railroads and real estate are the things I like," said Hetty. "Before deciding on an investment, I seek out every kind of information about it." "There is no great secret in fortune making," she continued. "All you do is buy cheap and sell dear, act with thrift and shrewdness and be persistent." It's as if Hetty Green were writing lines for Ben Graham and a legion of other value investors to come.

Railroads were the Internet of the day, promising growth to investors and huge economies of scale to shippers. Hetty Green liked the roads, partly because they came with the underlying value of thousands of acres of land grants and mineral rights. As Hetty's famed corner in the Louisville & Nashville showed, the market in rail stocks was a howling speculative wilderness.

The panic of 1873 was touched off by a run on the great banking house of Jay Cooke & Company. Jay Cooke had helped the Union finance the Civil War and was now heavily invested in the construction of the Northern Pacific Railroad. It was clear that Cooke was in trouble when a huge bond issue for the road failed to sell. Still another big investment bank, committed to the Central Pacific and the Chesapeake and Ohio Railroads, suddenly shut its doors and the panic spread like wildfire. In a few ruinous days, some 20 firms in New York and a dozen in Philadelphia were added to the casualty list.

Hot stocks like the Rock Island and New York Central were in free-fall. Railroad bonds shrank proportionately. Hetty Green cherry-picked the bargains, a tactic she followed right on through the successive panics of 1884, 1890, 1901, 1903, and 1907. "When I see a thing going cheap because nobody wants it," explained Hetty, "I buy a lot of it and tuck it away." "Then, when the time comes," she continued, "they have to hunt me up and pay me a good price for my holdings." Warren Buffett couldn't have said it better.

As in every panic, cash was king and Hetty had a lot of it. Suppliant borrowers quickly discovered she wanted collateral—a lot of it. Among those who came to her hat in hand were the principals in the dry goods firm of Hilton, Hughes & Company. They were headed by Judge Henry Hilton, a one-time advisor to merchant prince, A.T. Stewart. The Hiltons controlled the old Stewart building, a handsome white marble landmark at Broadway and Chambers Street. They needed about $1 million in short-term money—90 days or so—enough to tide them over some inventory problems.

Hetty wouldn't hear of it. She let the Hiltons hang for a month and finally closed the deal for more money than they wanted—a take it or leave it $1.25 million for five years at six percent. Green also demanded and got a mortgage on the Stewart building. As Sparkes and Moore relate in *The Witch of Wall Street*, Hetty's name appeared nowhere on the mortgage. Her proxy was one of her many accommodating banks, the Title Guarantee & Trust Company. When the Board of Taxes and Assessment slapped a $20,000 levy on the mortgage, it wasn't Hetty who paid.

Also among those to learn how protective of her assets Hetty could be was the old-line banking house of John J. Cisco & Son at 59 Wall Street. Hetty was family. Her father Black Hawk had long dealt with the Ciscos, and Hetty had been the bank's highest net worth client for more than 20 years. Husband Edward Green was also on the books.

So, when he came up $700,000 short on margin vaporized in an ill-timed speculative play, the Ciscos quite naturally turned to Hetty. The $550,000 in stocks, bonds, and other paper she had tucked away for safekeeping in the Cisco vault would go a long way to covering his debts, Hetty was told. An outraged Mrs. Green snapped that she was in no way responsible for Mr. Green's mistakes and demanded that her assets be shifted to the vaults of the Chemical National Bank. Faced down by that response, the Ciscos put their now-illiquid bank in the hands of a receiver, freezing Hetty's assets.

As fear of yet another run on the banks radiated through Wall Street, Hetty pushed her way through a death watch of newsmen. Wearing a black alpaca dress and a bonnet tethered to a blue veil, she stormed into the office of Cisco receiver Lewis May. "I have come for what belongs to me," she told him. When May gave her an ultimatum—pay your husband's debt or leave your securities as collateral—Hetty went through the roof. Raging, weeping, expostulating that her husband's borrowings were not hers, Hetty occupied May's office for the next five hours. She left when the vault was closed for the night and was back before it opened the next morning. After two weeks of haggling, Hetty caved. She wrote the bank a check for $400,000 and left in its custody about half of the $500,000 in paper it had been safekeeping for her.

Savage in defeat, Hetty began referring to herself as "Mrs. Green," dropping the Edward H. out of her name. Himself, the busted Edward H., listing his assets as seven dollars and a watch, took up permanent bachelor quarters at the Cumberland Hotel and spent most of the rest of his days shuffling between it and an armchair at the Union League

Club. Hetty was bedside when Edward Green died 17 years later at age 80. "The most important event of his life," the *New York Times* obituary read, "was his marriage to Miss Hetty Robinson."

In the workout of the Cisco bank, Hetty eventually got back about 75¢ on the dollar of the remaining $250,000 receiver Lewis May had grabbed as collateral. Fuming, she waited for payback time. It came when May was sued by other creditors for running up exorbitant administrative costs. He defended the $9,000 in legal fees that had gone into forcing Hetty to cover her husband's debt as achieving "one of the greatest things ever in the city of New York." If he actually had to sue Hetty, argued Lewis May, it was very likely that the case would have been thrown out of court.

Hetty pounced, dominating reopened hearings in which she launched her own claims against the receiver. Time after time she overrode her own lawyers to harass a witness. "Here are these letters where [your father] says none of my money will be used in anything, yet Mr. Green was using it all the time," she upbraided young John Cisco. Newspaper reports on the hearing hint at the fears that plagued Hetty. In one rambling accusation, she raged that the Ciscos' bullying tactics were aimed at causing a heart attack that would put her "out of the way" and enable them to "get all the money." "Didn't you expect to put me out of the way as they did my father?"

Hetty lived with the delusion that her father had been strangled and her Aunt Sylvia poisoned by a mysterious "they." It was one of the reasons why she moved so frequently from apartment to apartment under assumed names like "Mrs. C. Dewey" (after her Skye terrier, Dewey, titled in a fit of patriotism after the admiral and the battle of Manila Bay). Through the dark haze of her fears, Hetty saw clearly that Edward Green had for years been relying on her credit to back a series of disastrous deals, including a $2 million opium pool that went bust. Hetty ultimately withdrew her case against the Cisco receiver, but she had the satisfaction of tying him up for the better part of a year and a half and she had made her point. Hetty had been stung for the last time.

As part of this Pyrrhic Victory, she found a wonderfully receptive new home in the vaults of the Chemical National Bank.

Accompanied by two private detectives and a cab loaded with documents representing millions more than Chemical's $23 million in deposits, Hetty arrived to a warm welcome from President George Williams. He had set up a private office for her, which she promptly turned down. Fear of assassins kept her from having any visible permanent address, but so did fear of being triangulated by the tax collectors of New York, New Jersey, and Vermont. A permanent space in the bank would make her vulnerable to the fisc, one of the reasons why she instructed her son Ned "never to maintain an office." Her other motherly advice: "Never speculate in Wall Street; eat slowly; don't stay up all night; don't drink ice water; keep out of drafts."

Poaching an empty desk here and there, sometimes sitting on the floor clipping coupons, stowing bags and boxes of mortgages and securities in the Chemical National vaults, Hetty held court in the bank for almost a quarter century. Friends like Chauncey Depew, president of the New York Central, and financier Russell Sage dropped by to chat her up. So did a legion of promoters, tipsters, and hustlers.

She got some formal advice from other professional friends like Clarence Kelley, head of the Title Guarantee & Trust Bank, but many of her investment ideas came from the flow of courtiers who came in search of capital. Hetty was helped by a couple of young men thoughtfully provided by the bank to run errands for her, but otherwise played her hand close to the chest. She was so fearful of having her signature copied (post-trauma stress from her own forgery case?) that she rarely used conventional checks. She instead scrawled drafts on odd scraps of paper, a quirk that would make it easy for the protective Chemical National tellers to pick up any attempts to raid her accounts.

Hetty had extraordinary energy. Even in her 70s, she rarely delegated, chasing off to Chicago to testify against a clerk accused of forgery; whipping through Cincinnati where on one frenetic trip she foreclosed on a couple of mortgages, unloaded a block of business properties, picked up some raw acreage for development, and posed for pictures in the *Cincinnati Enquirer*.

Running a $60 million investment company that today would be staffed and computerized to the buttresses, Hetty kept the details in her head. She was credited with an uncanny memory—immediately, for example, locating needed papers she had not seen for years filed away at the bottom of an old trunk in storage. Money men like New York City controller Bird S. Coler, 12 years after her death, remembered Hetty as having "The best banking brain of anyone I ever knew. She carried all her knowledge in her head and never depended upon memorandum."

"She watched the money current so carefully," recalled the controller, "that when I went to ask her for a loan, she often knew how much I was going to require before I opened my mouth."

Hetty Green was a natural, nurtured in a demanding school. Her basic strategy was simple: Concentrate on hard assets like railroads and real estate bought on the cheap, rarely sell, reinvest the compounding cash flow. The only thing that Warren Buffett does better is play bridge. Except for her latter-day indulgences of son Ned as he got more deeply involved in the business, Hetty plowed all her income back into the portfolio. Her demons kept her from extravagances like the million dollar mansions made of marble that the Vanderbilts (cut dead by the Astors) were building on Fifth Avenue. No mansions or landmarks for Hetty. She wanted paying properties—lots of them. Hetty did not need Horace Greeley's advice to go West. She went where the growth was, investing in boomtowns and major railheads like Denver, St. Louis, and Cincinnati.

Her biggest bets were in Chicago, where the newspapers estimated that in the 15 years between 1885 and 1900 she bought some $17 million worth of property. As enumerated in *The Witch of Wall Street* her rent rolls included jewels like the Howland block on the southwest corner of Dearborn and Monroe, the Gower block at Monroe and Fifth, and "innumerable other small parcels in what is now the Loop."

Hetty shrewdly also bought heavily on the outskirts and waited for the city to come to her. Something of the values that strategy brought can be seen in a spread of 650 acres her father Black Hawk had picked up in the western Cook County town of Cicero in 1864 for $15,000. The land had been left in trust for Hetty.

In keeping with her general strategy of rarely selling, she had prevailed on the trustees to hang on to the acreage for almost 23 years. Then they were handed a court order to sell it. The order grew out of a tangled estate problem involving a partner who bought the land with Black Hawk. The partner had been unable to pay his share of the purchase. Although he later borrowed $100,000 from a Norfolk, Virginia bank on the strength of the land's growing value, he never repaid Black Hawk. The bank was suing to get back its $100,000 loan.

Hetty understandably got her dander up when Judge Loren C. Collins ordered an auction and established an upset price of $600,000. The trustees settled on a sale for $602,000. Hetty knew land values in Chicago like the back of her hand, which is what she gave the trustees.

A gain of 40 times on a $15,000 investment might have seemed a good deal to them, but not to Hetty Howland Robinson Green. She protested that she had already turned down a private offer of better than $800,000.

More acrimonious litigation, which Hetty lost after making yet another of her injudicious personal calls on Judge Collins. "My dear young man," she told him. You don't understand this case. Let me explain it to you." A choleric Collins showed her the door, thereby unwittingly setting himself up for yet another of the unforgiving Hetty's paybacks.

As Hetty explained it to Clarence Barron, soon to become owner of the *Wall Street Journal*, Collins' doom was sealed during another of Wall Street's sporadic money crunches. When a Clearing House Committee hit her up for a loan to reinforce a number of wobbly member banks, Hetty ingenuously allowed she was "just a poor lone woman" who knew nothing about investments. However, by some chance, did the Committee hold for the banks any demand notes on railroads terminating in Chicago? Did they ever! That's when Hetty's ever-ready cash reserves came into play.

As Clarence Barron reported, Hetty bought several million dollars worth of the notes at deep discount. She then abruptly told the roads she was calling the notes. Pandemonium! Hetty summoned the railroad treasurers east, and to their immense relief, told them she wasn't really interested in the money. What she wanted was cooperation in the interest of justice. To a man, the railroaders agreed with Hetty that Judge Collins, though otherwise a fine fellow, certainly did lack the judicial temperament. "Well," she told them, "you put him on the bench and you can now take him off, or you can pay your loans to me."

"They then piled a banquet board in Chicago with fruits and wines," reported Barron, "Dined the judge and nominated him for higher office while he resigned the lower one." "And then," continued Barron, "they left him to elect himself." It didn't take Collins long to learn what Black Hawk and her grandfather had drummed into Hetty's tutorials. "There's been dirty work at the crossroads," explained his advisers.

Hetty's acquisitive itch, in fact, had placed her at almost every major crossroad in the land. She owned significant chunks of at least a dozen railroads, including the Louisville & Nashville, The Rock Island, the Houston & Texas, and the Chicago & Northwestern.

The source of that inventory was young Edward Howland Robinson Green, then approaching 23. Hetty, after severe testing, had deputized

Ned as her representative in Chicago. It was 1891 and Ned, true to his mother's early injunction, did not have an office of his own. Speaking from rented desk space, he was talking to a reporter. Affable, conjuring cigarettes and matches from a secret compartment in his cane, Ned told the newsman that Chicago was spinning off to Hetty about $40,000 a month in rents, mortgage payments, and dividends. Hetty herself at the time intimated that she was worth around $50 million. Outsiders guessed that her nearly tax-free annual income was around $7 million. If so, Hetty was netting around 14 percent on her money at comparatively low risk— far better than the long-term yield of the stock market, and consistent with a growing cash flow compounded by steady reinvestment.

Ned Green made it sound easy. "This loaning business," he airily told the reporter, "is nothing more nor less than a pawnbroker's shop on a large scale, except that the borrowers have to hock a good piece of real estate instead of a watch." "Some men get mad when you call them pawnbrokers," continued Ned, "but loaning money as I do is nothing more nor less." Latter-day conglomerates may wince at the analogy, but Ned had it right. Skillful pawnbroking and skillful banking have the same solid principles in common: Know your customer, know your collateral.

The outspoken Ned himself was on a tight leash. When Hetty learned he had moved to a cheaper hotel to make his $6 a day allowance go further, she cut the per diem to $3. Ned knew pretty much what he was in for. Hetty had handed him a letter from the president of one of her carriers, the Connecticut River Railroad. It promised him a job "upon application." Ned was set to work clerking for $45 a month and at the end of the first month found himself $40 in debt. He wrote a "Dear Mom" letter and got a telegraphed reply, collect—"Not A Cent." Ned got the message, buckled down, and soon earned a modest promotion.

He was clearly being groomed for higher things when Hetty dispatched him to Chicago to deliver to her bankers a package she told him contained $250,000 in bonds. As Ned later recalled, "I stayed awake every foot of the way, putting the package under the mattress in my berth, and watching for robbers all night." Ned was relieved to get to the bank, demanded a receipt, and was chagrined to discover the bonds were actually a packet of expired fire insurance policies. "You know, mother always dearly loved a joke," recalled Ned, "but I'll say she had a very practical way of testing me out."

Some of the testing involved learning the real estate business from the ground up. As Hetty herself recalled, "I wanted him to learn what it cost to make a building and what went into it, so he would know something of what a mortgage on a building was worth." Hetty gave Ned a keg of white lead, stuck a paintbrush in his hand, and set him to work on one of the Chicago blocks she was putting up.

Hetty was giving Ned some of the hands-on education she got on the wharves of New Bedford. Curiously, she did not do the same for her daughter, Sylvia Ann. The daughter, after graduating from Sacred Heart Academy in New York, drifted aimlessly in Hetty's wake. Sylvia Ann was permitted a coming out party at fashionable Newport, but continually warned about the fortune hunters who might make up to her. Sylvia Ann was 38 when she married Matthew Astor Wilks, 57, a great-grandson of the moneyed John Jacob Astor. The bridegroom was pretty well-off himself, but Hetty got him to sign an airtight prenuptial agreement before the happy couple was whisked off by private rail car from Hoboken to the very social St. Peter's Episcopal Church in the countryside of Morristown, New Jersey.

Ned was not in attendance at a ceremony that drew rabid press coverage. Having proved his mettle in Chicago, he was moved up to the big leagues of Hetty's railroad portfolio. Part of her strategy was to pinch off relatively small but critical links that promoters like Collis P. Huntington needed to fill out their transcontinental lines. She was looking for premium buy-out candidates, rather like the building blocks absorbed these days by Cisco Systems and other high-tech conglomerates on the make.

Ned's upgrading was a real vote of confidence. A fretful Hetty urged him not to get married for 20 years, but thanks to his now proven business sense, turned a somewhat forgiving eye to his increasingly lavish lifestyle.

Hetty even took to bragging about Ned. Armchair psychologists could link her uncharacteristically demonstrative warmth to the trauma of Ned's cork leg. At age 13, Ned injured a knee sledding. It got progressively worse through a rough adolescence. Hetty's pinchpenny solution was to dress up in poorhouse clothes and take Ned on a round of Manhattan's free clinics in the hope of getting him treated as a charity case. They were quickly found out and told to pay up. Hetty resignedly shelled out for a doctor who insisted that the leg had to be amputated.

Ned later told friends it wasn't the cost of the operation, but hope of saving the leg that prompted a continuance of Hetty's ineffective home remedies. Eight years later, shortly before his twenty-first birthday, the leg was found to be on the verge of gangrene and amputated well above the knee.

That was why Ned, on crutches little more than a year after the operation, could so easily be identified as Hetty's proxy at a hotly contested shareholders meeting of the Ohio & Mississippi Railroad. The single-track road, linking Cincinnati and Louisville, Kentucky to East St. Louis, was heavily trafficked. Ned, backed by Hetty's 2,200 shares and $76,000 in bonds, was one of the three management nominees for the Ohio & Mississippi board, pledged to beat off a bid by the expanding Baltimore & Ohio for control of the road. The Greens, allied with financier James H. Smith ("Silent Smith" for his unreadable mien), were outvoted. Ned, in the thick of the battle, threatened to take the case to the Supreme Court. No one who knew his mother's litigious background could doubt it. After a two-year struggle, the Greens and "Silent Smith" finally got from the B & O what they wanted right along—a much sweeter price. Hetty's rule: Never take the first bid.

Also on Hetty's hit list was Collis P. Huntington, whom she blamed for deliberately running the Houston Texas Central into receivership, the better to pick up more than $250,000 of her mortgage bonds on the cheap. Hit by a flurry of lawsuits after a train wreck Hetty suspected Huntington of engineering, the road defaulted on its bonds and lurched into bankruptcy.

Among those seriously hurt by the default was the Cisco Bank, which then began looking to Hetty to cover her husband's loans.

The *New York World* reported that "Hetty Green's great fight has begun" when she refused to go along with a Huntington-inspired buyout of the bondholders. The *World* interpreted the buyout as an attempted squeeze on Hetty. There was no mistaking the bad blood between the two. "That woman," the imperious Huntington told reporters, "has no vision of this country's future. She is nothing more than a glorified pawnbroker."

With Ned again doing the bidding, Hetty responded by snaffling a key section of the Houston & Texas from under a Huntington agent's nose at a bankruptcy auction. Hetty's sense of hidden values once again served her well. The package came with a 277,000-acre land grant. More litigation and a bought Texas legislature. Huntington succeeded in getting Hetty's land grant invalidated, a move that cut seriously into her asset values.

Hetty was cheered on by Californians who hated Huntington and the depredations of his Southern Pacific "octopus." One band of malcontents sent Hetty a well-publicized gift—a six-shooter, complete with loaded cartridge belt and holster. Huntington had evidently not read the papers when he charged into the Chemical National and threatened an unyielding Hetty with having Ned jailed on a contempt charge. Defending her cub, an outraged Hetty reached for a revolver, shouting "Harm a hair of Ned's head and I'll put a bullet through your heart." Huntington bolted, losing his silk hat in flight.

Hetty always laughed when she told this story to friends. She had the last laugh, too. When the dust of the Houston & Texas reorganization finally settled, Hetty was sole owner and proprietor of a crucial 50-mile stretch of track renamed the Texas Midland (TM). It took years, but Hetty's initial vision was fulfilled. The Texas Midland was ultimately sold into Huntington's Southern Pacific at a premium. It was yet another triumph for Hetty's style of value investing—buy potential at a discount, wait for the market to come to you. Was Ben Graham listening?

The Texas Midland didn't look as though it had very much potential. It was a broken-down branch line, twin streaks of rust, running between the hamlets of Terrell and Garrett. Ned took over as president and quickly proved he was not a mamma's boy, but his mother's son. His first move was pure Hetty—a $500,000 certified check deposited to his personal account in the American National Bank of Terrell. The half million was more than twice the total resources of the bank. It warned Collis P. Huntington that Hetty was in the game to stay.

Ned, considerably more willing to delegate than Hetty, hired a couple of crack managers and highballed them into buying new locomotives, rebuilding bridges, and laying new track. He tied the TM into a connecting line and made it a through road, vastly improving rates.

On a roll, Ned attempted to poach cotton shippers from an adjacent Huntington fief and was almost shut down until Hetty intervened. She put the squeeze on Huntington by first depositing, and then threatening to withdraw better than a million from a bank that held some of his overdue paper. The bank responded by threatening to call Huntington's loans.

As the road improved, so did Ned's lifestyle. He installed his "housekeeper" in a refurbished six-room hotel suite in Dallas, acquired a private rail car designed by the great George Pullman himself, and by spreading quite a lot of Hetty's money around, became chairman of the Texas state Republican party. Ned's climb through politics considerably enhanced the TM's clout in the Legislature.

With political success came yet another upgrade in lifestyle. He and his housekeeper moved from the hotel suite to a newly purchased building in downtown Dallas, soon to be joined by a younger woman in a *ménage à trois* that continued on and off for years.

Hetty had not lost her keen eye for expenses. She acidly referred to Ned's housekeeper, Mabel Harlow, as "the harlot," but made no effort to cut Ned's spending back to size. In his early days in Terrell, Ned was held so short that he once imploringly telegraphed Hetty for $200 to go to the Chicago World's Fair. "Please, Mamma, I want to go so bad."

As to his business spending in Terrell, she had no complaints. The panic of 1907 struck at New York's Knickerbocker Trust Company, and touched off bank runs everywhere, including the Harris Trust Company of Terrell, one of Texas Midland's major depositaries.

There was a restive line outside the door and the bank had barely enough money to last an hour, when Ned pushed through the crowd, carrying a sizeable cardboard box. He dumped the box on the counter in a shower of bills. "$30,000," shouted Ned. "This is the safest bank in the country." Stopping the run wasn't pure altruism. As the Harris Trust's biggest depositor, the Texas Midland would have been hurt if the bank had gone down the tubes along with so many others.

Thanks to her super-sensitive antennae, Hetty had already sensed serious disarray ahead. The boom had been on for six years. Hetty, as early as 1903, had gone on record predicting a crash. "There were signs which I couldn't ignore," she later told the *Boston Traveler*. "Some of the solidest men in the street came to me and wanted to unload all sorts of things." "The New York Central quietly negotiated with me for a big loan," continued Hetty, "and that made me sit up and do some thinking." Looking at "an enormous inflation of values," Hetty quietly began to call in her money, "making few new transactions and getting into my hands every available dollar against the day I knew was coming."

It wasn't entirely a sixth sense at work. The market was getting too rich. Not many decades later, T. Rowe Price would sense the same inflation in his favorite growth stocks and startle colleagues by getting out of them. A band of latter-day contrarians began reacting the same way in

2000 to what they saw as identical warning signs. Bearish Laurence Tisch, for example, cochairman of Loew's Corporation, cut his stock holdings to only 10 percent of a $40 billion portfolio. As *Forbes* reported, the rest was in cash, short-term investments, treasuries, and other debt. "People look at a 10 percent correction, or 15 percent," Tisch warned. "They don't talk about 40 percent." From Hetty Green's day to this, it's better to be too early than too late in a market that looks grossly over-priced.

When the deluge of 1907 came, Hetty had cash, lots of it. Almost everyone else was holding what she mockingly called "their securities and their values." She put out money to almost all of New York's big department stores in what she called "legitimate business loans," but also backed speculative plays like an effort to push control of the Tennessee Coal Iron and Railroad Company into United States Steel.

One indication of how liquid Hetty became against the growing storm shows in the will she made in 1908, listing assets of at least $100 million. There was a slug of blue chips bought on the cheap, but a preponderance of first mortgages and other quality debt, with $20 million in cash out in short-term loans.

As Hetty's primary beneficiary (along with sister Sylvia Ann), Ned continued to liven up his lifestyle. He expanded his show-stopping rose garden in Dallas, talked about developing a residential community there, centered around a new mansion for himself, and gloried in the new title of military staff "Colonel" awarded him by a grateful Texas governor.

With Mabel Harlow the "harlot" in mind, Hetty, kept warning her heir against early marriage. She kept urging Ned to come back to New York, presumably with the hope that he would leave Mabel behind. "I need you every day. I implore you to be careful of your health. I have a bad cold," read one of her letters.

Ned fobbed Hetty off, arguing that he was too busy expanding the Texas Midland and pushing the family fortunes into the meat-packing business to leave Texas. He finally surrendered to Hetty's pleas that "they are robbing me." Ned told the newspapers (with a prudent eye on New York state tax collectors) that "I will always consider Terrell my home," climbed into his refitted private railway car, the "Lone Star" and checked into what the *New York Times* called a "specifically fitted-up" suite at the Waldorf-Astoria.

This combination of "office and living apartments," the Colonel soon expanded into 16 rooms, giving plenty of space to his entourage—Ned's housekeeper, now upgraded to "confidential secretary" and a semipermanent female "guest." None of this seemed to faze the frugal Hetty. The *Times* said she "appeared to be in excellent health when she greeted her big son." Ned predicted she would live for years, and with his customary good business sense, began to bring some organization to Hetty's affairs.

He set up an office (with no objections from Hetty) in the Trinity Building at 111 Broadway, put her assets into a couple of holding companies, and made sure that dividend checks no longer got hung up in one of Hetty's bags before deposit. Still, Ned chaffed at losing the free range of action he had been permitted in Texas. When it came to buying or selling suggestions in New York, he could often only say "wait until I've discussed this with mother." Even after a bout of pneumonia laid her low at age 77, Hetty did not let go. From time to time she even ventured out into high society, dressed to the nines, drawing surprised raves from papers like the *Boston Herald*.

At one reception, the *Herald* described her as wearing a "white satin modish skirt, with tunic effect of black satin entrain and a cloudy white chiffon around the shoulders." "To the amazement of the guests, she wore a pendant of diamonds, each stone the size of a pea and set in Roman gold," wrote a dazzled society page reporter. "Her whole manner was at variance with the generally accepted view of her personality," added the correspondent. "She smiled and chatted with guests who came to pay respects to the hostess."

At 80, Hetty finally relented to being ferried about in Ned's chauffeur-driven Pierce Arrow, dodging back and forth between digs in New York and Hoboken to wrong foot the increasingly bothersome tax collectors of both states. In a birthday interview with International News Service, the doughty Mrs. Green promised, "I'll live to be 100."

It wasn't to be. "Hetty Green Dies Worth $100 Million," read the page one headline of the July 4, 1916 *New York Times*. "Invested heavily in bonds and mortgages in recent years," continued a subhead. "Stock market not affected." At age 82, "generally believed to be the world's richest woman," Hetty Howland Robinson Green died after a series of strokes.

No one challenged the signature on Hetty's will. Except for four minor bequests to friends and her son-in-law totalling $25,000, Hetty left the rest of her estate to Ned and daughter Sylvia Ann, to be divided equally on the expiration of a 10-year trust. At six percent, Ned and sister figured to be sharing a gross income of around $6 million a year. The 10-year trust device seemed like a vote of no-confidence in Ned and his increasingly expansive lifestyle. It now included a number of young female "wards" in addition to his confidential secretary and semipermanent female guest. When it came time to pocket his half share, Ned would be 58 and presumably have sown all his wild oats.

The tax collectors of New York, New Jersey, Massachusetts, and Vermont (where Hetty also had a home) were quick off the mark at her death. So too were the editorial writers. With the huge public benefactions of other mega-rich like Andrew Carnegie and John D. Rockefeller in mind, they blasted Hetty for leaving nothing to good works. She was denounced as a miser and tax-dodger. The *Boston Transcript* sarcastically suggested that Hetty must have been convinced "she could do what no miser before had been able to do—take it all with her." "How much good Hetty might have done with her wealth if she cared to use it," sermonized the *Transcript*.

With Hetty gone and no one to keep him in the traces, Ned left the family business pretty much in the hands of professionals. He was on his way to mega-playboydom.

Ned drifted into marriage with the "harlot" after almost a quarter century of cohabitation, and subsequently set up $100,000 trust funds for his young "wards" (Uncle Ned hoped they'd all go to Wellesley). There was a million-dollar yacht (nine staterooms and a Louis Quatorze drawing room), a couple of million-dollar beach houses, and a clutch of expensive hobbies (stamps and coins, a radio station, an airport, a blimp) of which the "Colonel" generally soon tired.

Ned died in 1936 at age 68, ravaged by anemia and a series of coronaries. Ned's hobbies were high up in the *New York Times* obit. "As one whose life covered a wide range of interests, he became almost as picturesque a figure as his mother, Mrs. Hetty Green, eccentric financier," the *Times* reported. Ned had been spending about $5 million a year and left a considerably depleted gross estate of around $36 million, all of it ticketed to sister Sylvia Ann. The net was around $30 million at the comparatively low tax rates of those days.

Sylvia Ann was almost as eccentric as her mother. When she died at age 80 in 1951, it took a long, painstaking search through safe deposit boxes (a dozen) and wall safes before lawyers finally unearthed her will beneath a stash of Ivory Soap cakes in a kitchen cabinet. After the usual spate of litigation (the Girl Scouts of America were among the disappointed heirs apparent) the last of Hetty Green's fortune, $100 million, was given away—all of it.

The beneficiaries included such caregivers as hospitals (Beekman-Downtown of New York), the New York Association for the Blind, Seeing Eye Incorporated, and a number of homes for children and the aged. But there were also bequests of $100,000 or more to cousins Sylvia Ann had never met, and sizable sums to well-endowed prep schools to which she had no visible connection (Groton, Kent, Blair, and St. Paul's). Hetty often urged people to invest in "the world beyond." Sylvia Ann took Mamma at her word, driving a stake through the heart of demons that had plagued the Howlands and Greens for more than a century.

Professional heiress of Hetty Green,
Muriel Siebert decided early on to be her own woman.
Her success made Wall Street sit up and take notice.

Visit with a Billionairess
Muriel Siebert

IN NEARLY A HALF-CENTURY on Wall Street, Muriel F. Siebert has punched her way through many a glass ceiling. Among her distinguished "firsts": First woman admitted to the New York Stock Exchange, first woman discount broker, and first woman appointed New York State Bank Superintendent. And, to the cheers of feminists, the first U.S. working woman to become a billionaire on her own.

The latter breakthrough unfortunately proved more fleeting than Siebert's other achievements. Online trades are the fastest growing segment of the brokerage firm (Muriel F. Siebert and Company) she started over three decades ago. Spotting this connection early in the Internet craze, Web-happy speculators went wild. In the space of a couple of days, they pushed Siebert's holding company, Siebert Financial Corporation, from a low of $8.50 to a high of $70, giving the boss's 19.8 million shares a market of $1.4 billion. She segued in and out of the Big Rich for a couple of months until reality set in and the stock drifted through $55 on its way back to $13.50. "It's a good thing I didn't try to spend it," laughs Siebert, leaning over her at-the-desk lunch to drop a morsel of chicken to "Monster Lady," her long-haired pet chihuahua.

Almost all Siebert's capital is tied up in her firm (she owns 87 percent of it). From a pocketbook point of view, Siebert remains unfazed by this manic turn in her fortunes. "It's not as if I didn't have enough money to take care of myself," shrugs Siebert, who contributes heavily in energy and cash to such major feminist causes as the International Woman's Forum and the New York Women's Agenda. What really does worry her is the institutional side of the equation—the market dynamics that drove her stock and the way it bucketed all over the quote screen. For volatility and volume it beats anything seen in the Wild West markets of Hetty Green's time. "I hate to see innocent, misguided people get hurt," says Siebert. At its peak, the action was so frenetic there were days when the stock changed hands as many as three times in a single trading session, an incredible display of the bigger-fool theory.

Some people made money on the swing, of course, including Siebert's independently trusteed charitable foundation. "They sold a little in the 20s," she grimaces, "but that's not me." One of the reasons for the volatility in the stock is the fact that Siebert has held on to so much of it. Her stash leaves only about two million shares available for public trading, a scarcity value the Securities and Exchange Commission quickly looked into when online chat rooms began slavering all over it. "It's no longer the Lord who giveth and taketh, it's the day traders," snaps Siebert, banging her cluttered desk for emphasis. "That's the way it is these days."

In truth, of course, Siebert wasn't a billionairess at all. If anything, she and her fellow shareholders were victims of momentum players hipped on the illusion they could outgun the professionals, trading in and out on often grossly unfounded Internet gossip. It wasn't just Siebert Financial. Hundreds of other closely held stocks were on a moving hit list that gulled thousands of naïve investors into paying the price for trades they never should have made.

Thin floats like Siebert's—relatively few shares available for public trading—are easy to manipulate, and thus ready targets for hustlers. Siebert's anger—and the SEC's deep interest—centered on chat room punters zap trading in and out of Siebert Financial on rumors that the firm was a buy-out candidate. Or on the perception that it was a cheaper buy than bigger discounters like Charles Schwab and Company, also in heavy day-trade play. Or there were good auspices like the westerly direction of pigeon flights in Central Park. When online trading turned out to be the hottest business on the World Wide Web, any rationale would do. Probing for clues behind what looked like yet another online pump-and-dump scheme, the SEC zeroed in on the chat room bouncing to most of the noise. It turned out to be Tradingplaces.net, a Web site run by Chris Rea, 50, a Niles, Illinois-based stock caller. His trademark battle cry: "Let's rumble in the Wall Street jungle."

Self-dubbed "Merlin," Rea in earlier incarnations ran a home business that cranked out mailers for auto dealers. He peddled his electronic

services (including day-trading tutorials and broker recommendations) to subscribers at $279.95 a month. The cash brought access to a
cyberstorm of advisories, sometimes several a minute, flagging
"Monster Buys" and "Trade Alerts." "Value picking up, you chart watch-
ers. When you see the value go up bigger, this gonna explode," went
one typical Merlin call. Or, "Pull back alert: I would take profits here."
"Ghosts," like Warlock, Wizard, and Stoned, flitted across the screen,
blipping encomiums to Rea's trading skills, pumping chatter into a
frenzy that quickly radiated to other get-rich-quick sites. Count the
footprints in the millions.

So, the SEC questions for Siebert were those directed at dozens of
other episodes in which chat room gurus were suspected of trading in
front of their own subscribers. Corporate insiders have also been found
to dump stock into volcanic chat room moves.

Did Siebert know Rea? queried the investigators. Did she do business with him? Had she sold any of her stock on his calls? No, no, and
no were the answers. The question for shadowy Rea, whose puffed-up
resume showed no particular background in U.S. securities, and who is
not a registered advisor or broker: Had he been collecting reciprocal
fees from the brokers he highlighted for subscribers? Had he traded
against or worked outside deals on the stocks that he was touting? Rea
denied any wrongdoing, was never charged by the SEC, and Siebert
sees no foolproof way to protect traders from their own greed. Siebert
has been doing her bit by tightening up margin requirements—the
amount of borrowed money punters can trade on—and riding herd on
hyperactive accounts. Siebert is also moving her no-frills brokerage firm
into the advice and education business. She recently bought for about
$2 million two free-standing sites—dollar.com and the women's finan-
cial network—and wrapped them into her own Siebert.net.

The aim is to enrich her content with nuts-and-bolts pieces on topics like IRA legislation and 401k plans. It's not a purely eleemosynary
pursuit. Siebert hopes a strong educational bent will help her broaden
her product line beyond the bread-and-butter discount business to
include new branded offerings such as mutual funds, money market
funds, and insurance. Siebert thinks that putting serious financial information and planning tools into the mix will give her an eyeball edge over
the hundreds of other women's sites in the field. "No horoscopes, child-
rearing, or hobby pieces," she promises. Her hope is the educational

tack will generate enough trade to pay for the site. Despite her long commitment to women's groups, men account for the biggest portion of Siebert's commission business, and she is by no means ruling them off the site. But the heart of her new marketing pitch is that divorce, death, and other life changes demand that women "take control of their financial destiny." "We're going to help them do that, have some fun, and maybe make a little money," says Siebert. If it doesn't work? The irrepressible Siebert grins and feeds "Monster Woman" a bit of organic greens. "Hey, if it doesn't work, Uncle Sam is my partner."

There are competitive reasons for going into the advice business even if the expense of doing so cuts into profits. Traditional full-line brokers who have always offered advice of a sort are stealing market share from operatives like Siebert.

There is one other reason—self-defense. "A lot of people who have never been in a down market got hurt," says Siebert, "so we got hurt, too. We think people should be reminded of basic values like earnings and cash flow." "I've always been good at numbers," continues Siebert. "They light up the page for me."

That's the conservative analyst side of Siebert speaking. Her business success, though, shows that she is not afraid of taking risks. Siebert's first long shot—the one that took her from her native Cleveland to Wall Street—was a complete leap into the unknown. She had been studying business and accounting at Western Reserve College in her native Cleveland. When her father died of cancer after a long siege, Siebert chucked school and took off for New York. Her assets totaled $500, a beat-up old Studebaker, and about a jillion dollars worth of chutzpah. "If you are going to sit there and wait for other people to do things for you," says Siebert, "you will soon be 80-years-old and look back and say 'Hey, what did I do?'" "My mother," she continues, "had a God-given voice, and she was offered a place on the stage, but nice Jewish girls didn't go on the stage in those days. So, I grew up with a woman who was frustrated her entire life," continues Siebert. "I certainly wasn't going to continue that role. I vowed I would do whatever I wanted to do."

Strong stuff. Siebert first took it to the personnel office at the United Nations and got turned down—no language skills. She then took it to Merrill Lynch and got turned down again—no college degree, and no Wall Street smarts, either. Stocks were not the subject of conversation at the Siebert dinner table. Her only exposure to the stock exchange had been on a visit to New York years before. On to Bache and Company. This time Siebert played up her accounting studies, lied her way into a college degree—and got the job. It was 1954, Siebert was 22, and only Wall Street's big producers were making top dollar. As a $65-a-week analyst trainee on the wire desk, Siebert shared a $120 a month apartment in the East Side enclave of Tudor City, and after six weeks probation got a $5 a week raise. "It was $3.80 net, laughs the numerific Siebert, "so I had an extra 20¢ for lunch." Siebert broke in fielding stock queries from Bache branches and talking over the answers with analysts. She was learning fast. "The accounting background helped a lot," recalls Siebert. Soon she was covering industries cast off as less than interesting by senior analysts—radio, TV, movies, airlines. Riffling through memory, Siebert fastens on one study that particularly pleased her—a prescient look at the deep-discounted inventory value of Hollywood's old movies.

Siebert was doing well for a kid analyst—well enough to quit sleeping on her roommate's couch and move into her own apartment. But she was not doing so well as male analysts of similar attainment. "I fought like a son of a bitch to get ahead," she recalls. When she told Bache she deserved a raise and was talking to a competitor, Siebert was ordered to clean out her desk—pronto!

She moved to Shields and Company for something like $9,500 a year, definitely a step up the ladder. The quality of her research brought in three institutional customers. Siebert's modest annual bonus was keyed to the commissions they generated. Male brokers who brought in business got a 40 percent cut. That rankled. "I didn't create my business simply by pounding on the door and saying 'I'm a woman, I'm entitled,'" Siebert told journalist Beverly Kempton, "I made my success by slugging it out with the boys."

Women were a distinct minority in the upper reaches of Wall Street. Siebert recalls that most of her fellow analysts treated her "like one of the guys," but traditional barriers were slow to come down. At one point between jobs, for example, Siebert circulated a resume with her (Muriel) full name on it and got not a single response. She sent out her next resume with just her initials on it, and got an immediate call back. Further, companies scheduled analysts meetings at luncheon clubs where women were banned or sometimes weren't allowed through the front door (Siebert got in through the kitchen). And then there was the locker room atmosphere of a generally male world. "To me, the sexual stuff was just part of the game," says Siebert. "I remember telling some guys to go do the physically impossible to themselves."

Serious harassment and discrimination cases still pop up on Wall Street, but Siebert thinks "the protective laws have changed a lot of things." "Sometimes women are too sensitive," adds the tough-minded Siebert. "Places like the floor of the New York Stock Exchange are known to be animal farms," she continues. "When people work under a lot of pressure, the language can get rough. I learned all my foul language at the trading post. It doesn't mean a thing to me," she adds. "They're just words."

Siebert's quick adaptive ways are one of the keys to her success. She used to stutter and never thought of herself as a salesperson. But growing confidence in her analytical skills made it easier for her to deal with big institutional clients. She remembers doing a study of NCR, for example, seeing a period of rising earnings ahead because of projected cuts in depreciation charges. When one autocratic fund manager, disenchanted with the company, came in with a sell order on NCR, she persuaded him to hold on to a stock that he subsequently made good money on. "That established another customer," recalls Siebert. "So then I could call him and say, 'Hey, I think you should buy this because . . .'"

Wall Street research was far more objective in those days. Analysts now increasingly cut the cloth to land investment banking business. Siebert argues that when she was coming up, analysts were free to write buys or sells with little fear of retribution. These days sell recommendations are rare, partly because discounters such as Siebert have changed the way Wall Street makes its money. With tough competitive commission rates the norm, profit margins on that side of the business have been stretched paper thin. The real money is in huge fees thrown off by underwriting and merger and acquisition deals. Instead of being paid on salary and bonus (as Siebert was), compensation now flows mainly from the investment banking side. "We're talking about millions for analysts who get close to a company," says Siebert. "Nothing wrong about millions," she adds," but the issue of credibility puts the onus on the firm." The incentives almost invariably make for roseate recommendations.

That's one of the reasons why there are so many earnings "surprises," instantly picked by TV's financial commentators and magnified into erratic price swings. *Forbes* columnist David Dreman highlights the phenomenon, citing sell-offs of 50 percent in Intel and Apple Computer last year: when earnings fell below expectation. Dreman raises a critical question: "Wouldn't it be nice to find an analyst who warned you away from Intel and Apple with a sell recommendation?"

Chairman of the Jersey City, New Jersey-based investment advisory firm that bears his name, Dreman reinforces Siebert's view. Analysts looking to investment banking fees, he asserts, "cannot bring themselves to say the word 'sell.'" You have to learn to see through the code words. The closest most analysts come to the dreaded "S" word is to damn with faint praise: "accumulate," "neutral," "hold," or even "long-term buy."

Dreman interprets any such rating as a warning to bail out. These new assessments may seem favorable—a switch, say, from "aggressive buy" to "buy"—but Dreman interprets them as signaling "ditch the dog." His bottom line: "Read the research if you respect the analyst, but tear off the recommendation page and use it for kindling."

So, how is the investor to cope? As is clear from the new education.net Siebert has established, she thinks people should be doing their own homework and look at establishment research with a questioning eye.

Siebert is as contentious as her dustmop-size "Monster Lady" who has the run of the office and instantly challenges strangers. She was purged from Shields and Company for entertaining a partnership offer from a rump research group that was about to set up outside the firm. That deal did not gel, but Siebert did hook on as a principal with two small firms before setting her cap for a New York Stock Exchange seat. No major firm had yet taken on a female partner, so Siebert figured her only next step up was to crash the barrier of the totally male Exchange establishment and become a member. Nothing in the by-laws said she couldn't, but nobody made it easy either, says Siebert. Nine of the first ten members she asked to sponsor her turned her down flat.

Siebert by then had put together a thick book of institutional clients and was earning what the *New York Times* estimated to be a "a half-million dollars a year." That cut no ice with the banks. The Exchange demanded that she get a guaranteed loan for $300,000 of the $445,000 the seat would cost her. No bank would come up with the money until the Exchange formally agreed to admit Siebert. It was months before she was able to resolve this Catch-22, and become the first woman allowed to buy into the 1,366 member sanctum. So intimidating were the bars that she was the first woman even to apply in the Big Board's then 175-year history.

Siebert was taking on considerable personal exposure. A booming stock market had pushed seat prices to the highest level in 37 years. Muriel F. Siebert and Company started small in an office at 120 Broadway. Thanks to the publicity her breakthrough fanned, women looking for jobs or advice came by in droves. "They didn't have to look too far to find me," recalls Siebert. "The office was so tiny that all they had to do was open the door, and there I was." Siebert rarely worked the floor, spending most of her time, "upstairs," doing research and landing new clients. Siebert took a lot of kidding about the availability of plumbing when she did get to the trading posts. It was two years, she says, before anyone told her there actually was a ladies room tucked away in a corner of the Exchange floor.

Opportunistic as ever, Siebert again kicked up a ruckus when she became one of the Exchange's first members to plunge into the discount business. "May Day" 1975 brought the end of the fixed commission, pushed through by big institutional investors and the SEC. With negotiated rates now the rule, competition had come to Wall Street. It was a dramatic shift from the cozy way of doing business that dated all the way back to the Exchange's founding. Old, established, full-line brokers saw in this sea change severe damage to their profit margins and looked daggers at upstarts like Muriel F. Siebert and Company. When it comes to establishment slights, Siebert has a long memory. Wall Street's reaction to her discount initiative, says her Web site biography, was "quick and hostile." Her long-time clearing house dropped her and her firm faced SEC expulsion in 60 days if she could not find another house to clear her trades.

Though among the first out of the discount blocks, Siebert is these days dwarfed by such top dogs as Charles Schwab and Company and the Fidelity Management Group. The advent of electronic trading has sharpened price competition and at the same time fostered the opening of some 18 million Internet brokerage accounts. Despite the sell-off in high-tech stocks, some 35 percent of all trades generated by individual investors are made online, with bigger numbers still to come. The advantages: Trading is cheap ("no fee" brokers abound), convenient (trade from anywhere anytime), and offers ready-access to resources like instant stock quotes, initial public offering dates, and corporate earnings estimates.

Amid a blizzard of competing claims, Siebert notes that her firm has placed first or second ("That's not too shabby, is it?") among discounters rated annually by such consumer-oriented publications as *Smart Money* and *Kiplinger's Personal Finance Magazine*.

How to go about making a choice? Although increasingly rare as the industry grows through adolescence, Web site crashes and long telephone delays are still not uncommon, particularly on big volume trading days. One test: Call a couple of brokers several times over a couple of days and see how quickly you get picked up. Anything much over eight seconds (Siebert average) is below par. See what kind of answer you get to a question like this Kiplinger sample: "Are margin rates different in IRAs than regular accounts?" (Answer: IRAs can't be margined.)

Check ancillary services such as getting the year-end cost basis on your holdings, particularly stocks you have sold. Make sure you get real-time rather than delayed quotes. You want the stock price on your screen to be as close to the market as you can get it. Online trades, contrary to the advertising blarney, are not executed the second you tap the "Enter" key. Your order has to be routed through your broker to wherever it is being filled (floor trader, electronic market system), and may be executed away from the price you are expecting. One way to save yourself disappointment is to put in a limit order specifying the price at which you want to trade. Most discounters charge more (typically $5) to handle limit orders.

Some other threshold questions. Can your broker get you a meaningful crack at initial public offerings? (Don't count on getting a moon shot in any drop-dead amount.) What about inactivity fees if you don't trade? What does it cost to open and close an IRA, and what's the annual maintenance fee? As Siebert explains, advertised commission rates may seem low, but many discounters try to get some of their cost back by "tacking on a lot of fees." "They tack on postage," she says, "or they tack on the statement charges or charge you if you want to transfer and ship a security to a relative. You have to look at all the fees."

Siebert also suggests a check on the standard of the financial information you can access. Probably no more than a dozen discounters offer institutional-quality research, often only to high net worth customers.

Remember that commission rates are not all. Cheapest is not necessarily best. A low-ball broker may be fattening his profit margins with "payment for order flow"—typically a rebate of $2 or more a trade from the market maker to whom he has routed the order. This perfectly legal kickback may mean that you're getting lousy execution—unwittingly compensating the market maker by paying fractionally more on a buy and receiving fractionally less on a sell. Put those fractions together and you're paying a lot more than just the commission.

One way to check on the quality of an execution is to ask for the exact time of your trade. Punch in a one-minute intra-day reading on a Web site such as Bigcharts.com. If your price is worse than the trades grouped around the same time, take it up with your broker. Limit trades typically don't throw off order flow payments and thus are more likely to produce tighter trades. Though little known to investors, payments for cash flow are the mother's milk of the business, particularly for "no fee" discounters. "It's a rip-off," says Muriel Siebert, who claims to have "reduced payments to nothing."

Along with other discounters, Siebert thrived on the heavy trading volume of the bull market. Her prosperity represents a long gritty comeback. The business nearly foundered after she put it in a blind trust to take on a new challenge as New York State Bank Superintendent. It was no political plum. The portfolio included oversight of some 500 banking institutions with more than $400 billion in assets, and over 1,000 small loan companies, check cashers, and sales finance companies—all licensed by the state. For anyone with less drive than Siebert, taking on the assignment would have seemed quixotic. Siebert's newly formed brokerage firm, only two years into the business, was just finding its feet. The capital in the firm was mortgaged to the money she had to borrow to buy her Exchange seat, and the market was still in shock from the great sell-off of 1973–1974. "How could I refuse?" chuckles Siebert. "For a kid from Cleveland, it was a real challenge."

She was in the right place at the right time. Then Governor Hugh L. Carey was determined to put a woman in the job. Siebert's name kept coming up, making her a rare Republican ("social liberal, fiscal conservative") in a Democratic administration. It didn't hurt that Siebert had made some good Democratic connections through her work in women's organizations.

Siebert recalls her confirmation hearings with a triumphant laugh. The only written objection to her appointment came from a prominent financial journalist. How come? asked the head of the state senate banking committee. Siebert recounted how the journalist had breached a confidence, directly attributing to her sensitive background information she had given him on a brokerage deal. So? asked the banking committee chairman. "Well, I think he felt hurt when I called him up and told him he was a no good goddamn son of a bitch," answered Siebert, bringing down the house.

She was confirmed unanimously, just in time in 1977 to deal with New York City's failing Municipal Credit Union. Its total assets—$130 million—were much bigger than the insurance fund of the back-up government agency, the National Credit Union Administration. Siebert responded by taking over the MCU and running it.

It was a bad time for savings institutions of every kind, all too easily reminiscent of the bank runs of the Depression. Historic institutions like the Greenwich Savings Bank, chartered in 1833, were being drained by a mismatch in runaway interest rates. Forced to pay as much as 15 percent to hang on to deposits, Greenwich was stuck with about $1 billion in mortgages long on the books at about 8-1/2 percent. It was a desperate situation, mirrored in at least four other similarly stricken savings banks. With earnings registering zero, the Greenwich and its mates were heading for what would have been the first mutual savings bank insolvencies ever.

Billions in deposits were at risk. "I could cover one bank, but a whole industry?" asks Siebert, her voice trailing off. She fought commercial bank efforts to cherry-pick the mutuals and lobbied the Federal Deposit Insurance Corp for an orderly bailout. I buried four of them," recalls Siebert, ticking off the stronger thrifts into which she merged the sick banks. "We managed to do it with only modest cost to the FDIC and no losses to depositors."

At odds with the Carey administration on such touchy subjects as foreign takeovers of local banks (she was against), Siebert quit after five years, deciding the job had become one "for watchdogs, not creators." She went out on a high note, resigning to take a stab at the Republican nomination for U.S. Senator. Siebert finished third in a three-way race. She financed her campaign with $250,000 of her own money, leaving in the archives lasting images of her determination. There she is, in stocking feet, standing on an up-ended milk crate, peering over a lectern, exhorting a group of female supporters.

Siebert's sabbatical was over. She had learned a lot, picked up visibility, projected herself as a role model—and very nearly lost her business. It had done badly under a caretaker management during the five years she was grappling with the banks. There were some easy choices. Siebert could have sold her firm at a decent profit, and latched on to one of the several high-powered jobs she was offered. Being ("I am a fighter") Siebert, she of course forged on. She succeeded in rehabbing her firm into a nimble boutique. She has done all the right things— brought in experienced management, kept up with technology (although at a somewhat slower pace than some of her competitors) and pulled off a couple of useful acquisitions, with the usual contention along the way.

Siebert took a lot of flack from competitors, for example, over the shrewd unorthodox way she eased her firm into a public listing five years ago. In a typical opportunistic move, Siebert merged into J. Michaels, Incorporated, a down-at-the-heels inner-city furniture retailer that had run out of options. It liquidated paying $17 a share to its principals, and on the exchange wound up with a 2.5 percent piece of what instantly morphed into Siebert Financial Corporation. Siebert made no bones about her objective. She needed the currency of a publicly owned stock, however obscure, to reward employees with options, and to engineer the acquisitions she needed to spur growth. A clueless *New York Times* reporter, chin wagged that role model Siebert had shamelessly "decided to go public in a back-door way usually reserved for shadowy penny stocks," thereby opening the door to cheap shots from competitors. One of them harrumphed that hidden balance sheet problems no doubt explained why Siebert did not go public with a conventional direct sale and raise some capital.

Siebert didn't need capital because she was financing the firm mainly out of her own pocket. It's also likely that she shied away from a broader public offering because she didn't want to let too many outsiders into her own good thing. Siebert is her own best steward. She collects a modest salary of $150,000 a year (no bonuses, no options), and does not take down the 16¢ a share in dividends she is entitled to, thereby saving Siebert Financial $3.1 million a year.

It's the Siebert savvy at work. Dividends keep minority holders happy, but would be punitively taxable to her—a non-starter. The tax return she handed out to reporters during her Senate primary run showed that Siebert, like any sensible feminist, would rather augment her capital than share it with the Internal Revenue Service. Her earnings at the time were buffered by no less than 18 legitimate audit-proof shelters. Close attention to cash flow has enabled Siebert to bankroll her firm out of her own pocket. She has financed expansion with direct loans and by putting up her stock as collateral against bank loans.

Siebert is now in her late 60s and the time when she can continue to play one-woman band may be coming to an end. Competitive pressures are so intense and technology-driven capital needs so high, Siebert will either have to take on outside partners or merge into some larger organization.

Siebert says she has gotten offers and "might" sell out "if the price was right." This is a painful dilemma for Siebert at a late stage in her life. The firm is basically an extension of herself, a bully-pulpit that has given resonance to her fight for women's rights. It is also the prime source of municipal underwriting fees she has split with local charities and the cash she has put into projects such as small loans to female start-ups. "You've got to give back to the system," says Siebert with a conviction that underscores a troublesome question. Who could ever truly succeed the feisty Muriel Siebert? She has not married, has no family in the business, and has learned first-hand that a caretaker management is a sure ticket to oblivion. What to do? For the moment Siebert says only, "I expect to be around for a good while."

Siebert's quandary is endemic to most entrepreneurs running a personal business never quite permitted to become institutionalized. The lone hand approach is becoming untenable in the face of the changes sweeping the business. Traditional middle-tier discounters like Siebert, offering low rates and a modicum of service, long had the field to themselves. Then came the huge upsurge in bull market volume and the advent of online trading. Heavy volume is catnip for discount profit margins, but the increasing amount of it done on the Internet skewed the mix. Wiring the house raised capital costs, but improved efficiencies set off a rate war. Pure online brokers emerged, forcing hybrids like Siebert into the double bind of coming down on price and upgrading service.

Talking about the cost of installing new touches like a voice-recognition order system while shaving prices to $14.95 per trade, Siebert frets over where the price-cutting will end. "The online firms have been offering too much to get new accounts," she complains. "Seventy-five free trades if you open a new account? That's really saying we'll almost pay you to bring your account to us." "We don't make much at $14.95," continues Siebert. "Would I go to $8.00 to build more customers? No, I could not give them service."

So, the rope frays while yet another new force exerts its pull. Deep-pocket traditional brokers like Merrill Lynch, anchored to an expensively built sales and distribution system, have begun to change their look. Offering competitive discount packages with advisory hand-holding, the old-line firms have already bitten off almost 30 percent of total online assets traded. As online trading goes mainstream, moving from hotshot day traders to older, more conservative investors wanting advice, the onslaught will continue to build. Some of the expected growth (online traders are likely to triple to 14 million in the next couple of years) will be cannibalized from existing accounts, but the old-line brokers are on the move.

Bigger discounters have countered by backing into traditional portfolio management preserves via mergers like Charles Schwabs' combination with U.S. Trust Corporation. This potent blend of price and service is changing the contours of the business, hence Siebert's acquisition of the women's financial network and her dollar.com Web sites. Though limited by comparison with, say, E*trade's link to accounting firm Ernst & Young financial planners, the new outlets will offer the kind of unvarnished counsel that is a Siebert specialty.

Drawing on almost a half-century of experience on Wall Street, Siebert offers a sampler of advice: Forget about chasing hot stocks, however tempting they may seem. "I tell people, stick to your guns," says Siebert. "You will make money eventually. There is really no substitute for picking a company that your own research shows is going to increase its earnings and has a good outlook."

Discount brokers don't necessarily do it all. Siebert says her clients pay 6¢ a share for a round-trip buy-and-sell, while the same trade at a full-service broker may amount to as much as 50¢ a share, each way. But, "If that broker is giving you top-quality research," notes Siebert, "it's worth it." Her thought: Save money by voting a split ticket. "We have some accounts using full-service brokers who will trade some with them and some with us."

Straighten out your feeling about risk. If you're comfortable with risk, pick the best stocks in a "vibrant group with lots of momentum," says Siebert, but if "they are just today's game, watch them closely." For balance, throw in some companies you know are "not going out of business"—drug companies such as Merck and Bristol-Myers, for example.

Knowing when to sell is a lot tougher decision than what to buy. "If you find the reasons you like the stock in the first place are still there, you can be conservative and sell half to get your cost out," advises Siebert. "Or, if you expect a slow-up in earnings, sell more."

Siebert's personal investment program, of course, still consists of putting every last nickel back into her own business. "I'm still fighting like a son of a bitch," she laughs. Fighting to be what she has been from the start—an independent woman.

As the man who institutionalized venture capital,
General Georges F. Doriot performed brilliantly by following
a deceptively simple formula: Bet the jockey, not the horse.

CHAPTER 9

The Venture Capital's Capitalist

Georges Doriot

FOR OPENERS, THE business plan could not have been more ama-
teurish. It was four typewritten pages, reproduced on contact
paper, so that it read a funky white on black. The two engineers, both
in their thirties, had labored over it during many a lunch hour snatched
in the reading room of the Lexington, Massachusetts Public Library.
They lifted the format from a "How To Start A Business" section of an
economics text. It was molded on a case study of a made-up company
called Pepto-Glitter Toothpaste.

Sweating in their Sunday best, anxious over the pitch for $100,000
in start-up money they were about to make to a venture capital board
packed with prestigious names, the engineers tried to absorb some last-
minute coaching. The venture staff, sold by their own rigorous study of
the engineers' potential, wanted the deal to fly. Look, they counselled,
to convince the board, you've got to talk around the business plan:

❀ Don't use the word computer. Computers are losing money. The
  board will never believe that two engineers out of the MIT labs
  are going to beat IBM. Tell them you're going to make printed
  circuit modules.
❀ Don't tell them you're going to net five percent. Why would anyone invest in you for five percent? Tell them 10 percent; you have
  to show a better return than RCA.
❀ Tell them you're going to make a quick profit. Forget about the
  four-year projections. Most of the board is over 80 and they are
  not looking for long-term returns.

Improvising on their Pepto-Glitter script as they went, the engineers won a tentative okay: $70,000 in cash instead of $100,000, but with a $30,000 loan to follow if the front money produced results. Because the Boston-based American Research and Development Company (ARD) was taking all the risks, pronounced the board, it was only fair that the venture firm get a whacking 70 percent of the equity in the new company. It was understood, of course, that the two would plunge immediately into making digital logic boards. The strategy was to get up and running and generate the cash flow needed to support a more sophisticated product line further down the line. And by the way, get that word "computer" out of the company name. Let's call it the Digital Equipment Company (DEC).

This was 1957 and the beginning of one of the most fruitful collaborations ever in venture capital lore. In time, American Research shareholders cashed that $70,000 investment into more than $400 million worth of Digital Equipment stock.

ARD staffers were by no means certain that the DEC technology would fly, but they got the most important thing right—the brilliant engineering skills and work ethic of the two founders, Harlan Anderson and Kenneth Olsen. The decision to go with what was mainly a bet on the character of the two embodied the philosophy of Georges F. Doriot, for 26 years the driving force behind ARD, the United State's first publicly owned venture firm, and chief architect of organized venture capital as we know it.

Although the French-born Doriot died at age 87 in 1987, the unique stamp he put on venture capital is as high profile as ever. Consider:

❋ Executives Doriot trained at ARD—many of them prized students from the classes he taught for 40 years at the Harvard Graduate Business School went on to establish or to help run a number of top venture firms on their own. Among them: Greylock Management, Fidelity Ventures, Limited, the Palmer Organization, the Old Boston Capital Corporation, and the former Morgan Holland Partners. In the same ameboid fashion, these lineal descendants went on to finance a treasury of recent start-ups such as, Doubleclick, Incorporated, Copper Mountain Networks, and Preview Systems.

❋ Many of the 7,000 students he taught at Harvard brought Doriot's philosophy to the top of many of the United States' biggest corporations. Among them: James D. Robinson III, former chairman of

American Express; William McGowan, founder of MCI; and
Philip Caldwell, former chairman of the Ford Motor Company.

Thus, when Doriot needed a director to reinforce the board at
DEC, he could simply call talent like Philip Caldwell. Doriot's Rolodex
was "one of the best networking tools in the business," recalls a former
ARD executive. "It brought us deals and if we had a marketing or technology problem with one of our companies, we could tap some of the
best brains in the country."

The success of Doriot's start-ups, based partly on this ability to capitalize on the resources of major corporations, along with those of MIT
and Harvard, contributed mightily to the lower New England economy.
The evolution of Boston's famed Route 128 as a high-tech hotbed was
an early model for Sand Hill Road and Silicon Valley.

Bet the jockey, not the horse. That was the precept—along with rigorous preinvestment research and unstinting follow-up counselling—
behind Doriot's launch of more than 200 start-ups. They were winnowed
from more than 5,000 proposals. "When someone comes in with an idea
that's never been tried," Doriot told *Forbes*, "the only way you can
judge it is by the kind of man you're dealing with."

Some of the companies Doriot backed were losers in a high-risk
business, where five out of every six start-ups do not make it past year
five. Several million dollars, for example, evaporated in an early cast at
processing frozen apple juice and deveined shrimp. DEC was a once-
in-a lifetime hit, but Doriot brought in other storied high-tech winners
such as Transitron, Tracer Lab, High Voltage Engineering, and Ionics,
Incorporated.

The quality of Doriot's judgement shows in ARD's numbers. It was
put together in 1946 with the help of such institutional backers as
Merrill T. Griswold of the Massachusetts Investors Trust and Karl T.
Compton, president of MIT.

The handful of other venture pools around then were all privately
run for the benefit of families like the Rockefellers, Phippses, and
Whitneys. Thus, ARD was unique in its identity as a publicly owned
closed-end investment company. It offered two great advantages:
Outside investors of modest means for the first time could take a crack
at the potentially high rewards of venture capital, but without running
the risk of illiquidity, common to private venture deals.

ARD was formed in 1939 on the night that Germany invaded Poland. It grew out of a meeting between Doriot and ARD's backers. The consensus was that venture capital was too critical an element to be left in private hands. It should be institutionalized by putting money and advice together on a sustained, organized basis. The plan was pigeonholed by the outbreak of World War II.

Doriot came back to Cambridge and his lecture hall in 1946 after having been breveted a Brigadier General as Director of Military Planning for the Army Quartermaster Corps, and Deputy Director of Research and Development for the War Department. Part of Doriot's assignment was to see that war material was produced and shipped to the right place at the right time. Getting the job done included helping establish new companies to get rolling on specialty high-tech items.

With Doriot at its head, ARD started life with a public offering of $5 million. When ARD closed its books a quarter of a century later, the capital account stood at better than $400 million—not including generous pay-outs in portfolio stocks like High Voltage Engineering along the way.

Doriot was a lot more than just a brilliant portfolio manager. Money was less important than the social and economic impact of nursing new technology to maturity. Support talented people long term, build a company, and "the rewards will come," he insisted.

Sustained effort was very much part of the Doriot heritage. His father, an engineer, designed the first Peugeot automobile. He passed on the work ethic to young Georges with considerable force: If Doriot dropped below first in his lycee class, he got spanked. Young Doriot subsequently made it through the University of Paris and Harvard, but little wonder that in later years he almost always used a father-child analogy to describe his ties to his start-ups. He thought of them as his "progeny." Sometimes criticized for staying too long with losers, Doriot would retort: "If a child is sick with a 102-degree fever, do you sell him?"

Doriot carried the same fatherly feel into his classrooms, teaching an eclectic and wildly popular course at the Harvard Business School called simply "Manufacturing." It was about anything but manufacturing. The course centered mainly on Doriot's high ideals of how businessmen should behave and his humanistic views of solving such workday problems as how to structure a board of directors or what to do with a good early stage promoter who has no head for later stage operations.

Doriot was a commanding figure in class. He rarely took questions. He told his students that he would talk and that they would listen. He urged them to write down what they thought about his talks in the "Manufacturing" notebooks he asked them to keep. "Learn how to test yourself now," he told his students. "There will be no examinations when you leave school, and you'll miss them."

In his search for perfection, Doriot challenged everything. He pooh-poohed Harvard's famed case study approach, and regularly farmed out his students for on-the-job training. "Experience is the best teacher," said the General. Doriot was suspicious of numbers, warning students they could be manipulated to prove anything.

He inculcated in his students his own questing mind-set. Corporate guest lecturers were severely cross-examined. Disappointed that his students had not been tough enough on a visiting president of U.S. Steel, he told them they had missed an obvious point: "United States Steel doesn't understand what business they are in," he told the class. "They are in the materials business, not the steel business. They are completely ignorant of aluminum and plastics." As one devoted student later told *Forbes*, "Doriot was the first person to think in these terms. He had more influence on what happened in American business than the whole rest of the Harvard faculty put together."

Prize students like James Morgan, who became a senior vice president at ARD and went on to open his own venture shop, remembers the classload putting a heavy burden on married students. It was only theoretically leavened by the General's views on such outside topics as how to choose a wife, and his annual lecture cueing the women themselves on how to deal with the corporate culture.

The General's ideas on the subject, laughs Morgan, "would curl the hair of feminists." The ideal wife would clip newspapers and magazines for ideas her husband should be aware of, pack his bag for him on business trips and, in general, provide "unlimited support." The General himself could not have been more uxorious. He wrote innumerable love poems to his wife Edna. She, in turn, would slip notes into his pajama pockets as she—following the job description, of course—obligingly packed his bag for the road.

Jim Morgan nonetheless remembers anticipation of the wives' lecture as stirring almost as much anxiety as the bloodletting that took place when the General tore apart a business proposal. "My wife has a fiery temper," says Morgan. "She was pregnant. I'd been promising her I'd be home more, and here I was spending more time than ever in the library. I was afraid she was going to have it out with the General."

Morgan underestimated the General's charm. Morgan's wife Maureen came home dazzled. "What a wonderful man! The first thing the General told us to tell you is, 'you've got to work harder,'" she said approvingly. It was yet another example of the General's fondness for indirection, teasing ideas out of students and ARD's professionals in Socratic dialogue.

Charles Coulter, for instance, a retired ARD president, recalls biking over to the General's home in Boston's Back Bay to clear up some business one rainy Saturday afternoon.

As many of his old colleagues do when reminiscing about the General, Coulter slips into a French accent. Opening the door to Coulter's ring, Doriot asked "Sharlie, the bicycle when it rains, is it not dangerous?" "Yes," agreed Coulter, "the tires lose traction." "So," asked the General, "is it not possible to improve the bite of the tires? One could perhaps improve the traction with a new grade of rubber. Could not the gearing be improved? And as to the distribution of the rider's weight, could not the frame be altered?" "I know this sounds silly," laughs Coulter. "I'm standing there in the rain. The General is sheltered in the doorway and he's building a new high-tech bicycle company while I get wet."

Though not a technician, Doriot had what Jim Morgan calls a "philosopher's approach to science." "It was all in the questioning of that great inquisitive mind. The General would bore in like this," recalls Morgan, making a tight corkscrew motion with his right hand.

The General dug for detail. Morgan recalls one ARD associate who spent long hours sitting up with a sick electric motor company. The motors just weren't up to quality standards. The associate was flabbergasted when the General asked him what seemed to be a simple but germane question: "What about the bearings? Were they roller or ball bearings?" The MIT graduate and crack analyst had to confess he didn't know. Red-faced with embarrassment, the ARD associate "sat there in front of the General feeling about this big," says Morgan, holding out thumb and index finger a millimeter apart.

The General had a gift for aphorism that sometimes sounded sententious, but always stuck in the mind. Talking with *Forbes* on one occasion, for example, Doriot ticked off a number of convictions that are as valid today as they were in that interview 35 years ago.

❋ On careers: "There are three ways a man can go; to success, mediocrity, or oblivion. Of these, mediocrity is the most dangerous because it is enjoyable."

❋ On creativity: "A creative man merely has ideas; a resourceful man makes them practical. I look for the resourceful man. The man I want knows what to do with liabilities."

❋ Of trouble in small companies: "I like to see trouble come early in our little companies. Unless there is trouble, I worry. I want to know early how a man will behave under adversity."

❋ On hazards in small companies: "A little success makes some people get conceited. You can't run a small company on a 40-hour week."

❋ On capital gains: "I view capital gains as a reward for a job well done, not as a goal. The interesting ideas are research, development, production, distribution, and sales. If one can finance, produce, distribute, and sell right, he will get his reward."

The General's pursuit of the long term was thoroughly organized. From Wednesday to Saturday, he was all ARD; from Sunday to Tuesday, he was all Harvard. It wasn't as easy as he made it seem. He never made an evening business appointment or ate dinner the night before his classes, once confiding to an associate that even after 40 years, he felt nauseous before facing his students. Beneath all of that Gallic sang-froid was the young lycee student who had to get everything right, or face punishment.

Few students sensed this vulnerability in the General. If they had, it might even have deepened their devotion. Aging alumni regularly turned out by the hundreds for major birthday and anniversary celebrations, still showing what Charles Waite, one of ARD's Old Boys, calls the "missionary zeal" of Doriot's philosophy. "We believed we were doing something for the greater good, making America a better place," says Waite, who moved on from ARD to help found Greylock Management.

A sense of commitment was partly a response to the easy leap that the Doriot philosophy made from campus to start-ups. As late as 1960,

Waite recollects in the book *Done Deals*, venture capital was "still an academic experiment in some ways, because Doriot was head of it, and he was more than anything else a teacher." "He was in business to test a thesis," continues Waite. "Money really wasn't a very high objective."

Doriot's missioners trolled MIT and Harvard's labs, making converts among scientists working on technology initially related to defense or the space effort. Backed by modest research contracts from Washington, they needed the additional capital it took to bend spaceware applications to commercial use. One such find was Tracer Labs, a maker of analytical instruments, and a prime example of how a single ARD investment might generate dozens of others. As Charles Waite recalls, many Tracer Lab operatives came up with new applications their bosses wouldn't buy, so they'd "leave and come to us, or others, and get financing" to start their own companies.

Semiconductor producers such as Transitron, yet another ARD winner, showed the same branching phenomenon. "People poured out of Transitron, starting little companies, either in California or Boston," says Waite. "And if they weren't coming out of these companies," continues Waite, "there would be professors at MIT or Harvard, or elsewhere, that read the stock sheets and could see that there might be opportunities."

The ferment added significantly to the economic gains ARD's founders helped to bring about in the Boston area. One sure sign of that showed in the way that empty mill space, a relic of New England's dead textile industry, was filling up. The space—plentiful and cheap—was itself a catalyst to development. Ken Olsen and his partner, Harlan Anderson, for example, squeezing every last nickel out of their $70,000 ARD advance, headed straight for an old woolen mill in Maynard, Massachusetts. A double football-field-sized 9,000 square feet, swallowing the lawn furniture and leftover rolltop desk that demarcated the executive suite, cost them only 25¢ a square foot, including watchman service and heat. Thanks in part to its low overhead, DEC, much to the relief of ARD's older directors, managed to eke out a profit in its first year. Doriot, ever worried about flash-in-the pan triumphs, had a typical response. "I'm sorry to see this," he said, "no one has ever succeeded this soon and ever survived." The General did not want his children to leave the nest too soon.

When people talked of ARD, they thought of its most visible presence, the General. Doriot wasn't all business. He contributed generously to and helped run Boston's French Library. Doriot also painted, always using a palette knife on 7" × 10" canvases. This standardized dimension, he said, fitted precisely the amount of spare time he had. Doriot passed on his paintings, mainly landscapes and seascapes, to friends at Christmas time. He also sometimes "auctioned" his work to them at a standard maximum of 39¢ each. He boasted that two of his paintings hung in the National Gallery—one in the office of a former student, the other in storage as part of the collection of the late Robert Lehman.

Then there was the annual black-tie New Year's Eve party in the Doriot home. After dinner, the General would give a humorous talk, once mock-complaining that as a naturalized citizen, he could not become president of the United States. His only route to power, he said, would be as head of a union of computer programmers that would enable him to shut down Wall Street at will.

This was a whimsical turn for the General, who often used his sense of humor to diffuse ARD's internal tensions. Wall Street could not have been more generous to ARD. Its stock typically traded at a premium, partly because investors saw it as a cheap call on ARD's huge hoard of DEC. DEC's breakthrough success with the interactive minicomputer made it one of the fastest growing companies in the country. Reflected celebrity drew new venture proposals by the hundreds across the General's desk. Those that made the cut got a lot of handholding, often by the General himself. Denzil Doyle, former president of Digital Equipment of Canada, now long a venture capitalist himself, recalls the influence that Doriot's caring had on him. "I saw how the mentorship with Ken Olsen worked, and I got really intrigued by its role in managing a company," says Doyle.

Of course, he was experiencing what the General's hard-working staffers had known all along. Doriot tried to reward them with the same incentive that drove ARD's entrepreneurs—options—but was frustrated by government fiat. As investment company employees, the staffers were forbidden the incentives of options in either their own company, DEC, or any other portfolio company. Some staffers, not including the General, did get a chance to buy into the DEC shares

Harlan Anderson sold after a quarrel that ended his partnership with Ken Olsen. That left a few ARD senior people sitting comfortably on what turned out to be $50 million or more, while the rank-and-file worked long hours at low pay making millions for the managers of portfolio companies.

The General, focusing on the investment side of the business, pretty much left the day-to-day detail to others. That worked well enough—for a while. Charles Waite recalls having "good times," and felt he was "making the contribution that the great man wanted me to make." Then along came Optical Scanning Corporation. It was in deep trouble. Some ARD staffers wanted to pull the plug, but Optical Scanning was another child Doriot did not want to sacrifice. Acting with customary indirection, Doriot put a "still pretty green" Charles Waite on the board and let him advance the money that kept Optical alive for the next couple of years. Doriot did not "want to write the checks himself," recalls Waite. Searching for a consensus, the General wanted his senior staff "to want him to write the checks."

Set up as a kind of fall guy, Waite worked hard with the entrepreneur ("something the other guys didn't do") and finally got Optical in shape for a public offering. It was a very nice turnaround. ARD's potential loss of $3 million turned into a $20 million profit; the entrepreneur's net worth went from zero to $10 million. Waite's reward: a $2,000 raise. He agonized over that, loved what he was doing, but decided he should be "somewhere where he was compensated adequately." He followed his buddy Bill Elfers, who had been the Number 2 man behind the General for years, to help set up Greylock Management.

Given ARD's unrewarding regulatory structure and the entrepreneurial climate the General had helped to create, defections were inevitable. Doriot had put venture capital on the map, but in the 1960s it was still a very comfortable mainly East Coast business. There were probably no more than 50 principals involved in what was still very much a gentleman's game. Everyone knew everybody else, there was no direct competition, and plenty of sharing of deals. There was also plenty of time—time to check out the business on the ground; time to study the potential market and competition; time to follow the prime Doriot precept of digging into character. "Unless you were some great man— unless you were Dwight Eisenhower wanting to start up an infantry division"—remembered Charles Waite, "there wasn't much hurry to do the deal." One result was fewer mistakes than now and far more credible merchandise coming to the end-game of the new issues market.

ARD, always abundantly stocked with talent from the deep reserves of Doriot's Harvard classes, continued to thrive by nurturing good investments that also carried the kicker of economic good. One example: Ionics, Incorporated, another find culled from the chemical engineering labs of MIT. Its low-cost ion separation technology was a whole new look, with wide application, on desalting sea water. On ARD books at a cost of around $400,000, Ionics was by the early 1970s worth some $2 million. It was one of 45 stocks in a portfolio carrying 50 companies that had not yet gone public holding only three losers. One of the losers was a stylistic low-tech tic—a $500,000 investment in a chain of convalescent homes written down to a notional $1.

The long string of successes raised ARD's net asset value from $5 to a high of $90 a share (after a four for one split), not including earlier distributions of a number of portfolio stocks. Better yet, ARD stock often as not traded at premiums of 80 percent or more, partly because investors saw it as a cheap way of hopping on the DEC bandwagon. On the books at $61,400, with a market value of $354 million, DEC by the early 1970s had ballooned to more than 75 percent of ARD's assets.

Though not yet a director himself, the General worked tirelessly behind the scenes, helping Olsen over crises like the breakup with partner Harlan Anderson. "My job," the General liked to say, "is to watch, pray, and spread happiness."

Olsen's biggest problem was the double-edged sword of managing growth. DEC had gone public in 1966 at $22 a share, giving ARD in just nine years a return of more than 50 times its money. The number continued to multiply as DEC quickly capitalized on a technology that made its refrigerator-sized mini-computers cheaper, faster, and less complicated than IBM's room-sized main frames. DEC was fast outgrowing its old Maynard mill, creating new jobs in the area by thousands, and increasing revenues by 30 percent to 50 percent a year. Paradoxically, ARD was trapped in the dilemma of DEC's success. As the steward of both companies, the General was too sage a manager not to realize that he had a succession problem on his hands—his own. He was 72 and mortal. If he were to die without a successor, there was a chance that ARD's 65 percent control of DEC might fall into hostile hands.

Inextricably linked to the question of succession was how to sterilize the huge block of control stock that could destabilize both the market and DEC's management. Over brandy with a couple of ARD directors, the General explored the options. One was merger with another venture capital firm molded in the ARD style. That didn't work. Another was to lure one of Doriot's Old Boys from a different top venture firm. That didn't work either. Another suggestion did. Doriot and Bill Miller, President of Textron, Incorporated, long diversified out of textiles into conglomerate deal making, were good friends. The General sat on the Textron board; Miller on the ARD board. Thus, Miller was a known quantity, thoroughly familiar with the General's style. A Textron buyout of ARD would close all the right circuits; it would reinforce Textron's deal-making capacities; perpetuate the ARD name as a division; and keep the General on as chairman, with a mutually agreed upon venture executive as president and heir-apparent.

Equally elegant was the disposition of the DEC stock. It would be spun off, premerger, to ARD shareholders, who would also get a modest piece of Textron as part of the purchase package. However carefully structured, the Textron deal rankled some of Doriot's Old Boys. Who had been better trained than they to take on the succession? What's more, the DEC stock could have been spun off to shareholders at any time before. The General's strategy was to hang on to the crown jewels. They were, in effect, an advertisement for himself. DEC kept Doriot's reputation green, and the deals coming in the door. Off-loading the stock earlier, says one former executive, would have reduced ARD from "a big company to a small company with a mish-mash of venture investments." "I don't think the General had it in him to be that self-effacing," he laughs.

Actually, it was a good time to fold one's hand. Whether the General sensed it or not (as T. Rowe Price did), a runaway market was soon to go over the cliff. Thus, the spin-off had the timely advantage of upstaging a killer sell-off. The General's posting to Textron, on the other hand, was a less than happy event. Doriot was in good health, still full of zest for the job, but quickly decided that his agreed upon back-up—and designated successor—did not understand venture as he did. The two just did not click.

It was originally planned that Doriot could stay on as long as he liked. Caught in the impasse between Doriot and his presumed succes-

sor, Textron offered both a package. The General took his (there had
been no pension at his frugally run ADR), worrying how his company,
now a step-child, would fare under the new regime.

In fact, it grew awkwardly and far less spiritedly in the conglomerate milieu than it might have in its natural habitat. Under the presi-
dency of Charles Coulton, ARD made a lot of money for Textron, but
the fit was never quite right. Ultimately, ARD was surrendered to the
General's surviving Old Boys in a leveraged buyout.

The General kept himself busy as ever, and spending much of his
time helping Ken Olsen bypass the minefields of runaway growth. He
counseled patience over severe organizational problems, and talked up
Olsen every chance he got. Introducing the DEC chief at a Newcomen
Society meeting marking the company's 25th anniversary, for example,
the General told the group it was a good thing that Olsen had not been
around in 1712. That was when British innovator Thomas Newcomen
began making the improved steam engines that ushered in the industrial revolution. "Newcomen was a lucky man," Doriot told the group.
"If Ken Olsen had been alive then, he would have designed a better
engine, and today this would be called the Olsen Society."

So strong was the attachment that Olsen held several board meetings at Doriot's home while the General lay dying of lung cancer in
1987, at age 87. It was a generous gesture, and the General's pragmatic
spirit lingered long over his most rewarding progeny. Years later, when
DEC itself fell before the onslaught of the microprocessor, it was
Doriot-trained director Philip Caldwell who forced Ken Olsen to
resign. "People tried to help, but Ken just wasn't listening any more,"
says one Old Boy.

The Doriot influence continued well beyond the grave. Thanks
partly to the critical mass formed by his Old Boys, the number of venture capital funds in the field now has multiplied to more than 7,000.
The amount of money flooding into them over the last decade, mainly
from institutional investors, is up tenfold to $30 billion. The eye-pop-
ping incentive of big wins like ARD's early DEC investment is still at
the heart of the game. So is risk. Unwary investors following the rain-
bow of venture got clipped for billions in the recent implosion of
dot.com new issues, just as they had in earlier fads like biotechs.

Doriot saw change coming, lamenting that too many new venture
firms were bent on building stocks rather than sustainable companies.

His style of venture capital, time-intensive—make sure as best we can this company is viable—is being edged out by quick-hit operators, more interested in profitable exit strategies than building great companies. We've got a hot idea here, get it into the new issues market, quick! Doriot, a year or two before he died, summed up the trend:

He said he had just finished one of his stump speeches on the need for venture capital to create lasting companies when an enthusiastic young man approached and congratulated him on his talk. His own new company, backed by a brilliant business plan, the young man said, was already doing exactly as Doriot urged.

"Really," beamed the General, "what do you make?"

"Oh, about $1.32 a share," was the response.

Old Boys like Frank Hughes, a former president of ARD, chuckle sardonically over this tale. Many of them, edging toward retirement, have tried to instil the Doriot doctrine in the next generation, but find it an uphill fight against incalculable economic and cultural change. "Many young people do not much care about building substance, something that will stick in the fabric of the economy," argues Frank Hughes. "It's the way we are now," he adds. "Instead of being a by-product of work, cash has become an end in itself. It's the way people keep score."

What used to be a collegial environment is now big business. Huge pools of capital can no longer be profitably deployed into small start-ups. ARD style hands-on mentoring is vanishing, too. "How many boards can you realistically sit on and still have an impact?" asks Hughes. "Five or six, maybe, and then it all gets done by telephone." "You see it in these so-called skyrockets," Hughes continues. "Venture capital people work to make a quick killing on an IPO and then move on. Six to eight months later, the company is bankrupt."

How many of the more recent crop of start-up entrepreneurs would fit the General's description of the young Ken Olsen. "He was perceptive, he had managed people, he saw the relationship between production and distribution, he had a full understanding of the market two to three years out, and his ideas were not so far advanced as to be dangerous." Doriot may have over-praised Ken Olsen, but the job specifications could not be more sound.

In the end, DEC had a great run for many years, but failed to mature into a lasting company. Happily for the General, the downfall came after his death. A few years back, after shedding thousands of jobs, DEC was absorbed in truncated form into Compaq Computer. But if Georges Doriot leaves behind him no corporate monument, his legacy is perhaps prouder than that of those who did. He not only invented venture capital, he showed how it ought to be done. And that is a mighty contribution to American capitalism.

Closer to Wall Street than Broadway, Paul Bandrowski typifies the new breed of angel investors who trade long odds against hits.

A Venture of Angels

Paul Bandrowski

AT AGE 38, BUFFALO-BASED business angel Paul Bandrowski is something of an early start-up himself. Along with an informal band of fellow angels—family, friends, business associates—Bandrowski has helped to finance maybe a dozen new high-tech companies. He has become rich in the process but traces one of the most important lessons he learned about bootstrapping capital to fifth grade elementary school. "It's very simple," laughs Bandrowski. "You can get your business model right, your pricing right, your suppliers right, and then—wham—you get decked by the unpredictable."

Bandrowski is talking about more than just the cinnamon sticks he put up in his mother's kitchen and hawked at school for 10¢ a pack. He caught a sweet-tooth fad and rode it to the point where he was grossing $300 a month. Business was so good Bandrowski had to add his kid brother to the work force. That's when he was decked by the unforeseen.

It materialized in the form of a suddenly intolerant regulatory authority. "The principal suspended me for three days for neglecting my schoolwork," groans Bandrowski. Call it the parable of the cinnamon stick. The scourge of the unpredictable is all too common in what has become a full-time pursuit for Bandrowski—assaying small companies, helping to shape them, and rounding up the angel capital needed to get them off the ground.

Bandrowski and his fellow angels, cloaked in the Broadwayese for financial backers, are a new manifestation of private investing. Working outside the strictures of formal venture capital partnerships, they are freelancers, often operating in loose consort. By some estimates, they

number more than two million. Many, like Bandrowski, are entrepreneurs who cashed in on early business success, now reinventing themselves by channeling smarts and capital into fledgling companies.

The risks, lurking in X-factors such as product failure or skewed
market analysis, are high. The Small Business Administration figures
that five out of every six of the kind of early-stage ventures Bandrowski
midwifes never make it beyond year five. Bandrowski thinks the odds
are somewhat better than the SBA makes them. He puts the rate of
attrition at one out of every two—still high, but not prohibitive matched
against what the enthusiastic Bandrowski calls "Big hits that can bring
75 to 100 times your money."

The big hit potential led hundreds of freelance angel bands like
Bandrowski's to pump perhaps as much as $60 billion into 50,000 or
more start-ups last year. By some estimates that is more than 30 times
the capital mustered by deep-pocket professional venture firms, which
typically focus on lower-risk efforts higher up the development chain.
This stampede of angels, mainly high net worth individuals with business or professional connections, was galvanized by runaway tech stocks
now deader than yesterday's newspaper.

With big-name incubators like Safeguard Scientifics shrinking to
less than 20 percent of their bull market highs and grossly overpriced
dot.coms dropping like flies, haven't the angels scattered for cover? The
true faith runs deep, argues Bandrowski. Angel bands continue to grow
in number, as convinced as he, that prices have come down to bargain
levels. "I keep telling them not to stop," continues Bandrowski. "Keep
on buying." "Companies we passed on because they were too expensive
at $25 million are now selling for $2 million or $3 million," he says.

It is an old story, the third in the last 30 years. A huge speculative
wave builds ever higher, pushing venture tech companies to absurd levels; and then recedes piling them up on the rocks. These cycles have
savaged whole industry segments like biotech, and now dot.coms. That's
when shrewd investors like Bandrowski start picking up salvage, cheap.

He's typical of the many entrepreneurs who cash out of early success to put money and skills to work in loose alliance with other private
investors. They start ahead of the game. The arrangement is cheap—no
front-end costs or profit sharing with managing partners, as is the case
in formal venture capital deals. Coinvesting also makes diversification
easy in a high-risk business by pooling comparatively small pieces of

individual money ($50,000 to $100,000) over a number of deals. Typically, each of the pooled investments runs to $1 million or so, centered mainly on start-ups with revenues of well under $10 million. Most such companies have not yet developed to a point where they can attract venture capital—too risky, proportionately too small, and too costly to monitor closely.

This leaves an equity gap increasingly filled by angel money. The long-term aim (five years or so) is to add enough ballast so the company can pull in later rounds of financing, perhaps on its way to the big bang of a public offering. Angels like Bandrowski and friends swap cash for a minority interest (20–30 percent), and get to buy in cheap because they are taking on most of the risk. This first layer of cash helps to attract successive financing from establishment sources (banks, venture capital firms) that reduce risk and add significantly to the value of the angels' contribution. For the experienced executive, some of the value added is psychic. It comes from a chance to keep their management hands in. The touch has to be light, helping sensitive company founders over the rough spots without impinging on their freedom of action.

Bandrowski, for example, sits as vice-chairman of Sun Hawk, Incorporated into which he recently combined a fledgling start-up. The Seattle-based digital publishing company gave him a solid minority holding in a listed stock. Bandrowski plans to help reinforce the combination with an infusion of badly needed new capital. That doesn't mean he intends to run Sun Hawk. "It's very satisfying," says Bandrowski. "I get to help these guys. I may not know the technology and I'm not going to get in anybody's way, but entrepreneurs are surprised when I show them how pricing models work across different industries, and what it takes to get a banker to answer your phone calls."

Bandrowski's track record makes his soft approach an easy sell. Five years ago he was technology chief to his buddy Ron Schreiber, then chairman of Softbank Services Group, a technical support operation, and yet another majority-owned offspring of Masayoshi Son's globe girdling Softbank Corporation. Looking to squeeze more value out of the Buffalo-based affiliate, Schreiber and Bandrowski hit on the idea of spinning off some of the technology into encryption software designed to keep Internet intellectual property rights from getting ripped off. Competitors were already in the field, but there was clearly a fast-growing market in movie, publishing, and software companies deeply worried about protecting digital copyrights from hackers and pirates.

Schreiber and Bandrowski managed to sell the concept to Softbank, but burned up a $500,000 advance in less than six months. When the two went back for more, they were told the cupboard was bare. With a modest equity of their own riding on the outcome, Schreiber and Bandrowski started tapping on venture capital doors and came up empty. "Nobody understood what we were trying to do," recalls Bandrowski. "They said, 'Digital rights? What are they?'" "Also," adds Bandrowski, "At some level they figured we were just a couple of guys from Buffalo. Maybe we could do steel mills, but what did we know about the Internet?"

So, Schreiber and Bandrowski turned with fading hope to a band of local angels. They, in fact, had never done a tech deal, cautiously sticking to what they knew best—Buffalo's traditional industrial and metal-bending skills. The narrowness of that focus kept Schreiber and Bandrowski on tenterhooks as they auditioned. Were the angels, taking a cue from Warren Buffett, going to shy from tech propositions they wouldn't try to understand? Schreiber and Brandrowski worked their way through two breakfast meetings at the Buffalo Club. The lead angel was Ross Kenzie, "A rough, gruff military man turned banker," says Bandrowski, "who asked really tough questions." As Bandrowski anticipated, the romance of tech investing did not go down easily with Kenzie, who had done well in some 30 deals over the years, most of them hard asset buyouts. "What do you mean, you're not going to make money in the first 12 months?" demanded the burly Kenzie. Bandrowski and Schreiber eased the group slowly through the crypto technology and realized they were home free when one angel piped up with an epiphany: "Last time I read, Yahoo was not a bad early buy." With members of the group chipping in $50,000 to $100,000 each for a total of $3 million, Bandrowski and Schreiber were off to the races.

Their start-up, Reciprocal, Incorporated is a prime example of how angels network—one deal leading to another—and how angel money gets leveraged into bigger dollops of financing. Softbank's capital begat the Kenzie capital, getting Reciprocal to a working stage where Bandrowski and Schreiber could do missionary work on deeper pockets. This time around, venture capital firms realized they were looking at something more substantive than just two guys from Buffalo. So did

Microsoft, hot on the kind of crypto it takes to prevent repetitions of the massive computer break-in it suffered last year. Put it all together and you've got the $75 million in additional capital it took to make Reciprocal a going concern now employing some 200 and conservatively worth several hundred million dollars. At this writing, Reciprocal has not yet gone public, another big multiplier Kenzie's angels can look to down the road. Though they could have cashed out handsomely at several points along the line, Kenzie's angels still hold an extremely cheap slice of Reciprocal in what has become a transforming experience. Bandrowski says the group, having finally taken the plunge, has now gone in to invest in a number of high-tech deals with him. One of them is a ten-strike called OpenSite Technologies, a Research Triangle Park, North Carolina-based developer of online auction software.

While running Reciprocal as Chief Executive Officer, Bandrowski was giving a helping hand—as well as cash—to Michael Brader-Araje, OpenSite's founder. "When I first started talking to Michael," laughs Bandrowski, "he told me he didn't know a capitalization table from a billiard table." Brader-Araje learned quickly, but not without pain. As OpenSite developed, still hungry for capital, Brader-Araje, Bandrowski, and the Kenzie angels looked to a public offering. Ready to fly in the summer of 1999, they scrubbed because of a downdraft in the market. Early last year, they were poised for another try, but market turbulence again forced them to abort. "It was not exactly a happy experience," founder Brader-Araje told *Forbes*.

Eager to get on, he pulled a different exit card out of his sleeve—acquisition. When Siebel Systems brought out OpenSite in a $440 million stock swap, the Kenzie angels pocketed more than 100 times their money. It wasn't quite the Yahoo! that Bandrowski had seized on to fire their imagination, but it was a home run—and it was local. Part of OpenSite's operations were in Buffalo and word of the killing set a whole new band of wanna-be angels clamoring for admission to Kenzie's band. OpenSite was an open sesame for Bandrowski, too. His share of the loot ("I've got as much money as I'll ever need") enabled him to quit Reciprocal for full-time angeling and advising. Sidekick Ron Schreiber, also liberated, set up a company called Seed Capital Partners, an early-stage investment fund. "Ron's more into venture capital," says Bandrowski.

It's easy to tell where the separate paths these two long-time partners have chosen diverge. Angels tend to be unstructured free spirits.

Their ranks are populated with definitely hands-on types. Some are retired executives, determined not to spend their days yukking it up at the 19th hole. The younger contingent tends to be 40-ish, with leisure and money enough to be nearly full-time investors. Both commodities are spiked with the conviction that it's time to do something new. Paul Bandrowski is typical of this restless breed. "I knew I'd never be good at running a big company," he says. "Once you get it together, it's time to move on. My personal exit strategy is when you get to have 25 to 40 people on the payroll. That's when I'm out of there."

Thus, a critical distinction: Some 400,000 active angels (those who do three or more deals a year), in the main, are entrepreneurial-manager types who, so to speak, have got their hands dirty on the shop floor. Venture capital on the other hand tends to be staffed by financial-investor types with comparatively little direct business experience. The difference shows in the angel's willingness to take on higher risks and stick with them longer. They can be more patient because they don't have to kowtow to limited partners demanding quick returns or measure up to performance yardsticks to keep their jobs.

Logically, in terms of time and risk, angeldom should generate higher rewards. Winners like OpenSite get a lot of ink and certainly whet the appetite. Angels think big. They go in, according to a University of New Hampshire Venture Research Center survey, with the hope of quintupling their money in five years. That's the expectation. The reality may be quite different. Actual returns, spread over the spectrum from groups like the Nashua, New Hampshire Breakfast Club to the Silicon Valley angels, are hard to get at. The odds are they come in at no worse than the long-term 15 percent to 20 percent notched by the venture industry, and possibly higher.

That's better than the long-term stock market return, and of course, there's always the hope of a big hit. Two things are certain: Storming in where most venture capital firms fear to tread, angels finance some 75 percent of the nation's start-ups. That makes angeldom a huge social and economic phenomenon that has to be treated with respect. It's hard to see dilettantism in the mighty contribution angels make to job creation and the boost they give to the United States lead in world technology.

Angels have a long and honored history. Well before they picked up the vogue Broadway descriptive, they were known as private investors and helped to bankroll such groundbreakers as Alexander Graham Bell and Henry Ford.

Another certainty: Angels have more fun.

Much of the reward tends to be psychic—the buzz angels like Paul Bandrowski get from rolling up their sleeves and pitching in. There are social rewards too—bragging rights when a winner like OpenSite is booted home. The entry cost is not insuperable. "Accredited" investors, by Securities and Exchange Commission fiat, must be able to show a minimum worth of $1 million (including primary residence) or annual income thresholds of $200,000 ($300,000 joint). Angels come in all shapes and sizes. Some may chip in to only one or two deals; others may diversify across a number. Many are passive, quite willing to hand their proxies to the Paul Bandrowskis of the universe. Some, mainly cashed-out entrepreneurs with deep pockets, fly solo; most band together in more than 100 affinity groups like Ross Kenzie's Buffalo crowd. As Zina Moukheiber reported in *Forbes*, the syndication approach has been popularized by some of the big names surfacing at the top of many successful investments. Capital Investors of Washington, D.C., for example, includes such star quality as MCI World Com vice-chairman John Sidgmore.

The names are hotly pursued by promising entrepreneurs on the make. Group power means collectively bigger investments spread over more possibilities. It also makes for better networking, as in the cross-pollination that projected the Kenzie group out of its preoccupation with old economy buyouts into high-tech growth. Some groups, in the each-one reach-one fashion typical of angels, have recruited a 100 or more members. Others (Bandrowski, for one) keep it small. Inner-directed lead angels often just don't want to deal with too many other egos.

Most groups meet regularly to check out potential deals. It's often a bar and buffet scene, as was a recent monthly confab of the Texas Angels in the ballroom of Austin's Four Seasons Hotel. Some 90 members of the group have turned out for this $100 a head bash. After swapping business cards and high-tech tales, juggling drinks and hor d'oeuvres at the warmup reception, they get down to the serious stuff of the audition. The three start-ups pitching the crowd tonight have already survived two cuts.

They're among the half-dozen possibilities winnowed from more than 30 business plan summaries submitted to the group's steering committee. The first pass, aimed at picking three finalists who will do ten-minute standups before the crowd tonight, took place a week ago in the University of Texas auditorium before a five-person selection committee. It was by no means the hammer and tong inquisition nervous entrepreneurs clearly feared. They got encouragement and criticism in equal amounts. "You are lecturing and investors hate to be lectured," one entrepreneur was told. "We just want to know what the deal is." Yet another suppliant, deep into the innovations of his software package, was told to lighten up. "When you have a really technical product like yours, you have to discuss its benefits in layman's terms," was the instruction. "I hope this discussion will help you do that."

For the three who survived this cut, the preliminary offered useful cues as to how to package their ten-minute spiels for the formal presentation at the Four Seasons. The questions there also tended to center on technological feasibility, a crucial consideration for angels trying to figure out which horse they want to bet. There are some things the start-ups don't like to give away. "We'll have to plead the Fifth on that," was the response to one pointed query." "It's key intellectual property, and we can't reveal it right now." The topic was aired more openly in private discussion over coffee and dessert after the formal Q&A. Angels interested in follow-up booked additional time with the entrepreneurs. There would be weeks of continuing research before anyone started talking money. It was a satisfied group that headed to the elevators. "The social stuff is fun," smiled one angel. "But as you can see, it's also very, very professional."

The social side is definitely part of the appeal. What can be so wrong in a mix where you can make some money, perhaps big money, and give a budding business a lift, all in the company of kindred souls? Ideally, nothing. The threshold question is: Have you got the real angel stuff? The answer is partly a function of where else you've invested your money and how tolerant you are of risk. Seasoned hands like Paul Bandrowski can afford to put a big chunk of assets into private investing and expect to do well. If you've got some extra casino money that you can afford to lose, go for it! But only if you've got a balanced portfolio of other investments that will see you through the five to seven years it might take for a start-up to work out. The old venture capital wheeze applies here: Lemons ripen before plums. Thus, you should have enough free cash to diversify over a number of deals, and a reserve to put into follow-up financing.

If your hope is to add sweat equity to the cash, be realistic about the amount of free time you can spare. Equally important, check your temperament. If you're a Charlie-take-charge guy, you can be sure that any entrepreneur worth his salt will tell you to stuff it. If you do want to put energy into a deal, you'll likely be better off angeling with a couple of friends or in a small group.

The other side of the coin is, how comfortable do you feel about delegating big decisions to someone else? The point here is the difference between loose and organized groups. Both put on regular dog-and-pony shows for members. In the informal groups, individuals structure their own deals, taking on the whole burden of research, legal work and negotiations. Formal groups like the Washington D.C.-based Womanangels.net invest as a unit. Each of its members has agreed to chip in a minimum of $75,000 over three years, with the right to ante up more on the side if they so choose. This band of professional women, age range 30s to 60s, is fronted by a managing partner who takes on all the details. Typically, managers work for modest pay against a 15 percent cut of the profits. That's a lot cheaper than the 20 percent to 30 percent of the profit (plus two percent annual fees) imposed by the professionals in venture capital firms.

Formal or informal, many groups are often led to invest in a particular industry by common expertise. Paul Bandrowski's success with Reciprocal, for example, has nudged him into focusing on encryption technology. Investing in what you know is one way to reduce risk, and carve out a niche where you might be helpful. At the same time, be sure you're not investing in too specialized a property. If one product doesn't work out, is there a fallback application that might?

Finding a group that fits is all part of the networking process. Chat up professionals who might be plugged in: bankers, lawyers, accountants, university entrepreneur programs, investment bankers. Take a look at matching services that put angels and entrepreneurs together. There are probably 100 or so such outlets, many of them nonprofit or university affiliated. Most of them stage face-to-face venture forums, or tie capital and business together with the help of newsletters and the Internet.

One of the best shopping lists of matching services and angel groups, compiled with the help of University of New Hampshire's Venture Center, appears in *Angel Investing* by Mark Van Osnabrugge and Robert J. Robinson (Jossey-Bass, 2000).

Most angel groups screen potential members (if only to make sure that they meet the SEC's "accredited investor criteria")—a useful process that enables would-be members to ask questions, too. That's the time to look into items such as a group's risk tolerance, investment criteria, exit strategies management, and success ratio. Ask for brochures, annual reports, details on presenter forums. You are investing in a group as well as a portfolio, so talk to as many members as you can. It's nice to know you're among friends. If you don't seriously exercise this sort of due diligence, you may find yourself akin to Groucho Marx, who deadpanned that he would never join a group that was willing to let him in.

Part of the self-selection process—will this group and I get along?—turns on whether you are searching for the same kind of deals. Risk levels, the amount of money involved, the price of a venture all vary with the stage of development. The stages shake down like this:

Seed financing, usually involves only modest amounts of outside financing, but lots of sweat equity on the part of the founder. Typically, the cash goes to a product that looks good on paper, but has not yet been developed. At this stage of the game, for example, Amazon founder Jeff Bezos had put $10,000 of his own cash into Amazon.com and borrowed $40,000. Van Osnabrugge and Robinson, authors of *Angel Investing*, put the adjusted price of his stock at .001 a share.

Start-up financing is ticketed to companies rounding out development and market studies, but not yet a truly commercial operation. It was at this level that Bezos's mother and father tucked a total of $240,000 into Amazon. Their price: .1717 a share.

First (early) stage companies have burned up development capital and need another jolt of cash to set up full-scale manufacturing and sales. This is when two angels invested a combined $54,408 into Amazon. Their cost: .3333 a share. They were followed by a 20-angel syndicate that put up a little less than $100,000. Their cost was also .3333 a share.

Second (later) stage companies are generating revenues (but not necessarily profits), have a solid management crew in place, and need money for expansion. Two venture capital firms invested a total of $8 million in Amazon at this point. Their cost: $2.34 a share.

In its first public offering, not quite three years after Bezos put up his $10,000, Amazon.com raised $49 million at a price of $18 a share. That cheered the .3333 cents-a-share angels no end. In the early stages, Bezos, his family—and the angels—were taking most of the risk, so they got in cheap. They also harvested the biggest rewards. The later arriving venture capitalist firms, investing in what was a going concern, paid considerably more for a still handsome but lesser return. It's a classic demonstration of risk-reward ratios and how each layer of financing builds a base for the next.

The risks and rewards vary so that you should be sure that any angel band you might want to join is in sync on the stage that suits you best. Further, if you hope to help the entrepreneurial launch, is there room for you to do so? Other points to explore: industry concentration (typically high-tech), minimum investments, and overhead costs like the manager's cut—if any.

Networking puts angels together; networking brings them the deals they invest in. Computerized matching services do this out of a confidential database submitted by both sides. Some screen start-ups for minimal standards before putting them on the date list; others do not.

All matching services fade out after making the introduction. Angels do a lot of prospecting on their own—Ross Kenzie and the Buffalo Angels' willingness to talk to Paul Bandrowski, for example, even though he came from the Ultima Thule of technology. The early filtering process is important in the way that time is important. In angeldom, as elsewhere, you have to kiss a lot of frogs before you find a prince. So, one threshold question, always, is a cautious "who brought this deal in?" Finders are not always objective; they are often selling. Is a brother angel trying to aggrandize his brother-in-law under the corporate guise of something like Superengineionics.com?

There is almost always a certain amount of judicious exaggeration in such presentations. In their pitch to the Buffalo Angels, Bandrowski and Schreiber leaned heavily on Yahoo! and the financial rewards that high-tech investment can bring. That certainly caught the group's attention. What really clinched the deal, though, was Bandrowski and Schreiber's demonstrated management skills, and a detailed explanation of the market they were shooting for. Anyone can cobble together a glitzy business plan. The dot.coms that destructed like a string of Chinese firecrackers were all plausible enough to find backers. The angels' imperative is to cut through the paper and ballyhoo to the reality (if any) behind the business plan. Thus, Bandrowski says Ross Kenzie "checked all of our references and talked to everyone to learn the technology." "It was one of the most painstaking pieces of due diligences I have ever seen," adds Bandrowski.

So, Kenzie did not permit the Bandrowski-Schreiber charm offensive to distract him. That puts him one up on the general run of angel. University of New Hampshire research suggests that entrepreneurial enthusiasm and personality weigh heavily in angel investment decisions. Good vibes are nice, particularly if you hope to work directly with the entrepreneur. But the higher virtues lie in demonstrated expertise and some concrete display of management skills, not always easy to find anywhere, let alone in a largely untried start-up.

One measure of those qualities is how sedulously the founder bootstrapped his firm before looking to outside help. Basically, how much hustle has he shown? Is he logging the requisite 80 to 100 hours a week? How much of his own money is at risk? Is he leveraging—and regularly paying off—credit card and home equity debt to keep himself afloat? Is he working out of his garage, or in rented space that eats up capital? Is he working with used or leased equipment rather than splashing out for new? Why not insist on dedicated frugality and fully utilized sweat glands in a wanna-be you're going to give your money to?

Think of Paul Bandrowski's background as a model for the kind of entrepreneur you want on your side. Put temporarily out of business by regulatory authority—the principal in his fifth grade elementary school venture—Bandrowski tried again two years later. No cinnamon sticks this time. "I talked to my dad about wholesale margins on candy bars—he was always in business—and the markups looked good," recalls Bandrowski. Using some of the capital from his cinnamon stick gig, Bandrowski bought $200 worth of Snickers and Milky Ways at a discount outlet for 12¢ each. He sold them for 30¢ each (a nickel over then retail) during the lunch hour through a gang of 20 kids, splitting with them the 18¢ markup. "It was a good business plan," laughs Bandrowski. "There was immediate cash flow and the marketing costs were quite low."

Bandrowski spent almost all his subsequent school years in one business or another, including a software company he put together with a group of fellow students at Central Michigan University. "That's where we did have marketing problems," says Bandrowski. "Nobody wanted to buy from us because they thought we were just a couple of college kids." They persuaded an angel—one of his friends' fathers—to put some cash into the venture and handle the marketing. The switch worked. "We wound up selling out to another group and actually made some money," recalls Bandrowski.

Central Michigan was one of the six colleges Bandrowski attended and left. "I was always arguing with my professors," he says. The last of those arguments erupted at the University of Chicago, where Bandrowski took exception to a case his professor was presenting. "You think it actually works that way?" queried Bandrowski. When the academician insisted it did, Bandrowski asked him if he'd ever been in business. "No. What difference does that make?" came the answer. "I walked out and never looked back," says Bandrowski. Eight ventures later, Bandrowski had enough cash to reinvent himself as an angel.

A probing mind and a precocious interest in business are typical of many top entrepreneurial names; something to look for in your search for talent. Take Amar Bose, whose experiments on loudspeaker design led to the founding of Bose Corporation, a state-of-the-art audio products company. He set up a home radio repair shop in Philadelphia at age 13 during World War II when his father's import business faltered. At that time, almost everyone who could repair radios was in the military. Soon Bose's shop (employing seven other students at 50¢ an hour) was one of the biggest in town.

Similarly, as a 14-year-old during the German occupation of Greece, George Hatsopoulos, founder of Thermo Electron, built radios on the sly and sold them mainly to the Underground. He filled a notebook with inventions, hoping he could one day build a business around them. That's precisely what Hatsopoulos did. An inspiration on how thermionic emissions could be harnessed to convert heat into electricity with no moving parts became the core of his Thermo Electron empire.

Granted those are exceptional talents, but the early commitment to business is not. Such predictive experience is one of the first things to look for in a prospective entrepreneur. Passive angels often don't make a point of sitting in on early talent interviews. That's a mistake. In early-stage companies, you're investing first in people, then in a product. One common angel regret is failure to truly size-up a founder. Will he stand up when things go wrong, as they invariably do? Can he put a real management team together, or does he feel comfortable only with yes-men?

Feeling and intuition frequently control how angels invest. Often there is very little else to go on. Financials aren't very much help in assessing a company with very little history, but they should nonetheless be challenged. Business plans should be screened as part of the early due diligence, too. Treat them as sales documents. Take no entrepreneurial projections for granted. What you're looking for is a unique product in a fast-growing market that will preempt the competition. The search should be focused. Your group should be playing to its own industry strengths, with savvy lead angels running an independent check on market potential.

You can hire outside experts to do the grunt work, but that adds to the cost of what is by definition already an expensive, time-consuming process. Preliminary screening should be rigorous enough to allow only the very best bets to get to the formal due-diligence stage. Once you get there, take a cold look at traditional items such as cash flow and potential rate of return. Do they look promising enough to make this investment worthwhile? Angels often do not do as much deep research as they should—one of the reasons why they make decisions far more quickly than venture capitalists and, as a result, get to repent at leisure.

Without deep thought, it's hard to resolve one of the toughest questions in venture finance: Could this company work out and how big a piece of it are you entitled to for taking on most of the risk? It's important to hammer out those issues in the precontract bargaining. Since they intend to live with the entrepreneur for half a decade or more, few angels haggle to the last for an extra two percentage points of equity. But who gets what for how much can become an everlasting bone of contention, even in such great success stories as the creation of Digital Equipment Company. Friends say that Kenneth Olsen, founder of the computer maker (now part of Compaq Computer) to this day feels that he gave up too much of his company for too little—70 percent of it for a $70,000 seed investment that ultimately netted shareholders of Georges Doriot's American Research and Development Company more than $400 million.

Business angels often feel that they've been taken too, regretting that they didn't push for better terms. You don't want to be too aggressive. But don't settle for less than a meaningful minority position (20 to 30 percent), and maybe a seat on the board like Paul Bandrowski's vice-chair position at Sun Hawk.

A grab for control is a no-no. Why strip a fledgling company of what may be its most valuable asset—the entrepreneur's incentive to build? And why worry about equity anyway? Convertible debt is probably a better option. If things do go badly, debt will give you at least a claim on assets. Other considerations before you go to contract: Illiquidity is one of the great drawbacks of investing in start-ups. How do you get your money out? In an outright failure, you might be able to salvage something from the bankruptcy court. If the business merely bumps along at subsistence levels, the customary escape routes are trade sales, management buyouts or mergers (like Paul Bandrowski's combining his start-up into Sun Hawk). Cashing in through the new issues market is every angel's dream exit, but a long shot. In effect, angels run a farm system, happy to get from semipro to the minor leagues, knowing only that exceptional talent will make the leap to big time.

Careful monitoring is the best way to help your entry move up in class. Make sure that you're getting maximum mileage out of every new dollar in capital you put up. Keep pay scales tight, and make stock a major element in compensation packages. Doing so saves start-up cash and pushes incentive from the top right on down through to the mail room. Fight any temptation to hire expensive management from the outside. Cultivating talent in-house is bootstrapping by other means and part of the satisfaction of plunging into venture investing.

There are other ways to do so, of course. You can invest—passively—in publicly traded incubators such as Safe Guard Scientifics or Soft Bank Ventures—both selling for a lot less now than a year ago. You can invest in publicly traded business development companies, or even in venture-oriented mutual funds. You can do that, but you'll never feel the creative buzz that Paul Bandrowski talks about. "Angeling sure beats working," he says.

Among the national hookups that will help you delve deeper into Angeldom are: the Small Business Administration access to Capital Electronics Network (http:\\ace-net.fr.unh.edu.\) and the MIT Enterprise Forum, Incorporated (http:\\web.MIT.edu\entforum\www\chapters\

chapters.htm). The Ace-net (sometimes known as the Angel Capital Electronic Network) has links to more than 30 affiliates across the nation. The MIT Forum has 15 chapters in the United States and four abroad (Toronto, Jerusalem, Mexico City, and Taiwan).

A geographic smattering of angel groups includes Technology Capital Network (617-253-7163); Gold Coast Venture Capital Club (Florida, 561-488-4505); New York Angel Investors (212-785-7898, extension 300); Private Investors Network (Virginia, 703-255-4930).

A NOTE ON SOURCES

M OST OF THIS BOOK, as cited in the text, is based on interviews, public documents (court records, Securities & Exchange Commission filings, and the like), contemporary reminiscences, newspapers, and other periodicals, particularly *Forbes*.

I am grateful for the work of others embodied in the following books:

CHAPTER 1 ❧ VALUE AVATAR: BENJAMIN GRAHAM
For the chapter on Ben Graham, I have drawn on his own classics, Graham & Dodd *Security Analysis* (McGraw-Hill, 1934), *The Intelligent Investor* (Harper & Row, 1949), and his delightful *Benjamin Graham, The Memoirs of the Dean of Wall Street* (McGraw-Hill, 1996, copyright Graham Memoirs Grandchildren's Trust). Janet Lowe's *Benjamin Graham on Value Investing* (Dearborn Financial Publishing, 1994) offers further insights on Ben's family life. His evolution as an analyst is described with telling anecdotes by Irving Kahn and Robert D. Milne in *Benjamin Graham, the Father of Financial Analysis* (copyright Financial Analysts Research Foundation, 1977).

CHAPTER 2 ❧ VALUE WITH A DIFFERENCE: MARTY WHITMAN
Chapter 2 owes something to Martin Whitman's own works: *Value Investing* (John Wiley & Sons, 1999) and *The Aggressive Conservative Investor* (with Martin Shubik, Random House, 1979). Hilary Rosenberg's *The Vulture Investors* (Harper Collins, 1992) is a sharp reportorial look at Whitman and a clutch of other deep-discount operatives in action.

CHAPTER 3 ❖ GROWTH AVATAR: T. ROWE PRICE

This chapter draws from an unpublished company history, particularly helpful for its wide use of entries from the T. Rowe Price diaries.

CHAPTER 4 ❖ EXTENDING THE GROWTH CULTURE: TOM BAILEY

For the first time, Tom Bailey and the Janus culture are caught between hard covers for the first time. Press coverage has been copious, but few reporters have managed any sustained interviews with Bailey, who modestly prefers to keep his portfolio managers out front. One notable exception, apart from this book, is Tom Easton's *Forbes* cover of Aug. 23, 1999.

CHAPTER 5 ❖ SWINDLE OF THE CENTURY: ANTHONY DEANGELIS

The definitive work on Tino DeAngelis is *The Great Salad Oil Swindle* (Coward, McCann, 1965), by Norman C. Miller, who won a Pulitzer Prize for his coverage of the caper in the *Wall Street Journal*. The chapter also draws on the author's unpublished manuscript.

CHAPTER 6 ❖ INVESTOR BEWARE: A CAUTIONARY TALE

The travail of Henry F. Silverman is probably best explored in a novel. Early warnings of hyper-accounting were sounded in a number of pieces by *Forbes* staffers Howard Rudnitsky and Michael Oznanian.

CHAPTER 7 ❖ THE RICHEST WOMAN IN THE WORLD: HETTY GREEN

Hetty Green was richly covered by the reporters of her day. The two definitive works are *Hetty Green, The Witch of Wall Street*, by Boyden Sparks and Samuel Taylor Moore (Doubleday, Doran, 1935), and *The Day They Shook the Plum Tree*, by Arthur H. Lewis (Harcourt, Brace & World, 1963). The latter pushes the story forward from Hetty's death to the dissolution of her outrageously won fortune.

CHAPTER 8 ❧ VISIT WITH A BILLIONAIRESS: MURIEL SIEBERT

Muriel F. Siebert is still writing the history of women on Wall Street through the workings of her discount-brokerage firm.

CHAPTER 9 ❧ THE VENTURE CAPITAL'S CAPITALIST: GEORGES DORIOT

The recollections of Charles Waite on his days with General Georges Doriot appear in *Done Deals* (Harvard Business School Press, 2000, copyright President and Fellows of Harvard College). Edited by Udayan Gupta, the book is an overview of U.S. venture capital and its growth, as seen by more than 30 foremost practitioners.

CHAPTER 10 ❧ A VENTURE OF ANGELS: PAUL BANDROWSKI

An outstanding work on angel investing, packed with valuable how-to's, is *Angel Investing* by Mark Van Osnabrugge and Robert J. Robinson (Jossey-Bass Inc., 2000).

ACKNOWLEDGMENTS

Thank you and a deep *ojigi* to James W. Michaels for a characteristically deft editorial hand. It is typical of the finesse and judgment he put into shaping *Forbes* for almost a half century. Thank you also to Nicola Pullen of *Forbes'* hard working library staff for skill and good humor in putting together a cabinet full of raw research. Thanks again to the *Forbes'* Info Tech gang (Carolyn Buonocore, Louie Torres, and Juliana Vendramin) from a guy who needed a lot of help at the keyboard. And a tip of many hats to CAM for insight and touch on a work-in-progress.

New York, 2001

I N D E X